Backcountry Bikepacking

Backcountry Bikepacking

By WILLIAM SANDERS

Stackpole Books

Published by
STACKPOLE BOOKS
Cameron and Kelker Streets
P.O. Box 1831
Harrisburg, PA 17105

Other books by William Sanders
  The Bicycle Racing Book
  Guide to Inflatable Canoes and Kayaks

Cover photograph © 1981 by Greg Siple, courtesy League of
American Wheelmen, P.O. Box 988, Baltimore, MD 21203

Library of Congress Cataloging in Publication Data

Sanders, William, 1942–
    Backcountry bikepacking.

    Bibliography: p.
    Includes index.
      1. Bicycle touring.   2. Bicycle touring —
Equipment and supplies.   I. Title.
GV1044.S26   1983   796.6   83-326
ISBN 0-8117-2258-9 (pbk.)

Printed in the U.S.A.

for my father
William Newton Sanders
1896-1980
who knew about roads

Contents

*Now I see the secret of making the
best persons,
It is to grow in the open air and to
eat and sleep with the earth.*

—Walt Whitman

Introduction

It was a warm, bright October day, and the midday sun was making me sweat a little by the time I pedaled the last bit of dirt Forest Service road and turned onto the blacktop. The grade had been steep and the gravel loose coming down off the mountain where I'd spent the night, and I'd had to go slowly and use the brakes a lot, so I didn't have many miles to show for the morning's efforts. But that was all right; it usually took me all day to cover the same route on foot—to say nothing of a lot more hard work and sore feet.

The old two-lane road was almost deserted as I rode along, with no traffic beyond the odd pickup truck, and the houses miles apart. Big, glossy crows flew up off the road as I approached, cawing irritably; up near the crest of the great ridge I'd just left, half a dozen vultures wheeled in stately circles, probably hoping for a hit-and-run driver to pick me off. Once a wild turkey flapped clumsily across the road and disappeared into the forest, looking as if he ought to be on a bourbon-bottle label.

Fifteen miles and a bit under an hour later, I pulled into a tiny crossroads community—two houses, a store, and a fishbait purveyor—and paused to pick up some bread, cheese, and fruit,

1

and to refill my water bottles. With the unfailing reserved courtesy of all mountain people, the lady at the store asked no questions about where I was going or why I had chosen such an outlandish way to get there.

Down the wide main highway a few more miles, I found a nice spot in a grove of bright yellow beech trees and got off to eat lunch. While I sat peeling an orange with my old Ka-bar pocket-knife, a big hairy tarantula came out of the bushes, scuttling along in that low-slung, prowling desperado way they have, and gave me a wide detour before rustling off into the underbrush again.

One of the handlebar-end shift levers had been feeling a little loose all morning; I got out the little screwdriver and tightened it up. Back on the bike, I took advantage of a fresh tailwind and a clean road to snap the chain onto a higher gear combination and wind it up a little, enjoying the sensation of speed and grace after my hypercautious morning. This was farm country, nice enough, but rather dull compared to the hills, so I worked up speed and stayed down in a crouch rather than fooling along checking out the scenery.

There were a few big trucks on this road, but the lanes were wide and there were no blind curves or crests; the drivers all gave me plenty of room, and most of them waved. A big hound ran out at me from an unfenced yard, but I brandished my pump and let off a loud karate shout and he hit his brakes and ran back into the yard.

Late that afternoon, rolling down an unmarked dirt road, I crossed the river on an old one-lane, concrete-slab bridge, where an old man looked up from his fishing long enough to grin at me. A few miles beyond the bridge, a rough but passable side road led off to the left through dense, second-growth pine-and-hardwood forest, and I followed it down to the river. There was a little cleared area I remembered well; I'd spent a lot of nights there over the years, on my way through the mountains on foot or coming down the river in various craft. This was the first time I had come there on a bicycle, though. I sighed with relief to see that there was nobody else around and no litter.

I got out the little butane stove from the left pannier bag, along with a few packets of dehydrated food picked up at the supermarket back in the last town. Soon there was a pot of iodine-purified river water coming to a boil while I got the tent from the other pannier and set it up in my usual spot under a couple of big sycamores. It took only a few more minutes to undo the straps, get the sleeping bag off the rack and out of its stuff sack, toss it through the tent door, blow up the tiny air mattress, and do the other jobs that become routine when you do this sort of thing often enough. By now the noodles were done, and I hunkered down to eat.

Later, the noodles long gone and the instant pudding a fond but fading memory, I sat beside my tent in the deepening evening and listened to the gurgle of the river and the sounds of little wild things starting to come out on their night's business.

"Anna Marie," I told my bike, "we're going to have to do this sort of thing more often. . . ."

*   *   *

The bicycle has passed through some remarkable developments in its history, not just technological developments— though these have been spectacular enough—but changes in the essential concept of what the bicycle itself was and what it was for. The original inventors of the bicycle were looking mostly for an answer to the transportation problems of Europe, especially Great Britain, during the last quarter of the nineteenth century. Expanding populations and increased urbanization had made it necessary to use available farmlands to grow food for people; feeding large numbers of horses as well had become a serious problem. As we would put it, they had an energy crisis—indeed, there are amazing parallels with some of the problems of our time, though this is not the place to go into them.

The bicycle was intended, then, as a substitute for the horse, primarily for the working man—expensive to buy, but cheap to maintain without need of stable or pasture. But the leisured classes discovered the bicycle and turned it into, to put it baldly, a faddish toy. A minority of the cyclists and engineers of the late nineteenth century did indeed try to develop the machine's potential as a serious vehicle, but for most people it was merely, in modern terms, the "In" thing to do. This lasted until the first automobiles appeared; the bicycle then went back to being the working man's personal transportation—as it remains to this day in much of the world, something we in our motorized culture tend to forget.

In the United States, the most internal combustion-happy of nations, the eclipse of the bicycle was almost total. During most of this century, any adult American who rode a bicycle was assumed to be either too poor to own a car or, most likely, some sort of lunatic. American tourists overseas goggled in amused

astonishment at the sight of grown people—even policemen!—
riding bikes as a normal thing; the phenomenon was, in fact,
widely cited as another proof of the superiority of the American
way of life.

   The famous—or infamous—"bike boom" of the early
1970s, part of a general awakening of interest in exercise, fitness,
and sports, at first created a situation not unlike that of the Gay
Nineties. The primary focus of interest in the bicycle was as a
device for getting exercise (a kind of mobile gymnasium,
perhaps), as a toy for casual recreation, or, all too often, simply
as a trendy status symbol. Later, environmentalists and social
planners began to agitate for the use of bicycles in solving the
problems of mass urban transportation, and an actual political
ideology evolved around the bicycle. Others became interested in
racing, and Americans began to appear in European and Latin
American race packs.

   But actually *going* somewhere by bike took much longer to
catch on in this country, though Europeans have been doing it for
a century. Even when the concept of "bicycle touring" began to
take hold, the American bikie developed a rather original
approach: ride a stripped-down, near-racing bike and ride in
groups with a van or car following along to carry everyone's food
and supplies. (The support vehicle, poking along at its slowest
and smokiest speed, invariably bore a bumper sticker reading,
"BICYCLES DON'T POLLUTE." As Mark Twain said in another
context, "Nobody smiled at these colossal ironies.")

   More independent souls did indeed begin cruising around
the countryside on their bikes, but most of them stuck strictly to
populated regions and good highways, carrying only a change of
clothes and a few toilet articles, staying in motels or hostels and
either eating in restaurants or buying no-cook food along the way.
Carrying camping gear along was usually considered a rather
desperate alternative to motels, and not many people even tried
it; those who did nearly always stuck with paved highways and
"official" campgrounds. To a great many Americans at that time,
"camping out" bore distinctly unpleasant associations of their
youth—leaky, fetid pup tents, inadequate blankets, heavy, unreliable air mattresses, and attempts to get a fire going in the rain. As
it happened, this was also a time of considerable change and
invention in the camping-equipment industry and in the whole
concept of camping itself; and, as in all revolutions, there was an
accompanying cloud of confusion and misinformation.

The great breakthrough came in 1976. In honor of the nation's bicentennial celebration, a group of cyclists and hostellers organized the now-legendary "Bikecentennial" cycle tours. Thousands of people rode on the various excursions; astonishing numbers made the coast-to-coast run, which had long been considered the exclusive turf of a handful of super-fit athletes and fanatics. These rides, and the publicity that followed, did much to awaken Americans to the potential of the bicycle as a means of covering respectable distances and seeing beautiful scenery.

Participation in the Bikecentennial and similar organized tours tended to be quite expensive, so a good many of the riders elected to carry camping gear and sleep outdoors rather than pay for accommodations. But a remarkable thing happened. Very soon most of them discovered that saving money was the smallest part of it—bicycle camping turned out to be a whole trip in itself. Recent advances in modern lightweight camping equipment had made it possible for any moderately fit cyclist to be self-contained and independent, carrying bed, kitchen, and house along wherever he or she chose to ride. No more being locked into merciless schedules, having to make the next town before dark no matter what; no more of the soul-slaying business of pedaling around a strange town at night, trying to find a vacant room while cross-eyed with fatigue; no more snotty desk clerks telling you you couldn't take that dirty thing in the room with you . . . and above all, no more being tied to the main highways and the towns, with their noise and pollution and ugliness and, oh God, their murderously dangerous traffic. With a simple, light, compact camping outfit that could be carried on any bike, you could leave all this behind and ride into a clean, quiet world of trees, streams, birds, and nights under the moon and stars.

All great liberations start with simple ideas.

When the Bikecentennial project was announced, many people wondered what bicycles could possibly have to do with the Declaration of Independence. Well, if nothing else, a very considerable number of Americans on bicycles discovered a whole new approach to "life, liberty, and the pursuit of happiness."

Nowadays, of course, there's another side to the cycle-camping phenomenon. It's not just the bikies getting into camping; it's also the campers finding out about bikes.

It will hardly be news to anyone that the U.S. is experiencing a great wave of interest in outdoor sports such as backpacking, canoeing, ski touring, and the like. Thousands of people each year flock to wilderness and near-wilderness areas. Ordinary department stores routinely stock sophisticated equipment once found only in specialized expedition-supply houses. And for all the problems of overcrowded trails and rivers and the frequently irritating behavior of the "wilderness chic" crowd—who often seem to see the outdoors as a kind of disco floor with trees—this is a fine thing, because this heightened awareness has been a decisive factor in preserving some magnificent stretches of wild country from exploitation and destruction.

Now it may be hard to understand where the bicycle fits into this. Even with the expanded interest in bicycle camping, most American bikepackers tend to operate primarily in built-up areas and on paved highways. The bicycle does seem at first to be a rather limited and marginal proposition as a backcountry vehicle; it looks fragile, with its skeletal frame and webby wheels, and many otherwise expert cyclists automatically associate it with good, smooth-paved surfaces.

This misconception probably originated in conjunction with the kind of high-speed, no-load "touring" mentioned earlier in this chapter, but it is true that many Americans are nervous off the pavement, even in cars. Indeed, during World War II, the Germans discovered to their joy that American tanks would invariably advance down a road rather than spread out over the fields and forests! Even the rugged U.S. cycle racer, who takes heat, fatigue, and high-speed crashes in stride, complains bitterly if a course is not glass-smooth—while his European counterpart thinks nothing of racing at close to 30 miles per hour over dirt, gravel, and ancient, eroded cobblestones. And modern tourists forget that people were making long journeys on bicycles—bicycles far less sturdy than ours—before paved highways were even invented.

Once you try it, you'll discover that the bicycle is a superb instrument for bikepacking. Riding along in the open air on silent wheels, you see, hear, feel, and even smell your surroundings as totally as any hiker, canoeist, or skier; speeds are low enough that you don't have to miss anything, and there is no exhaust to dirty up the air, no noise to ruin the peace of the outdoors, and no problem of fuel supplies.

Yet even a rather poor cyclist on a clunky bike can cover very easily more ground in a day than any hiker or paddler alive. The bikepacker can operate over a range undreamed of by any other self-propelled traveler. The bike's speed can be used to hurry through uninteresting or unpleasant places—towns, industrial areas, land subjected to obscenities such as clear-cutting or strip-mining—and yet the bike can be ridden at a walking pace when the cyclist wants to take in the scenery.

There are many other advantages to the bicycle. While hikers have to carry all their food and other expendable supplies, the accumulated weight often being enough to take all the fun out of the day, the bikepackers can usually pick up groceries at rural stores or on the outskirts of small towns. Except on really off-the-map runs, the cyclist has less to carry and can have all sorts of goodies that the hiker sees only in frustrated dreams—fresh fruit, cold drinks, fresh, canned, or frozen meat and vegetables, even booze.

A certain amount of physical effort is involved, yes, but most people find cycling less fatiguing than hiking with a heavy pack. Even when a hill is too steep and long to pedal, or part of the way unrideably rough, you can still let the bike carry a lot of the weight as you walk up, pushing it like a wheelbarrow. Going downhill, you get to take a break and coast; loaded backpackers usually find downhill walking as fatiguing as climbing. True, a canoe or raft will carry you along with the current, but rivers flow only in one direction, which creates the need for complicated car-shuttling arrangements—and maneuvering in rapids can be plenty tiring too.

It is true that a certain element of risk is involved too; riding on roads with automotive traffic can be frightening and dangerous. But carrying your own camping gear and learning to ride on back roads will enable you to get away from such routes. (If you are an avid cyclist but traffic is scaring you out of your fun, you definitely ought to try backcountry bikepacking; it may be the answer to your prayers.) Even when riding along highways with motor traffic, sometimes an unavoidable situation, the danger is far less than many imagine. It's *city* traffic that can kill you. I've been hit four times by cars in the city, having two bikes trashed under me, but I've never even been bumped by a car on the open road.

And while we're talking about safety here, a cyclist with a decent map and compass doesn't have to worry about getting lost—and bikies very rarely have to swim for their lives after a crash.

As for the myth of the frail, road-bound bicycle, forget it.

Lightweight touring bicycles have been ridden across the Sahara, through the Khyber Pass, from Alaska to Tierra del Fuego and back, and just about everywhere else except for the polar regions. These trips were made using bicycles in no significant way different from those sold at any ordinary bike shop. Bicycles have been used in jungle warfare (the Japanese in Malaya and the Vietcong in Indochina made them a decisive weapon) and are routinely used in undeveloped countries where paved roads are virtually unknown.

Certainly anyone who can ride a bike at all can learn to ride on dirt or gravel roads, given proper equipment and a basic knowledge of the technique—and these matters are a good part of what this book is about. This opens up great possibilities in itself. For example, most National Forests are crisscrossed with networks of excellent dirt roads with hardly any motor traffic or human settlements to be encountered.

If you want to go beyond that, there's what the British call "rough stuff"—riding the bike (with maybe a bit of pushing and carrying here and there) clear off regular roads of *any* kind, down logging tracks and cowpaths and trails and—well, the limitations are mostly determined by the individual cyclist's guts-to-brains ratio.

Expensive? Yes, somewhat; good bikes are not cheap, and neither is the lightweight camping equipment suited to bike-packing. Still, there are ways to reduce the expense (again, we'll be talking about this throughout this book), and it is certainly not necessary to own the most expensive makes and models of bike, tent, sleeping bag, and so on. The cost is fairly comparable to that of most other forms of outdoor travel. A suitable bike can be had for about the same price as a good canoe or kayak, a cross-country skiing outfit, or for not too much more than a quality backpack and a pair of really good mountain boots.

Certainly the price of even the finest custom touring bike with all accessories is very far below that of such motorized toys as vans, trail motorcycles, four-wheel-drive trucks, and power boats. That's without even figuring in the cost of gas.

There is also a hidden saving with a bicycle. Usually a hiker or a paddler has to calculate the expense of getting to the trailhead or launching area, and back home afterwards; float trips add the complexities of car shuttles. With gas prices rising, this can be a real sting, to say nothing of wear and tear on the car and the terrible increase in vandalism and theft of parked cars in such areas.

The cyclist, on the other hand, will often find it possible to make long and interesting trips that start right at his or her front door. Within a radius of as much as several hundred miles, your home *is* your trailhead. If you should be in the position of not owning a car at all—an increasingly common situation, and I think an admirable one—the bicycle is obviously your best way to go.

Taken on the whole, I don't know of any other form of backcountry travel that's in a class with cycling for sheer versatility. It combines the freedom of hiking, the grace and technical satisfaction—the elegance, if you like—of canoeing or skiing, and a range of operation not all that far below that of the motor vehicle. It's faster than a horse and infinitely less trouble, and does not present the environmental, aesthetic, and economic problems of the internal-combustion engine. You can even stay in shape and save money by using your bicycle to ride to work or around town when you're not using it for camping; this is something that might be extremely difficult to do with a canoe or kayak, or a pair of skis.

As a final bonus, cycling offers great health benefits and is highly recommended by doctors and fitness experts. Personally, I don't like to push this aspect very hard—there are plenty of easier and cheaper ways to get some exercise, if that's all you're after. Still, it *is* nice to know that you've got that going for you too. And there's something very appealing about anything that's genuinely enjoyable, yet isn't illegal, violates no religious teachings, contains no cholesterol, and has never been linked to cancer in laboratory mice.

No, the days aren't all like the one described at the beginning of this chapter. Flat tires, hostile motorists, nasty dogs, sunburn, and a sore, sore bottom—these things happen. If you stick with it long enough, you will have moments when you profoundly feel that you ought to have your head examined for ever getting involved in the whole business. But then this is true of any human activity, isn't it, including life itself?

Willie Nelson wisely says, "Nothing works every time."

So I can't guarantee it will always be perfect. What I *am* going to do in this book is to show you what you need and how to make the best use of it, in order to go bikepacking with a minimum of bad times and a maximum of good ones.

A word here about the orientation of this book. Many readers are going to find some parts rather basic; you may be an expert bicyclist who wants to try camping, or a highly experienced backpacker who is interested in getting into cycling, and so you may already know some of this stuff. Do not be offended; as part of the nature of things, a book like this *has* to be written for the person who is pretty much a novice all around. I think it's better to tell one person something he already knows than to fail to tell somebody else something he doesn't.

It is also possible that your own experience will in time lead you to form entirely different conclusions on some matters; it is even possible that the author might be *wrong* about something. Individuals differ widely in a zillion ways; nothing in here should be construed as The Final Word.

Enough checking the maps and tightening the straps. Let's get this thing rolling on down the road.

The frame thereof seemed partly circular
And part triangular—O work divine.

—*Edmund Spenser,*
The Faerie Queene

CHAPTER **1**

The Beast
with Two Wheels

To begin with, of course, you've got to have a bicycle.

The bike itself represents the bottom line in more ways than one. It is usually the most expensive single item in the bikepacker's outfit, and certainly the most complex. So we will begin with a detailed look at the bicycle—but if you're on any sort of budget, and who isn't these days, you'd better read the whole book before making any big purchases, or you might not have enough for the other things you'll need.

A couple of words, too, before we get into the nuts and bolts. The following remarks are very general and should *not* be taken as a lot of stuff you have to have. The American cyclist is already given to excessive concern with hardware and the relative status of various brands and designs.

The information in this chapter is meant to serve as a set of guidelines for the beginner who is about to buy a bike and is hopelessly confused by the plethora of makes and marques and the conflicting claims made about them. It is also meant to help the person who already owns a bike and who wants to know whether or not it will be suitable for cycle camping or can be modified for this purpose.

I've also tried to indicate some of the less excruciatingly expensive alternatives for the benefit of those who have to watch their bucks. Bike dealers and well-intentioned affluent cyclists often lead novices to believe that they have to have this or that super-costly item, and there's nearly always something cheaper that works just about as well. But this should not be taken to extremes. Backcountry camping is rough on equipment, and you don't want to be off in the boondocks with a lot of cheap junk that's going to break or malfunction.

One more point: Specific makes are for the most part mentioned as examples, or as possible suggestions for the guidance of readers who may be really at sea. This is not a consumer-reports or product-review publication; for detailed evaluations of current products, consult cycling and outdoor magazines. While from time to time I may give positive and even glowing endorsements to various products, this should not be construed to mean that these are necessarily the only choices, or even the best ones. Usually I have merely described the makes and models with which I am personally familiar or which have been widely used by cyclists and/or campers in recent years. I have also given some weight to the availability of these items, and, where relevant, to cost.

In other words, just because I mention an item in this book, no one should assume it's something you *have* to have, and if I don't mention a product, it shouldn't necessarily be taken as criticism. There's just too much stuff on the market to get it all in these pages.

There are exceptions; in some cases I do think certain products offer significant advantages, and when I come to one of these, I will make it a point to say so—as will be the case with stuff I think genuinely stinks.

The Clunker Option

Almost any bicycle can be used for bikepacking; some are more efficient than others, that's all. Only you can say whether you're prepared to accept the penalties of less than ideal equipment, either for economic reasons or because you simply enjoy the challenge of doing things with improbable tools—rather like those hunters who use muzzle-loaders or crossbows.

The cheapest, crudest type of bike in general use is the one-speed, coaster-brake, balloon-tire roadster, alias bomber, alias tank, alias clunker. These ungainly but admirable beasts turn up at throwaway prices in Goodwill stores and garage sales. Sometimes, in fact, they literally *are* thrown away, and it is possible to scrounge up enough discarded parts to assemble one. (There's certainly something worthy in the idea of a recycled bicycle.) If you're really in a world of hurt for cash, this might be the only way to go.

While sturdy and fairly reliable, clunkers are damnably heavy and sluggish, and coaster brakes are dangerously inadequate. On a long downhill with a load of camping gear, a coaster brake can literally burn up. If you take a clunker into the hills, at least figure out some way to fit it with caliper-type brakes.

Don't be misled, either, by the apparent ruggedness of the clunker. That massive-looking frame is really weaker in many ways than a seemingly frail lightweight. The low-quality metal and cheap, welded construction make it necessary to employ heavy-gauge tubing, which is unwieldy and dead-feeling without being particularly strong.

Clunkers are something of a fad in some circles right now, and some people are doing a lot of off-the-road cycling on them. Often these "mountain clunkers" are highly modified and specialized machines, however, with caliper brakes, derailleur or hub gears, and so on. In some cases there is even a custom frame, so that what you get is not a clunker at all, but a special-purpose, rough-terrain custom bicycle that can be as expensive as a good lightweight.

The clunker, or its hot-rod brother, may be fine for off-road use—though it can't be a barrel of laughs humping something that heavy over a fence or fallen tree, or wading a waist-deep creek with it on your shoulder—but most of us prefer to be able to ride with reasonable speed and efficiency along the highway, so we have more time to spend in the woods. To me, the clunker, or even the super-clunker mountain bike, lacks the versatility that is so much of the bicycle's charm. Either you sacrifice range of operation, or you have to use it in connection with a motor vehicle. Still, it's up to you. And it's certainly better to go on a clunker than not to go at all.

Three-Speeds
and Five-Speeds _____

Three-speeds are considerably better than clunkers, and not just because of the added gears. The better European-made three-speeds have very strong lugged frames, steel cotter-pin cranksets with good bearings, and narrower, higher-pressure tires than the coaster braker. The internal hub gear is simpler and easier for some people to operate and adjust, and many like the upright position and the soft saddle. Such bikes often turn up at secondhand stores for very little. I once acquired an old Dutch three-speed for 13 bucks and used it for various applications, including squirrel hunting, for years. (Check the gears on these bikes very carefully—old three-speed gears are very prone to slippage.)

A quality three-speed such as a Raleigh, a Hercules, or a Batavus will be marginally adequate for touring and camping if you're willing to live with its limitations—a somewhat limited range of daily travel and frequent walks with it up the steepest hills. However, if you're really going off the map, a three-speed handles well on bad roads, and it has no derailleur to catch brush or be damaged by mud and dirt.

Basically, though, this is not a bike for serious travel. The lowest gear isn't really low enough for the big hills, considering the weight of the bike and the inefficient power transmission in any planetary system—you lose a lot through the friction of those little gears inside. The high gear is too high for riding on the flat and too low for downhilling with a load, and the whole bike is terribly heavy, clumsy, and unresponsive. The upright position is pleasant at first, but over the long miles it wears you down. The braking, especially when wet, leaves a lot to be desired.

Now, if you've got a good three-speed and can't afford anything else, or simply love it and don't want to replace it, ignore all of the above remarks and *ride* it. It will certainly be a lot more bike than one of those cheap, discount-store ten-speeds.

Most of the above observations apply as well to the so-called "tourist" bike, not to be confused with a touring bike. This is the "five-speed" so popular in some circles; novices sometimes buy them thinking the bikes will be more versatile than three-speeds but simpler than ten-speeds. It rarely works that way. Despite their more sophisticated gear system and slightly wider range of gears, most stock five-speeds are closer in handling qualities to the three-speed: gaspipe frame, mattress saddle, upright bars, and so on. Yet they're virtually as mechanically complex as the ten-speed. They are called "tourist" bikes because they are commonly employed as rental bikes in certain European resort areas, not because they are good for cycle touring. They're a bastard breed; I do not recommend them at all.

The Bikepacker's Bike

The bicycle camper will almost always get best results and maximum satisfaction from a modern, lightweight, derailleur

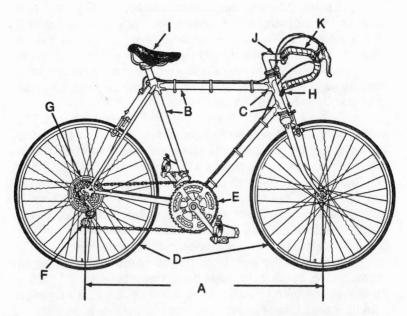

A—Long wheelbase (40"-42")
B—Slack angles (70°-72°)
C—Fully lugged frame
D—27" x 1¼" clincher tires
E—Cotterless crankset taking wide-range double or triple chainwheels

F—Wide-range derailleur
G—Wide-range cog cluster
H—Handlebar-end shifters
I—Comfortable saddle
J—Short-throw stem
K—Randonneur handlebars

Features of a touring bike that would be suitable for backcountry cycling.

bicycle—what most people call a "ten-speed," though of course other gear setups are possible.

Not all bikes in this class are equally suitable. The cheap "ten-speed racer" produced by various U.S. concerns and sold in discount and hardware stores is especially bad, lacking either the performance of the fine bike or the ruggedness and cheapness of the clunker. Except for Schwinn, which makes strong bikes at all price levels, most cheap U.S. bikes are toys.

A very expensive bike may not necessarily be a good choice either. The true racing bike is built for speed and maneuverability rather than comfort and stability; less expensive "stock" machines, whose owners use them for everything from commuting to novice-class racing, often are much better for our purposes. You wouldn't ride a thoroughbred race horse to punch cows. (True, my own bike, Anna Marie, is a rebuilt Gitane Tour de France that was originally supposed to be a racing bike, but she goes back to an era when racing frames were much longer and looser than today, and she's softened up over all those miles. Anyway, we're used to each other.)

The ideal camping/touring bike should be:

— sturdy in design and construction, capable of carrying an adult rider and 35 pounds of gear on poor roads, but *not* excessively heavy or clumsy;

— stable, with or without loads, and free from any tendency to shimmy, vibrate, or snake on long, fast downhills;

— comfortable to ride for long distances, within the limits of reasonable efficiency;

— equipped or compatible with wheels and tires suitable for extended riding over a variety of surfaces;

— capable of handling fairly wide-range gears, with emphasis on low gears for mountain and dirt-road riding;

— designed to accept carrier racks, bags, and (if desired) fenders, with all accessories mounted securely;

— mechanically reliable and simple to maintain and service, preferably with a minimum of specialized tools;

— compatible with components readily available in the country where the bike is to be used. This last is particularly important with regard to tires and tubes.

Naturally there are compromises implicit in all of this. Individual tastes and preferences come into it; some will be willing to sacrifice comfort for speed, others vice versa, and so on.

Novices will have to be guided by experience as they gain it.

It might be well to digress a little here and point out that there are basically two different groups of people who are interested in bicycle camping. One type is the avid cyclist, the *tourist;* he or she basically regards riding a bicycle as an end in itself. To such a person, the primary point of the whole business is to enjoy cycling for long periods in pleasant surroundings, and camping out is chiefly an adjunct or means to this goal.

The other type—represented by the author of this book, among others—is primarily an outdoor person who is devoted to spending as much time as possible out in wild and scenic country and, in Walt Whitman's words, "living and sleeping with the earth." This person is probably into things like backpacking as well. To the hard-core bikepacker of this persuasion, the bicycle is a means to an end—perhaps a much-loved means, but a means all the same.

All this is rather oversimplistic; most people fall somewhere between. The cycling enthusiast usually enjoys the time in camp too, and the camper gets a kick out of cycling as much as anyone. Still, it's worth trying to consider where you fit in.

The point is, your orientation will influence your choice of equipment, particularly the bike itself. If you're interested mainly in cycling, you'll want as fine a bike as you can afford, even if you have to skimp a bit on the camping gear. If you're a really hot cyclist, chances are you'll spend as much time as possible on the road, and your camps will be rather hasty little bivouacs in which you sleep and eat, period.

If you're primarily a backcountry camper who wants to do your traveling by bike, then you'll probably be just as happy with a fairly basic sort of bike. You'll want it to be comfortable, and you'll want it to be capable of carrying a good deal of cargo because you'll tend to go into more remote areas and be more self-sufficient. (On the other hand, you probably already own some good, lightweight camping equipment, so you may have more money to put on the bike.) Keep this principle in mind throughout this book—think about where you, personally, are coming from.

Let's pick the bike to bits and see what we've got here.

Frames

The frame is the body and soul of the bike. Its geometry and construction will determine the performance of the whole machine; any other component can be changed. Unfortunately, the admitted importance of the frame has led some contemporary Americans to become very silly about the fine points of frame geometry, and there is an actual pecking order in some circles, in which status is determined by the frame you ride. "Decal sniffer" is a common pejorative lately, as well it should be. Luckily for you, nearly all of this mumbo jumbo relates to racing frames—for cycle camping, the fine points are far less critical.

The regular *diamond frame* is standard for most serious cycling, for riders of either sex. The old-fashioned "ladies'" drop-frame bike is very inefficient, weak, and whippy, and since society has dropped its stupid demand that women wear skirts at all times, the step-through frame is no more than an anachronism, like whalebone corsets.

Still, very short women—and men—have special problems. For complex geometric reasons, it is very difficult to build a standard diamond-style frame in 20" or smaller sizes without creating either an excessive forward reach or some weird angles. In fact, a decent 19" frame is really a special-order job, while too big a frame is especially dangerous on a rough road.

There is an alternative. The *mixte frame* uses two narrow tubes that run straight from the top of the head tube to the rear dropouts, passing on either side of the top tube. The frame looks funny but is very strong and stiff, and this design is very suitable for small sizes. It is also somewhat heavier because of the extra tubing, and there are some problems with mounting certain accessories. But for short people who don't want to go to the expense of a custom frame, this is clearly the answer. Gitane, Peugeot, and Raleigh make very good, inexpensive mixte-frame bikes. Some custom frame builders such as Bob Jackson and Mercian make very fine mixte frames to order.

Most good frames are built with *lugs.* These are little steel fittings, rather resembling pipe elbows, where the tubes come together. They do not hold the frame together; their function is primarily that of distributing brazing heat and riding stresses.

But there are perfectly good lugless frames, such as the lower-priced Raleighs or the Viscounts. There are also some very expensive lugless frames made by custom shops; a true master builder can actually make a stronger joint this way, as there is a more even flow of brass, though this is mostly encountered in racing bikes.

Any quality frame will be *brazed* at low temperatures, not welded. Welding involves high temperatures that weaken the metal and mandate the use of heavy, dead tubing. The finest frames are silver brazed (incorrectly called "silver soldered" by many). This costs more, but it's worth it, since silver brazing is done using lower temperatures and thus does not weaken the metal so much.

The best frames are made of *double-butted* tubing—the tube walls are thicker at the ends than in the middle. This shows only on the inside, like a bottleneck; you can't see it from the outside at all. The metal is therefore stronger at points of stress—the joint areas—yet lighter and springier over its working length. This saves weight, makes the frame stronger, and makes for a very lively, pleasant-riding bike.

Double-butted tubing brands include Reynolds, Columbus, Vitus, Tange, Ishiwata, and a few others. For anything but racing, one is as good as another. But note that these companies also produce special, super-thin tubing meant for racing that's totally unsuitable for touring. Stay with normal gauges, such as regular Reynolds 531.

A double-butted frame is definitely worth having if you can afford it. But if you can't, any decent hi-tensile seamless tubing will do perfectly well. Some well-known names are Truwel, Durifort, or the straight-gauge Reynolds 531 used in the utterly delightful Dawes Galaxy.

In determining the performance of the finished bike, materials are less important than the geometry of the frame. In general, a bike will be more comfortable to ride and more stable with a fairly long wheelbase (40" or 41"), generous fork rake, and relatively slack frame angles. To be more specific would require another book as long as this one; these factors interact in a very complex way. For example, the optimum fork rake will be determined in part by the angle of the head tube; with a 72° head tube 2 inches of rake will be about right. And so on.

Frame angles may need to be explained a bit to some readers. There's nothing very complicated about it: The more the seat and head tubes tilt back from the vertical, the more comfortable the ride will be. However, there will be a corresponding drop in maneuverability and pedal efficiency. Racing bikes have very steep angles, 74° or more, for sprinting and zipping around corners; but their ride is quite harsh, and the more extreme designs are tricky to handle. Most touring frames run 72° fore and aft; 71° or even 70° would be better, but frames this shallow are hard to find. This is the legacy of a generation of U.S. cyclists divided between racers and people pretending to be racers. It also reflects the excellent quality of modern paved highways and the compulsion of most American cyclists to stay on them. A 72° frame is just fine.

There's certainly no sense in having 73° angles or steeper in a bike made for touring; you could use it, certainly, but I can't see why anyone would buy such a frame specifically for that purpose. Yet I have before me catalog listings for expensive "touring" frames with 73° angles, and no information at all on fork rake or wheelbase! For the price of such a frame, you could buy a complete bike that would be much more suitable and pleasant for camping and touring.

One important detail to watch for is the clearance between the frame and the tires. Some bikes meant for racing will not accept anything but tubular tires. Most of these will take European 700C clinchers, but these are unobtainable in most parts of the U.S. If you expect to mount fenders, you will need additional clearance for them.

Be sure the dropouts—where the wheels attach—have eyelets for rack supports. Without these, it's nearly impossible to mount a carrier rack properly, and many racing frames do not have such eyelets.

Of course, the frame has to fit you; far better a cheap bike that fits you than an expensive one that doesn't. Stand in your bare feet, straight-kneed, and have somebody measure from crotch to floor. Subtract 10 inches from this, and you'll have your frame size within about an inch. More than an inch too small, and you'll have to raise your seat too high, resulting in a cramped, crouched-over position. Too big, and you might be in for some great pain. (If male, they say that in time you'd sing tenor beautifully, but it's hardly worth it.) If you happen to be a border-line case and there are two different standard sizes you could ride—if, say, you fall midway between a 23″ and a 24″—go for the smaller one. It will handle better and be safer.

If all this seems too complex and technical, don't let it throw you. Just use your eyes and common sense. Does the frame look solid and well made, without roughness or gaps at the joints? Sit on the saddle; can you reach the handlebars without an exaggerated forward-leaning position? (Remember that this can be corrected somewhat with a shorter stem.) Does the whole bike look very upright and eager (bad), or does it seem to be leaning backward (good)?

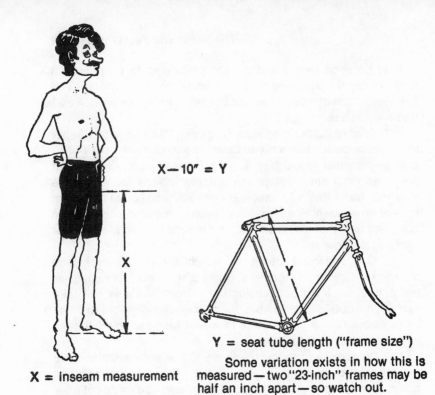

X — 10" = Y

X = inseam measurement

Y = seat tube length ("frame size")

Some variation exists in how this is measured — two "23-inch" frames may be half an inch apart — so watch out.

Eyelet for mounting rack

Some very fine racing frames lack eyelets

Common frame rear fork dropout

Racing frame rear fork dropout

To determine correct frame size, subtract 10 inches from your inseam measurement. This is only a rough rule and no substitute for personally trying out a bike. Note that your bike must have eyelets on the dropouts if you intend to attach touring racks.

If they'll let you test-ride the bike at all, try to feel whether it tries to pound you. It should have enough give to absorb road shocks, but it shouldn't feel spongy or whippy, because this will induce instability under load. Does it track steadily, or do you have to fight it all the time? In other words, do you feel comfortable and relaxed on this bike?

If they won't let you test-ride the bike, my main advice is to take your business elsewhere. If this isn't feasible, try this test. Standing beside the bike, grasp the seat post firmly in one hand and the stem in the other. Put the near pedal in the bottom position, put your foot against it, and shove pretty hard down and away from you. Don't overdo it; you can bend a cheap bike out of shape permanently! A good bike frame will push back against your foot; it will feel springy and alive. A clunker, with its dead, heavy tubing, will have no resilience at all; a racing bike will feel very stiff. Try this with several different bikes and you'll get the idea.

Most standard "club" bikes in the medium price range will have at least acceptable frame geometry, and some of the economy models, such as the Raleigh Grand Prix or Schwinn LeTour, are actually more suitable for our purposes than many of the very expensive bikes. It's mostly in the upper price brackets that the true racing frame appears, and that's the main one to watch out for. For that matter, some of the older racers, such as the Gitane Tour de France or the great old Peugeot PX-10, can be turned into very good touring bikes. These often turn up for sale secondhand.

Should you go the custom route, I suggest British builders, such as Bob Jackson or Jack Taylor; they have a long tradition of making bikes for just this sort of thing. If you've got the money and think you're going to get really serious about cycle camping, this might be your best answer. One nice thing is their readiness to braze on various fittings for racks, bottles, lights, fenders, and the like for very reasonable additional charges. These are fine things to have because they anchor the accessory solidly, and you don't chew up your paint with clamps and clips.

Wheels

Wheels are right up there with the frame in importance. Rotating weight will slow and fatigue you more than dead weight. Racers know that a heavy bike with light wheels is faster and easier to pedal than a light bike with heavy wheels.

But we can get too carried away with this idea. The racer's bike weighs only 22 pounds or so and carries no weight besides the rider, and its function is to win in a contest of speed in which fractions of a second mean victory or defeat.

For touring and camping, it's another story. When you hang 30 pounds of camping gear on the bike, a few extra ounces on the wheels just won't be all that critical. I don't mean that you can't tell the difference, or that you shouldn't try to keep wheel weight down, but don't go to the point of compromising reliability. Nobody's going to give you a trophy for getting to the campsite five minutes sooner, but you'll certainly feel stupid if you keep getting stopped by flats or broken spokes—and under some conditions you might get hurt, too.

Tires for cycle camping will almost certainly be the familiar "clincher" or "wired-on" type. Some touring is done on tubulars, but only by affluent cyclists on excellent paved roads. Even then it's a pretty impractical business.

Not that tubulars are necessarily flimsy or unreliable; good ones, like Clement silks, are very strong and puncture resistant, more so than some light clinchers. They're damnably expensive, but not everybody has to worry about that (or so I hear).

Tubulars present other problems on anything but smooth pavement. The high pressures and narrow profile that give them their remarkable low rolling resistance also give them a harsh ride, and the narrow tread is hard to control on gravel. They must be glued to the rim very solidly, and changing a tubular tire in rain, mud, or cold weather is a hellish, hellish job.

Some light, narrow-profile clinchers are now made. The more extreme designs, such as the famous Michelin Elan, are similar to tubulars in riding qualities and have just about the same problems, including a certain fragility. Most require a special rim, and if you destroy one a long way from a bike shop, you will play hell finding a replacement. To me, they represent the worst of both worlds.

I suggest you stay with regular 27" × 1¼" clincher tires. But don't be stingy and try to make do with those junky discount-store tires; get a good strong make such as Michelin or (my own usual choice) Schwinn LeTours.

There are 700C metric tires and wheels, the chief advantage of which is easy interchangeability with tubulars. But these types are not sold in the U.S. except at bike shops that handle

European equipment, and the rims won't take any standard American tire size, so you could have replacement problems if you ruined a tire on a backcountry tour. (If you're planning to tour Europe, though, this is their standard size.) The regular 27" × 1¼" can be found nowadays in hardware stores and even supermarkets in small towns all over the country; this is important on a long trip. True, you might have to use something pretty grim as a replacement—those cheap Taiwanese 27" tires sold in discount stores are terrible, and you can't pump them up very hard or they'll blow right off the rim—but it beats walking home. Or spending a week in a small town in Montana while your buddies back home mail you a new tire.

The 26" tires and wheels used on three-speeds aren't just for kids and Dutch housewives; they make an excellent rig for really rough country. The lower center of gravity gives superior handling qualities on dirt, gravel, or mud, and the wider-section tires give greatly improved traction. The ride is very comfortable, and the wheels are strong. They can be mounted on a regular frame, but you may have problems getting the brakes to reach the rims, and the bike will look funny. (Fenders will help mask those big gaps.) These wheels are very popular with tourists who travel in Mexico. Incidentally, 26" wheels are of some help to the short person.

Rims must be strong, but steel rims are unnecessary. Any good alloy rim, such as Super Champion, Weinmann, or Araya, will hold up under even very hard use if the wheel is correctly built. Ian Hibell, one of the great bikies of our time, has ridden all over the world on execrable roads—from Tierra del Fuego to Alaska, across the Sahara, through a Panama jungle where he had to hack a path with a machete—often in places where a broken wheel literally would have meant his life. He uses Weinmann alloy rims. Defense rests.

Steel rims are not just heavy, they're dangerous. When they get wet, they don't brake worth a damn—and it's in wet weather that you're most in need of reliable brakes. If your bike has steel-rimmed wheels and you can't afford to replace them, so be it, but a pair of alloy-rimmed wheels would be the best single modification you could make.

Until recently, steel rims were all you could get in 26" size, but the new mountain-bike movement has led some makers, such as Araya, to bring out excellent alloy rims in this useful size. A pair of 26" alloy-rimmed wheels should allow a bike to operate on dirt and gravel with great surefootedness and security, without inducing any really severe penalty in highway performance.

Hubs come in large-flange and small-flange models. The small-flange hubs will give a somewhat softer ride at the cost of a higher incidence of spoke breakage. A compromise: Use a large-flange in back and a small-flange up front, if you can find anyone willing to sell you a mixed set. Personally, I would rather put up with a little more road shock than fool with broken spokes, but others may feel otherwise.

As for makes and models, I like Dura-Ace because the bearings seem to keep out water and dirt unusually well, but it's really no big deal. Other premium brands are Campagnolo Record, Avocet, and SunTour Superbe. Less expensive but perfectly good touring hubs include Normandy, Campagnolo Nuovo Tipo (a very nice little hub for the price), and SunTour VX, among others. Some like the sealed-bearing hubs, such as Bullseye or Phil Wood, which do keep out water and dirt well, and eliminate maintenance problems—but they're quite expensive and roll a teeny bit stiffer.

Wheels with 36 spokes laced 3-cross are standard, and these are fine for any reasonable use if properly tensioned and kept true. On very long, rough trips with a heavy rider and lots of gear, the British system of 40 spokes in back has merit, but 40-hole rims and hubs aren't easy to obtain in the U.S. nowadays.

Again, don't let all the technology buffalo you. If you own a good bike of any sort, it probably came with perfectly good wheels—barring the matter of steel rims just discussed—and you may never have to replace them. If the ones you have give good service, leave them alone. In my observations, most of the broken spokes and other wheel failures one sees are due to improper construction by self-taught amateur "mechanics" rather than any particular choice of components.

The Power Train

Looked at objectively, the derailleur system is ridiculous. The idea of shoving a drive chain off one moving cog onto another is as scientifically absurd as—well, as the idea that a human being could sit atop a two-wheeled vehicle without falling over. . . .

Most bikes used in camping and touring employ a ten-speed setup: two big chainwheels up front and a five-cog cluster in the back. Actually, this creates eight usable combinations, not ten. Owing to mechanical problems induced by excess chain offset, the big chainwheel should not be used in combination with the biggest cog, nor the small chainwheel with the smallest cog.

Some riders are now using a six-cog cluster, which gives two more speeds. (They call it a "12-speed," but actually, due to the problem just mentioned, it's simply the first *real* "ten-speed.") This arrangement, however, tends to weaken the back wheel and increase spoke breakage. The new Sun Tour Ultra Six system is supposed to get around this problem, but it does require the use of a special thin chain. There are even seven-cog blocks for real fanatics. The chief problem so far has been the tendency of manufacturers to build up these multiple blocks as racing sets, with the extra cog used to develop a higher gear rather than a lower one. However, the Ultra Six is apparently now available in a touring block with a 34-tooth low. I think I'm about to buy one myself. The advantage would be having closer spacings between high and low gears, which should be more comfortable to pedal.

In theory, you get 15 speeds with three chainwheels. This enables you to use very low gears without unpleasant wide jumps between gears. There is also a certain mad "class" in owning a 15-speed. (With a seven-cog block, you could tell everybody you had a 21-speed bike.) Actually, you don't get 15 speeds; not only is the chain-offset problem increased, but some duplication is almost unavoidable. Setting up a 15 involves considerable math and a lot of knowledge of cycling mechanics.

You might like the 15-speed, though. It's a lot of fun to play with if you enjoy complex mechanisms but a nightmare if you don't. I had one once, and I suspect I'm about to convert Anna Marie to one. But don't even think about it if you're still new to cycling. A 15-speed is very much a handful, and the conversion can run into quite a few bucks.

The old-fashioned, cottered, steel crankset seems to have been removed from the scene, except on the cheapest bikes, though you might acquire a used bike with one. It had its virtues—notably strength—but it was heavy and an absolute beast to work on, and sometimes it liked to rust.

Most good bikes now come with alloy cotterless cranksets, and these are generally very well made and serviceable—though a few of the cheapest stamped-and-swaged Japanese cranks may be a bit too weak for big strong riders in rugged country. Most of the flimsier ones, however, have pretty much vanished from the U.S. market.

If you want even reasonably wide-range gearing for mountain travel, the cranksets designed for racing are very frustrating. The otherwise incomparable Campagnolo Nuovo Record goes no lower than 42 teeth, owing to the length of the spider arms; the same is true of Campy copies such as Sugino's popular Mighty Compe sets. With such a setup, the only way you can get low mountain gears is to fit a big heavy "granny" cluster in back, with a long-armed derailleur to wrap all that sloppy chain, and even then your lowest gear won't be all that low. With the biggest cog on the market, a 34-toother, and a 42-tooth chainwheel, your lowest gear will only be 33.3", which is far from wall-climbing class. (If you don't understand all this stuff about gear ratios, hang in there; we'll be explaining the Great Gear Mystery in the next few pages.)

Other makes are more appropriate, if you've got a choice. The fine old Stronglight 93 went down to 38 teeth, the same as the newer Stronglight 105 and 104. (The latter is found as stock on the Peugeot UO-10, which is a *very* decent little bike for cycle camping at a reasonable price.) Sugino makes a Mighty Tour with a 34-tooth minimum, which is getting down there, and the SR Super Apex can be had clear down to 28 teeth; both of these makes can be set up as triples if you want a 15-speed, and both are low-priced units—real bargains in fact.

Most versatile of all is the T.A. Cyclotouriste; chainrings are made in a fantastic range—55 to 26 teeth—and it can be set up as a triple. The average casual cyclist may not want to get that involved, but if you're building up a really fine touring/camping bike, you couldn't go wrong with the T.A. Cyclotouriste. And it isn't a particularly expensive unit. As we keep seeing, expensive isn't necessarily best in this business.

Freewheels in themselves are not a critical item, in that one make seems to work as well as another. (A technical note of possible interest: Do not screw a splined Shimano freewheel onto a Dura-Ace hub or you'll play hell getting it off.)

What *is* important—and this is something you may well want to change even if your bike is otherwise okay—is the size of the cogs on the freewheel cluster. If you're going to ride anywhere but on the plains, you will want to have a bottom gear low enough to get up any mountains within reason; you will also want high enough gears to take advantage of tailwinds and downhills, though this last can be carried to dangerous extremes. Somewhere in the middle there should be a moderate gear that is comfortable for you to use on level ground over long periods. You'll find you do 90% of your cycling in this gear, under most conditions, so it deserves some attention.

Ideally, all of your gears should be evenly and closely spaced, within the limits of the possible, so that you can get a comfortable combination for most normal situations. That is, you don't want to get stuck with one of those setups that constantly force you to choose between breaking your legs in a gorilla gear or overspinning like a mad hummingbird. Great big changes in pedal resistance can be pretty painful to the legs.

It is *not* vital that the gears be set up so as to give exact jumps according to some formula or to make an elegant pattern on a graph. Despite the Alpine range of tables, figures, and formulas published on this subject, most of it is "paper cycling," theoretical exercises only. Most cyclists do the greater part of their cycling in one or two favorite medium gears that they find comfortable, shift all the way up on steep downhills and all the way down on steep climbs (and, no matter *what* they've got, they wish before they reach the top that they had something lower!), and use the other gears for somewhat oddball situations or to compensate for wind conditions.

I go into all this because a lot of "authorities" have made very doctrinaire statements about what gear setups you should use, and as it happens, no two of them agree, so beginners tend to get confused. Don't. Most of these people are simply very avid cyclists who enjoy fooling with their bikes and playing with different gears. Nothing wrong with that—you may be that sort yourself, in which case you'll have endless fun, as will the guy who sells you all this stuff. But don't be misled into thinking you're in trouble if your gear setup doesn't match Professor Gearloose's neat little table in the latest issue of *Obsessive-Compulsive Cycling*.

Let's pause here for a short explanation of terms, for the benefit of those who are still new to cycling. In discussing bicycle gearing, what we are talking about mainly is the ratio between the front (chainwheel) and rear (cog): The greater the difference between the number of teeth fore and aft, the higher the gear; and the less the difference, the lower the gear. This is, of course, very important in setting up a bike for mountain touring. If you had a 34-tooth chainwheel and a 34-tooth cog, the wheel would go

Number of teeth on rear cog

Number of teeth on chainwheel

Rear cog \ Chainwheel	28	32	34	36	38	39	40	42	44	45	46	47	48	49	50	51	52	53	54
34	22.2	25.4	27	28.5	30.1	30.9	31.7	33.3	34.9	35.7	36.5	37.3	38.1	38.9	39.7	40.5	41.2	42	42.8
32	23.6	27	28.7	30.4	32.1	32.9	33.8	35.4	37.1	38	38.8	39.7	40.5	41.3	42.2	43	43.9	44.7	45.6
30	25.2	28.8	30.6	32.4	34.2	35.1	36	37.8	39.6	40.5	41.4	42.3	43.2	44.1	45	45.9	46.8	47.7	48.6
28	27	30.8	32.7	34.7	36.6	37.6	38.5	40.5	42.4	43.3	44.3	45.3	46.2	47.2	48.2	49.1	50.1	51.1	52
26	29	33.2	35.3	37.3	39.4	40.5	41.5	43.6	45.6	46.7	47.7	48.8	49.8	50.8	51.9	52.9	54	55	56
25	30.2	34.5	36.7	38.8	41	42.1	43.2	45.3	47.5	48.6	49.6	50.7	51.8	52.9	54	55	56.1	57.2	58.3
24	31.5	36	38.2	40.5	42.7	43.8	45	47.2	49.5	50.6	51.7	52.8	54	55.1	56.2	57.3	58.5	59.6	60.7
23	32.8	37.5	39.9	42.2	44.6	45.7	46.9	49.3	51.6	52.8	54	55.1	56.3	57.5	58.6	59.8	61	62.2	63.3
22	34.3	39.2	41.7	44.1	46.6	47.8	49	51.5	54	55.2	56.4	57.6	58.9	60.1	61.3	62.5	63.8	65	66.2
21	36	41.1	43.7	46.2	48.8	50.1	51.4	54	56.5	57.8	59.1	60.4	61.7	63	64.2	65.5	66.8	68.1	69.4
20	37.8	43.2	45.9	48.6	51.3	52.6	54	56.7	59.4	60.7	62.1	63.4	64.8	66.1	67.5	68.8	70.2	71.5	72.9
19	39.8	45.4	48.3	51.1	54	55.4	56.8	59.6	62.5	63.9	65.3	66.7	68.2	69.6	71	72.4	73.8	75.3	76.7
18	42	48	51	54	57	58.5	60	63	66	67.5	69	70.5	72	73.5	75	76.5	78	79.5	81
17	44.4	50.8	54	57.1	60.3	61.9	63.5	66.7	69.8	71.4	73	74.6	76.2	77.8	79.4	81	82.5	84.1	85.7
16	47.2	54	57.3	60.7	64.1	65.8	67.5	70.8	74.2	75.9	77.6	79.3	81	82.6	84.3	86	87.7	89.4	91.1
15	50.4	57.6	61.2	64.8	68.4	70.2	72	75.6	79.2	81	82.8	84.6	86.4	88.2	90	91.8	93.6	95.4	97.2
14	54	61.7	65.5	69.4	73.2	75.2	77.1	81	84.8	86.7	88.7	90.6	92.5	94.5	96.4	98.3	100.2	102.2	104.1

around once each time you cranked the pedals, and you could just about ride up the side of a house, an entirely possible and not unknown arrangement.

There are various ways of expressing this power ratio, but the most common in this country is the Equivalent Wheel Diameter (EWD) system, in which gears are expressed in inches. This is a hangover from the old days when they rode those high-wheel jobs with the pedals directly attached to the wheel; the size of the wheel determined the rider's leverage and pedal efficiency. When they invented drive chains, they used the EWD system to relate the new drive to what people were used to, and it stuck.

So when we speak of a 67″ gear, we mean you get the same linear travel per pedal rotation as if you were riding an old-fashioned bike with a 67″ front wheel. Sounds silly, of course, but then a "foot" was once the King's shoe size!

There is a common misconception that "inches" refers to how far the bike rolls with each pedal rotation; this is entirely wrong. (Europeans do figure gears that way, but in metric.) EWD inches can be determined by the following formula:

$$\frac{\text{teeth on chainwheel}}{\text{teeth on rear cog}} \times \text{wheel diameter in inches} = \text{EWD}$$

Obviously, to get a lower gear, we can either use a smaller chainwheel, or a larger rear cog, or both, and there will be several possible combinations that will give the same ratio. To some extent, this will be determined by the limitations of our other equipment, such as the range of chainwheel sizes available for a given make of crankset, or the capacity of the derailleur. How much money and work we want to put in will influence our decision too.

Derailleurs (to get ahead of ourselves a minute) are limited in two interrelated ways. A given make of derailleur will have a listed "range"; the catalog or spec sheet will say, perhaps, "capacity 14–28, total capacity 30 teeth," or the like. This may look complicated, but it isn't. The first figure simply tells you how big a cluster it can handle, that is, how large a cog the

Chart on opposite page shows gears in Equivalent Wheel Diameter (EWD) for most commonly available combinations with standard equipment. However, not all chainwheel or rear cog sizes are available for all makes; check specifications.

derailleur can make the chain climb onto. If you exceed this limit, you may damage the mechanism and probably won't get it to shift anyway. "Total capacity" refers to how much slack chain the derailleur can wrap up. This is determined by the length of that swinging arm with the little pulleys on it that hangs down there, and by the tension of the main spring.

So, using the case just listed as an example, 14 from 28 is 14, and 14 from 30 is 16, which tells us that the pair of chainwheels up front can't be more than 16 teeth apart. For example, if the big chainwheel is a 52-toother, the little one cannot have less than 36 teeth if we want the whole weird-looking mishmash to work right.

But note that it doesn't matter what size the chainwheels are, as long as the total *difference* is the same. So here we get back to what we've been talking about with the gears: If we want a lower gear, we could replace *both* chainwheels and not have to worry about any of this other stuff. If we wanted a lower gear than 36 × 28 teeth (34.7"), in the example, replacing the cog cluster with anything bigger would force us to buy a new derailleur as well, to say nothing of various mechanical problems; but if we replaced both chainwheels with, say, a 48 and a 32, everything would continue to work and nothing else would have to be replaced, assuming our crankset will take chainwheels that small. Also, of course, going to smaller chainwheels makes the bike lighter, while adding big cogs and a long-armed derailleur makes it quite a bit heavier, and more complicated. Now you see why we went on so much about cranksets.

Of course, you lose gear range at the top this way, but what of that? Factory bikes nearly all come with a 52 × 14 top gear (100.2"), but this is unnecessary and even dangerous for touring; you can only wind it up on a downhill, and you shouldn't do that with a loaded bike. Something in the low 90s or upper 80s is plenty high enough. In fact, a cycle camper whose top gear is only 82" or so will not be really handicapped.

How low should your gears go? Most people find that in anything but flat terrain, something in the low- to mid-30s is needed, or at least awfully nice to have. The 34.7" gear in the above example is okay for moderately hilly country with a minimal load of equipment; in real mountains or on a long trip with a lot of cargo, something lower, around 30"–32", would be even better. A glance at a gear chart and a study of catalogs will show you that only a few makes of crankset will let you get into this range without using a big 34-tooth cog, and only a few derailleurs will handle a cog that big. (Economics do come into it here. It is admittedly cheaper to replace the freewheel cluster and rear derailleur than to replace the entire crankset—though if your crankset is such that you can replace just the chainwheels, this is the option cheapest of all.)

But take heart if all this is getting you down. Most stock bikes of the nonracing variety come with a 14–28 cluster, a big chainwheel of 52 teeth, and a small one of 40 or occasionally 42 (39 in a few lucky cases). This setup, while not ideal for true Alpine conditions, is fully adequate for most U.S. roads, except in the really big mountains. Indeed, it can be used anywhere in the country, if you're willing to walk the bike up some of the longer or steeper pitches. This is not a felony; in fact, it gives your back, and backside, a nice rest. A 40 × 28 arrangement gives you 38.5″; you can climb some pretty big hills in that gear if you're in shape. Just concentrate on eliminating unnecessary weight from your camping kit.

Super-low gears below 30″ are rarely necessary, and in fact, it's hard to balance a loaded bike while twiddling along so slowly. But they're kind of fun to play with, and if you're going on dirt roads in the hills, you may need something like this—dirt roads are graded much more steeply than paved ones, and loose surfaces call for lower gears.

As I keep saying, individuals must consider their own needs. A strong young rider, one who rides a lot and perhaps does some racing, may feel even a 35″ gear is effete and unnecessary. But a middle-aged man with bad knees (such as the author) may well have a real need for the stump-puller "grandmaw" gear, and should not feel embarrassed about getting it.

A rough rule to keep in mind: On a long trip, with the bike fully loaded, you will usually find yourself needing to gear one "jump" lower than you would for the same situation on a no-load, Sunday afternoon ride with the local touring club.

Derailleurs

We've already seen how these things affect our gearing setup. As we saw, with the correct chainwheel set it is possible to go on using a light, fast-acting, narrow-range racing derailleur, such as the Campagnolo Nuovo Record. Such a unit will work better and require less adjustment and maintenance.

(continued on page 36)

Gearing for Backcountry Touring

Your basic suffering overloaded bikie

Your basic steep hill

In order to get low gears for this . . .

we must decrease the difference in size between

this   and   this . . .

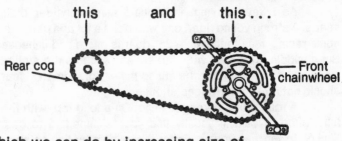

Rear cog

Front chainwheel

which we can do by increasing size of

this . . .

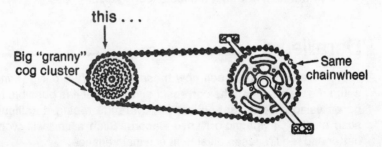

Big "granny" cog cluster

Same chainwheel

which, however, adds weight and mechanical complexity —
and is easily damaged or fouled by mud and brush . . .

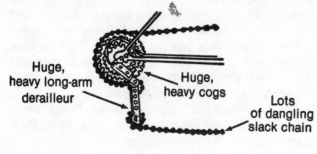

Huge,
heavy long-arm
derailleur

Huge,
heavy cogs

Lots
of dangling
slack chain

or . . .

we can instead make this smaller . . .

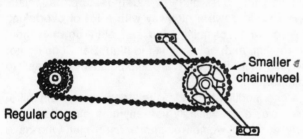

Smaller
chainwheel

Regular cogs

producing light, compact, reliable set-up —
rugged and easily maintained.

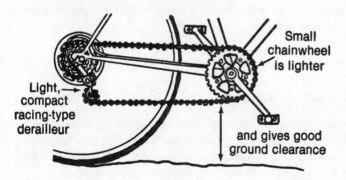

Small
chainwheel
is lighter

Light,
compact
racing-type
derailleur

and gives good
ground clearance

Still, most camper-tourists want a bit more range. SunTour makes a line of inexpensive and well-made touring derailleurs that should be the choice of anyone who has to watch expenses. If you've got more money to spend, try the Campagnolo Rally (the Rolls-Royce of touring derailleurs, and priced accordingly) or the Shimano Crane GT. Either of these will handle a wider range of gears than anyone is likely to need—they'll go to a 36-tooth cog, which nobody even makes any more—and they work very smoothly for a derailleur of this type. But a SunTour VX-GT or a Shimano Titlist will cover the same range at a fraction of the cost. I use the Titlist myself and can't understand why it isn't more popular; it's a very fine unit at an attractive price.

Don't get more derailleur than you need. These wide-range units are intended to be used with wide-range cogs; they perform very, very poorly with close-range, small-cog clusters.

Whatever derailleur you use, I strongly recommend getting a set of Sun Tour Bar-Con shifters, which mount at the ends of the handlebars. They let you shift gears without removing a hand from the bars. Obviously this is a wonderful safety feature, especially when you have to ride down a highway with a lot of overtaking auto traffic. Also, when climbing, you can shift down without breaking your rhythm, and, being mounted high, Bar-Cons do not get fouled by mud or brush. They are inexpensive and easy to mount and adjust.

This is one modification I definitely endorse for *any* bike-packer's bike. I would not willingly use anything else. Bar-Cons are particularly good for women or short-armed men who have trouble reaching down for regular frame-mounted shifters. (Shift levers mounted at the handlebar stem are very poor; they give imprecise shifts and form a hazard to the groin in the event of a crash or sudden stop.) And they are the only shifters that really work well on a mixte frame.

Pedals

Pedals should be wide for comfort, especially if you wear Batas or joggers. Some racing pedals are uncomfortably narrow. "Rat-trap" teeth, seen on older designs, are unnecessary with cleats, but provide some useful grip with uncleated shoes.

Lyotard makes some first-rate touring pedals at rock-bottom prices. Steel pedals are cheaper than alloy and more durable, and the difference in weight is not really all that important.

Toe straps and clips greatly increase pedaling power and efficiency, and reduce knee soreness, by holding the foot in the same position all the way around the stroke. There is also less chance of the foot coming off the pedal, a very good safety feature when the shoe or pedal are slippery with rain or mud. Get them and learn to use them, but make sure the clips are long enough for your feet.

Toe clips and straps are not dangerous, nor will you have trouble getting your feet out for a sudden stop unless you foolishly jerk the straps down way too tight. Just a sharp tug up and back, and out you come. Nothing to it. Getting into the things may take a little practice, but it's well worth it. I have even fitted toe clips to clunkers, such as my old Dutch three-speed, and was greatly impressed by the improvement.

Seats

Seats are another controversial matter—I almost said "sensitive area"—that too. Narrow racing saddles of bare or thinly covered nylon are out, of course. Even the type of racing saddle with a leather covering and foam padding is not much better. The problem is that racers and tourists just don't sit on their bikes in the same way. Weight comes on a different part of the saddle and the body, so shape has to be quite different. Makers such as Avocet now offer contoured and padded saddles designed especially for touring use, and this is probably the best answer for most people. Some of these companies also make saddles meant for women. Since women definitely do have special needs in this area, for reasons we hardly need go into, they should look into these products. But be sure to get the models made for touring.

Leather saddles have enormous class and will break in to fit any build or style, if you can stand about a year of pain in the process. I use the old Brooks Pro and wouldn't use any substitute, but I've been breaking mine in for seven or eight years now—if I lost it, I don't know if I could face a new one, or, rather, back up to it. Ideale is another good make of leather saddle, said to be a good choice for women.

The trouble with leather for cycle camping is that it is easily ruined by the wet and mud; if you ride a leather saddle while it's wet, you can ruin its shape forever. A plastic bag and a rubber band will help, but basically I'm afraid I have to recommend something else, despite my own practice.

Fat mattress saddles are no good for long rides, as they chafe the thighs and weigh a ton.

Saddle problems often arise from improper adjustment in position rather than any particular make or material. A micro-adjusting seatpost, such as Campagnolo or SR, is very much worth having.

There was a song, "Don't give me no plastic saddles," but I don't think it had anything to do with bicycle camping.

Bars and Stem

Modern dropped handlebars, as we have so often been told, provide the most comfortable, efficient, and versatile range of positions for the average rider. You can assume several different positions with these bars, which relieves back fatigue and hand numbness; you can sit up to look around or hunker way over to burrow into a headwind. Unless they suffer from back trouble, people who find dropped bars clumsy or uncomfortable usually have the bike set up wrong—saddle too far back, stem too long, or the bike may simply be too big. Check these things before giving up.

The most common style of dropped bar is the Maes road-racing pattern. This is the kind in which the top part is absolutely horizontal and then swings down and around to form the hooks. This is a good, serviceable design, but a better bar for touring is the "randonneur" style. In this type, the horizontal part of the bar sweeps upward somewhat before turning down. This allows you to sit up quite a bit more, giving your back some relief and making it easier to look around at the scenery; yet you still have the full-dropped position available for headwinds or down-hilling. Few bikes have these as original equipment, but they don't cost much; the Schwinn LeTour bikes do come with randonneur bars, and a Schwinn dealer can get them for you and usually will sell the bar alone. People with small hands may have trouble reaching the brake levers with randonneurs, since the curvature is rather peculiar.

Short women who ride inexpensive stock bikes may not be able to live with dropped bars at all. Except for mixtes, the forward reach on most 19″ stock frames is excessive, even with a

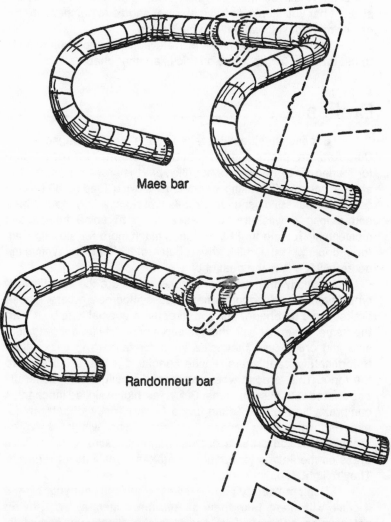

Maes bar

Randonneur bar

Two types of handlebar configurations. The Maes bar (top), which is standard on most ten-speeds, has a straight top part. The randonneur bar (bottom) has a top that is upswept, permitting a more upright position. With either type, bar width should be at least equal to shoulder width.

minimum-reach stem. It may draw the scorn of the trendy, but if you find a regular flat bar more comfortable, use it and the hell with them. Tourists do 90% of their riding on top anyway. On a rough-surface road, the straight bar may even give you a bit better control. The bar found on French mixtes is a good design, as is the British "all rounder" or North Road style. But if you use a straight bar you'll have to have a softer saddle to compensate for having more of your weight on your behind.

As for stems, the make is irrelevant. The important thing is to get the right length. More on this in another chapter.

Brakes

Expensive sidepull brakes, such as Campagnolo and Dura-Ace, are pretty and light, but they're better for racing than for touring. They do work beautifully, but they aren't great for the steady on-and-off braking needed to slow a loaded bike on a downhill. Tourists *must* have *excellent* brakes; a fully loaded bike and a long downstairs run can add up to some humongous momentum. Touring brakes are used much more for slowing than for stopping. I still think the regular old Mafac or Weinmann centerpull brake is the best choice.

Actually, the very finest brakes of all are the "cantilever" type favored by tandem owners and cyclocross racers. These brakes have no bridge, but bolt directly to special lugs built onto the frame. Leverage with them is enormous, they do not get full of mud and brush, and their clearance for fenders is unexcelled. Unfortunately, cantilevers require special lugs that are brazed to the forks. This is done when the frame is built, and is generally associated with custom bikes. But, a few highly skilled mechanics can braze lugs to an existing frame (a very tricky job, strictly for experts, which also means that the frame will have to be repainted). If you order a custom frame, be sure to have them braze on the fittings for cantilever brakes—you'll never regret it. They're light, too.

Don't fit "safety" brake lever extensions onto your bike; if it came with them, take them off and throw them away. They do not develop adequate leverage to brake effectively, especially with a loaded bike, and in any case, they interfere with fitting a handlebar bag. If you can't reach a pair of conventional brake levers, your bike is set up wrong, or you need to go to a flat handlebar.

Brake cables must be first quality, such as Campagnolo or other braided cables. Don't trust your life to those twisted-picture-wire cheapo cables. One very good product is the Teflon-lined brake-cable housings made by various companies. These improve brake action and require little maintenance.

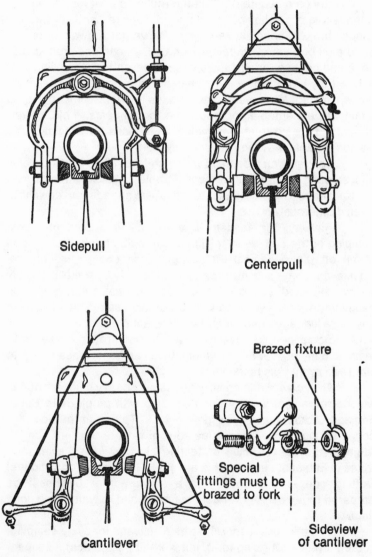

Sidepull

Centerpull

Brazed fixture

Special fittings must be brazed to fork

Sideview of cantilever

Cantilever

Three types of bike brakes.

Odd Stuff

Before closing this discussion of the touring bike, here's a word or two about some of the farther-out alternatives.

Tandems are fascinating machines that have a technology all their own. Couples often find the togetherness of a tandem very appealing; it seems like such a romantic idea to go cycling about the country on a two-seater. But the reality is a bit less romantic. A tandem is a mechanical nightmare. It requires special wheels, special brakes, special everything. You've got the weight of two people on one set of wheels, which causes endless problems. A good one costs a fortune and a cheap one isn't worth having; and only a truly expert bicycle mechanic has a prayer of keeping a tandem rolling. Moreover, many couples have difficulty arriving at a mutually acceptable approach to riding tandems. A big, powerful, gutsy type up front may make life hideous for a small, timid person in back; they may never really work it out.

Tandems also demand very high-level bike-handling skills, and steering them requires considerable physical strength and coordination. They build up tremendous speeds on downhills, often dangerously so.

Anyway, the tandem is pretty much a bust for cycle camping of the sort we're talking about in this book. It's no good at all off the pavement—it will give you enough mechanical trouble as it is—and its great weight and bulk make it terribly awkward around a camp. There's really no way to carry enough camping gear for two people on a tandem since it doesn't have any more luggage space than a single-seat bicycle.

Some people have managed to get around these problems, and my helmet is off to them, but in all conscience I have to warn you away from tandems.

Tricycles in this country are usually heavy clunkers ridden around retirement villages by old ladies with purple hair. But in England, some master builders—Jack Taylor in particular—construct wonderful three-wheeled lightweights that are comparable to the finest racing or touring bicycle. (They even race trikes in England; I am told it is a sight to take years off your life.) Getting one in this country is a special-order business; be prepared to lay out a great deal of money and to wait a long, long time.

The trike is not entirely to be dismissed for cycle camping. In fact, it has a lot going for it. If it weren't for the cost, I suspect

I'd have one myself by now. Its three-point stability must certainly be an advantage on bad roads. You can get off it, and it just stands there, with no need for a kickstand or anything to lean it against. The layout of the back end is such that quite a lot of luggage can be carried in a very stable, solid manner. (I've never seen it done, but there can't be any real reason why you couldn't work out a way to carry a regular frame backpack on a tricycle—something a lot of us would like to be able to do on our bikes, and which has resisted the best efforts of many people to date.) Since the weight is distributed over three wheels instead of two, there should be less spoke breakage, the tires should last longer, and a sudden blowout shouldn't be quite as catastrophic as on a bike. You've even got those big wheels right there to fend off heel-snapping dogs.

Despite what you might think, though, the trikes' advantages do not include ease of handling. They corner like nothing on earth—you have to lean to the outside on turns, against all bicycling instinct. Maintenance and repair are a whole different ball game—parts are almost impossible to get in this country except through import, and few American cycle shops are capable of servicing trikes. Nor is the three-wheeler easy to carry atop a car, take up an elevator or stairway, or store in an apartment, to say nothing of putting it in the trunk of a VW. It's definitely not a purchase to make lightly.

Now that we've got you fixed up with your bike, let's take a look at *you.*

CHAPTER **2**

_____ **Threads**

What to wear? As with the bike and its accessories, there are conflicts, complexities, and compromises inherent in the final choice, with much depending on individual circumstances.

The bicycle camper is in a peculiar position here, and in fact there are problems that have no parallel in any other branch of camping except perhaps ski touring. He or she has to have clothing appropriate for two totally different situations; what is comfortable for riding may be very awkward to wear around camp, and vice versa. Yet the cyclist does not have a lot of room to carry much in the way of changes of clothes. To keep weight and bulk to a minimum, every single item carried has to serve as many purposes as possible, truly a knotty problem.

Admittedly, plenty of bikepackers and other nonracing cyclists do not find this any problem at all. They simply hop aboard the bike in whatever is handy—a T-shirt and a pair of running shorts or cutoffs, or even simply an ordinary outfit of street or work shirt and pants. The same sort of rig they'd wear for a casual hike, in other words, with perhaps a pair of running shoes or even sneakers. Within limits, this remains a valid approach. I do it myself quite often on short trips, or on rough-country runs where clothing takes a beating. It's certainly a cheap way to go, and clothing of this type is easy to care for and can be washed and dried in any laundromat. These same clothes can be worn in camp, so only one change is needed over all.

On the other hand, dedicated cyclists, for whom high-performance cycling is the main point of the whole trip, go the opposite route. They copy the road racer's outfit: knitted jersey, chamois-lined black shorts, and cleated leather shoes. This type of ensemble is very expensive (as many a novice racer has been appalled to learn) and demands considerable special attention and care, particularly in keeping the shorts clean. It is also rather uncomfortable off the bike and, indeed, totally impractical for most of the activities the average bikepacker must carry out. The shoes in particular are miserable beyond belief for walking even a few steps. So an outfit of extra clothing must be carried for in-camp wear, and this additional weight distinctly reduces the possible added efficiency.

Still, that added efficiency is there, and it's hard to ignore. The snug fit of jersey and shorts greatly lessens wind resistance,

Two approaches.

something to think about on a trip across open, windy plains. The shoes transmit power without wasting it, and the whole rig is supremely comfortable *on the bike*.

A lot of us, maybe most, fit somewhere between these extremes. We use some racing-type items, or something similar, where the advantages clearly outweigh the problems. Yet we're willing to sacrifice absolute efficiency for greater convenience and versatility, not to mention economy. So, let's look at the picture a bit at a time, as we did the bicycle.

Shoes

As with the hiker or jogger, shoes are *the* critical item of clothing. The shoe, after all, forms the interface of power between the rider and the machine, a bad place to lose energy. Also, stresses on material and construction are considerable. But for the bikepacker, this is a very difficult problem to resolve. Unlike the racer or even the day-tripping tourer, we *have* to be able to do a fair amount of walking. Walking and cycling do not have anything like the same requirements in footwear design, nor do they impose the same stresses. So any one of the various alternatives must necessarily involve some degree of compromise.

In terms of pure cycling efficiency, there's no question about it. The traditional cleated leather shoe worn by racers has it all over everything else. Its rigid sole, stiffened by a metal or composition shank, transmits *all* of the power of the leg muscles to the pedal, without wastage. Its nailed-on or built-in cleats grip the pedal cage in order to fix the foot in a solid, unchanging position that induces a smooth, strong pedal motion and eliminates slippage. Once broken in, these close-fitting shoes of soft, supple leather are extremely comfortable while riding. Ventilation holes allow sweat to evaporate in hot weather and allow rain water to run out, eliminating squishiness.

Unfortunately, once the rider dismounts and takes a few hobbling steps, the disadvantages of this fine item become painfully obvious. It would be hard to devise a more uncomfortable and, indeed, downright painful shoe to walk on or even stand around in, and there is a considerable risk of slipping and falling on your keister on most surfaces. As far as walking in them goes, the shoes seem to have been designed by a professional sadist.

Nor is it just a matter of personal comfort. Cycling shoes of this type are not made to be walked in, and if you subject them to very much pedestrian activity, they will quickly become soft, loose, and floppy, thereby losing any real advantage over ordinary tennis shoes. And cleats will crack or come off if walked on very much.

Despite these and other problems (for one thing, as Lord Chesterfield said about something else, the expense is damnable), many, many hard-riding bikies use racing shoes exclusively. They carry a second pair of shoes for walking or wearing in camp and consider that the added power and efficiency more than compensate for the extra weight and trouble. One such die-hard said to me, "Half the time when you see a tourist doing any real walking, he's having to push his bike up a hill that he could have *ridden* over if he'd worn proper shoes"—rather overstated, but a good point withal. Cyclists who plan to cover really big distances—coast-to-coast, say—or to cross major mountain ranges, or those whose primary interest is in cycling for its own sake, will probably end up going the cleated-shoe route.

If you do, be very careful in fitting yourself. Most of these shoes are made on the Continent and tend to be quite narrow, and metric sizes are a Byzantine labyrinth in which strong men have broken down and wept. Detto Pietro is a popular and reasonably priced brand; Adidas racing shoes are nice but rather light for touring (and they self-destruct if walked on). Dutch Medalists are cheap and solid.

Deep-grooved, hooflike cleats are unnecessary and clumsy. The alloy track type is adequate and cheap; even nylon cleats can be used if you're very careful not to walk on them. Some experimenting is necessary to get the cleats positioned correctly. The ball of the foot is supposed to go right over the pedal spindle, but many tourists like the toe just a tiny bit farther forward than this. (If the toe clip gets in the way, you can space it out with a few washers.) On longer trips, carry a spare set of cleats and a supply of nails.

Some old-school tourists modify the basic racing shoe by adding a low heel (any shoe shop can do this) and sometimes a thin rubber sole. They leave off the usual cleats and instead nail a couple of strips of leather to do the same job, or they file a shallow groove in the sole. Such improvisations seem to work all right, but don't expect miracles—no racing shoe will ever be fun to walk on.

People who can't accept these problems have until recently had to wear some sort of sneakers or running shoes. These are indeed very pleasant and comfortable to walk in, but there is a considerable loss of efficiency during cycling. Every time the foot pushes the pedal, it has to compress the sole material before any power gets to the bike. This wastes much energy. And if you spend your days stomping a loaded bike over mountains or windy flats, you get to be very stingy about your personal energy supply. In addition, the toe straps and clips tend to chew holes in these shoes, which can become expensive over the years.

Spongy-soled tennis shoes or the cheapest sort of pseudo-running shoes are pretty hopeless. The sole is just too thin and soft to protect you. With every stroke, the sharp-edged pedal

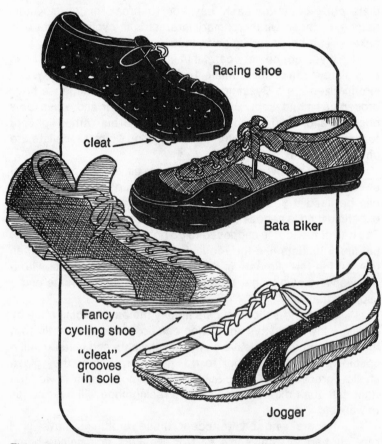

Racing shoe

cleat

Bata Biker

Fancy cycling shoe

"cleat" grooves in sole

Jogger

Three styles of cycling shoes compared to popular jogging style.

cage presses painfully against the sole of the foot. Also, the flimsy materials and construction may leave you barefoot halfway through your first trip. Such shoes aren't even much good for *walking* anywhere except on a gym floor. Even a pair of leather street shoes would be better.

Somewhat better "joggers," usually made in Korea and sold in discount stores under such names as Pro Champ, are not too bad and will do reasonably well for all but long, severe trips—though they won't last more than one season if you ride much. The top-grade running shoes, such as Puma or Adidas, are quite good; the sole is stiff enough to give you some solid support while pedaling hard up a hill, yet the shoe is very comfortable to walk in and durable enough for any normal cycling use. Medium-priced jogging or running shoes are probably the overall favorite among most U.S. bike campers today, partly because such people often jog or run as well and like to be able to use the same shoes for both.

In recent years, a third alternative has appeared. Various makers now offer sneakerlike shoes specifically designed for cycling, with stiffened soles and reinforced uppers. The idea has caught on very strongly in touring circles as a combination of some of the advantages of both worlds, and new makes seem to appear every month. The most popular make currently is the Bata shoe, with its ugly black canvas uppers and functional, no-frills design. As they say, not much for pretty but hell for stout. Batas are quite cheap as such things go. I consider them an outstanding buy, especially if you have a tight budget or are going into muddy areas where shoes may be ruined.

More sophisticated shoes of this general type are made by such well-known concerns as Avocet and Detto Pietro. These models usually have suede uppers, though smooth-finished leather would repel water better and be much easier to keep clean. They probably would be better for winter wear than the canvas Batas. The Detto Pietro version even has a grooved Vibram sole designed to grip the pedal cage, so that you have a kind of crude "cleat" effect. Prices, as you might guess, are quite high, comparable to regular racing shoes or the better joggers. But for long-range or heavy-duty use, these are probably the best answer, if you can afford them.

For most cycle camping trips, these combination shoes—either the basic Batas or the fancier versions—are what I recommend. Efficiency is still less than with cleated racing shoes, but the improvement over regular sneakers or jogging shoes is enormous. You can wear the same shoes for riding, pushing the bike over unrideably rough or steep bits, exploring the area on foot, or poking around camp. (I've even done some pretty fair low-level rock climbing in a pair of Batas, though I certainly don't recommend it.) I've never seen it worked out on paper, but I'm sure it could be shown that the weight saving—not having to carry a second pair of shoes—more than compensates for any slight loss in pure pedaling efficiency.

Whatever kind of shoe you wear, make sure it *fits*. Loose shoes give you blisters and tight ones cut off circulation in the toes. You can't be too fussy in this area, which is why I advise against buying shoes by mail if you can help it. Make sure you try them on with the same kind of socks you'll be wearing when you cycle.

Seat Covers

Racing shorts, with their chamois-lined seat and crotch, are the most comfortable choice for any cycling wear. The chamois absorbs sweat and reduces chafe, and there are no seams to create soreness. The knitted legs fit snugly and do not flap in the wind, yet permit full circulation. Because of their lining, it is not necessary to wear underwear, which means one less thing to have to carry and fool with.

This is speaking strictly of *good* cycling shorts, and there are some horrendously shoddy efforts on the market. Seams that come open after moderate use, undersized chamois inserts, thin material you can almost see through, and other unpleasantries make these things no bargain. (Not that they are necessarily priced any lower than the good stuff; in fact, some of the worst junk has been sold at exorbitant prices.) Even wool, long a sign of quality, no longer proves anything. A few years ago, I was given some new "100% Finest Wool" shorts that proved to be so thin and shoddy as to constitute indecent exposure; I was actually afraid to wear them for fear they'd come apart in public.

For longer camping trips, these specialized shorts present one serious problem: maintenance. They must be kept scrupulously clean to prevent saddle sores, and this means hand-washing and air-drying to avoid ruining them. The chamois also tends to dry out and get stiff with repeated washing, so you have to rub in lanolin to keep it supple and soft. This adds up to a lot of trouble on a camping trip; in rainy weather you may find it impossible to dry them at all. The hassle of washing them properly· may tempt you to wear a sweaty, dirty pair just one more day, which is a good way to get a nasty infection. There are racing shorts made of cotton (Sergal is a good brand) that are easier to wash, but you still have the chamois to fool with, so you can't do them by machine.

Ordinary walking shorts, or cut-off work pants, can be used, if you make sure there isn't a big thick seam right where you sit. Some like to sew a terry-cloth lining into these, making them almost as comfortable as racing shorts and much easier to care for. Shorts of this type, with or without the terry insert, can be washed and dried at laundromats in small towns or at the more developed public campgrounds. With reasonable care, they can even be dried by a campfire.

Inexpensive jogging shorts are okay if you get them long enough to come about halfway down the thigh, which may not be easy. You must avoid any kind of short shorts that put the bottom hem up where you sit on the saddle; you will be chafed raw. Don't even think about cutoffs—denim is unpleasant when wet and dries stiff, and jeans have big nasty seams in the very worst places. If you can get them, U.S. Army khaki uniform shorts are quite good. Excellent wool shorts can be made by cutting the legs off a pair of tropical-weight U.S. Air Force woolen uniform trousers; these also make very fine woods pants when left as is.

There is, of course, no law that says you have to wear shorts at all. If it isn't particularly hot weather, you may prefer long pants, which keep your knees nice and warm—a lot of knee soreness is caused by people wearing shorts in chilly weather; 70°F. should be the bottom limit of shorts weather for most people. Long pants will also protect your legs from brush and insect bites, and on a gravel road your legs can get very raw from little bits of grit flying up from the wheels if you don't cover them. In this case I really endorse military surplus stuff, except Navy bell-bottoms, which are rather impractical for cycling. Another good place to find tough, well-made outdoor pants is a police uniform supplier.

A very comfortable outfit, top and bottom, is a regular old-fashioned floppy gray sweat suit. It looks very sloppy, but it's comfy beyond words, and you can sleep in it too. Good, soft cycle shorts can be made by cutting the legs off of sweat pants.

Do not wear a belt while cycling; it will chafe you and interfere with circulation. Get suspenders. Shorts of the more traditional type should have a drawstring, preferably, rather than elastic.

Tops

Here it is definitely worth imitating the racing practice if the budget will stretch to cover it. The road-racing jersey is a marvelously handy garment. With its row of big pockets across the back, you can carry all sorts of things—snacks, wallet, rocks to throw at dogs—without having them fall out every time you bend down to brake, as happens with regular shirt pockets. And you can dispense with carrying stuff in your pants pockets, which is always uncomfortable. Though it looks hot, a good wool or part-wool jersey is really very comfortable and cool in any weather, as it wicks sweat away from your body and creates a cooling effect through evaporation.

Again, however, watch out for the junk. The same people who made the shorts I mentioned earlier also cranked out a line of spectacularly wretched jerseys; you wear one twice and you no longer need to wear anything else, because it reaches your knees. If you carry anything in the pockets it nearly drags your rear tire.

Luckily for Americans, this country turns out some very fine jerseys indeed. Emily K. of California is my favorite. I have an Emily K. jersey that was one of a batch made up for the staff of the now-defunct tabloid, *Competitive Cycling,* and after seven years of hard use, including some bad crashes, it is still the best jersey I own.

Watch out for slick-finished synthetic fabrics, which do not breathe well. Most of these are intended for track or criterium racing, and some do not even have pockets.

If you don't want to spring for a jersey, a T-shirt will do okay. But a T-shirt will get sweaty and sticky, so you'll have to change pretty often. Regular shirts usually flap and drag, creating additional air resistance, and do not come down far enough in back to cover your kidney area when riding in the full-dropped position. Close-fitting knit pullovers of the style favored by golfers or tennis players are excellent for cycling and are easy to wash. And if the weather isn't too hot, you can't beat a sweatshirt, though the lack of pockets is an annoyance.

Wear *something* above the waist, even if male. You might look very dashing and get a good tan, riding around bare-chested, but you'll also run the risk of a bad sunburn, which can ruin the whole trip. If you have a fall, even a minor one, you're going to be very unhappy picking gravel and grit out of your lacerated upper torso. For serious cycling, I don't think much of tank-type tops, or halter tops for women. The shoulder is usually the first thing that hits the ground in a crash; a shirt or jersey won't really protect it, but it will at least lessen the abrasive effect.

If a jersey is worn, a T-shirt underneath will be more comfortable and provide a bit more protection in a fall. Most women cyclists of my acquaintance agree that a bra of some kind is essential to prevent soreness, especially on bumpy roads.

Headgear

Here I am going to be completely dogmatic: **Get a good helmet and wear it.** There are just too many crazy people driving around on the highways today. It's worse in town, no doubt, but out on rural roads some of these characters really crank it up and go. If one of these speeding maniacs hits you, you're going to need all the armor you can get. Even in a simple, minor fall, some extremely nasty things can happen to the human brain. People have been killed in such seemingly trivial accidents as slipping on wet leaves. I was once consulted as an expert witness in a court case in which a man had been permanently paralyzed in a fall resulting from a burst front tire—this on an open, level road. Head injuries can cause paralysis, brain damage, blindness, epilepsy, and the ever-popular favorite, death.

The old-fashioned leather-strap racing helmet is pretty poor, though no doubt better than nothing. Since it's also uncomfortable, expensive, supremely ugly, and provides no protection from the sun, why bother? There are better helmets available for equal or lower prices.

The best choice is one of the modern, full-bowl, hardshell helmets. The best designs work by absorbing impact through a layer of crushable, *not* resilient, foam lining. Suspension straps are nowhere near as good, while resilient foam pushes back against impact and may actually increase brain damage. The two current makes that I am most familiar with, and the odds-on favorites with American cyclists, are the Bell and the Mountain Safety Research helmets.

Bell helmets are very popular, almost a fad, and justly so. This was the first really effectively designed helmet, and some devotees would go so far as to say it is still the only one. Certainly the record is impressive and the design admirable. The unique air-scoop system makes it a good choice in hot weather, and weight is reasonable.

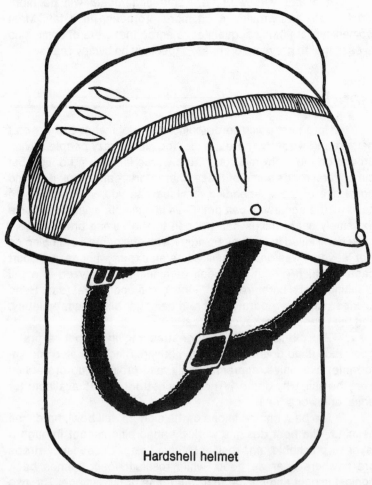

Hardshell helmet

Your best protection in rough terrain—a hardshell helmet.

Mountain Safety Research also makes a good helmet, which everybody calls simply the MSR. Originally developed from a rock-climbing design, the domelike yellow MSR is a bit heavier than the Bell and may not be quite as effective in extreme situations, depending on whose figures you believe. It is considerably less comfortable in hot weather, but much more pleasant than the Bell in cool air. Despite the added weight, the MSR feels more comfortable to me.

Helmets meant for hockey and similar sports are best left to the activities for which they were intended. Hockey helmets tend to be very hot and do not give adequate protection.

Some like the light Skid-Lid design; I must say it fails to impress me for bikepacking use, at least in rough country. The holes on top are too big to give adequate protection against rocks and other debris in a fall. The manufacturer asserts that this is a rare or overrated problem; this may be, on paved roads or city streets, but on a gravel road it's a real hazard. I personally have been badly cut through the interstices in a leather Cinelli helmet, and I know of other similar cases. Still, I suppose *any* helmet is better than none at all.

Some people say they "just can't stand" to wear a helmet. This is silly. People too weak to wear helmets are too sick to be cycling anyway. Little kids playing football, adolescent girls on mopeds, and overweight construction workers wear hard headgear and don't seem to die of it. What such people mean is that they find helmets uncomfortable or think they look foolish. But if you worry about comfort or appearances, what are you doing on a bike to begin with? If you want to be comfortable all the time, stay home and drink beer. If you want to avoid criticism of your appearance, become a model for a fashion magazine. If you want to ride with me, put your helmet on.

Gloves

Fingerless cycling gloves are a lot of protection for a little money. In even a minor fall, bare palms can be badly skinned, and then it is very painful to grip the bars. Cycling gloves protect the palm and reduce finger numbness, yet leave the fingers free to work the brakes and gears, and to make appropriate gestures at officious motorists or persons making comments about your helmet (see above). Gant is the best brand I know.

Regular cotton work gloves are worth carrying except in summer. On a cool morning, those aluminum handlebars can be a real heat sink and very unpleasant to touch with the bare skin, and windchill on exposed fingers can be nasty. Such gloves also have many uses around camp. They wear out fast but are easy to replace. Rural stores invariably carry them, usually for less than a dollar a pair.

Bad-Weather Gear

Some kind of protection against rain is essential except on desert rides. (Even then you can get a nasty surprise.) Ponchos are the usual answer. Handy and versatile in camp and fairly effective against falling rain when on foot, they aren't worth a damn for bike riding. The wheels throw water up from the road and drench you from beneath, and fenders do not entirely cure this. Ponchos also have a lethal habit of suddenly flying up to cover your face, which is one of those things that sounds funny until it happens to you.

The best answer, in my opinion, is a simple rain suit of waterproof, coated nylon. Many criticize this approach because you can sweat like a pig inside such a suit and probably get just as wet as you would from the rain. This is entirely true, but the point is missed. The primary function of the suit is *not* to keep you dry, which is virtually impossible anyway. The real danger is hypothermia; the wind from your forward speed causes evaporation from your wet clothing and skin, and this can quickly induce a very dangerous chill, even in relatively warm weather. Hypothermia can hit very fast and without warning, and even can be fatal, so it's nothing to kid around with. A waterproof windbreaker or anorak and a pair of rain pants will prevent this evaporative effect. Your skin may be uncomfortably wet, but at least it's *warm* moisture; your body heat is retained and you stay warm, using the same principle as that of a wet suit. This outfit will also come in handy on cold, windy days—it's really a wind suit as much as anything.

It's hard to find a good durable waterproof outfit that isn't too heavy. (Cheap vinyl rain suits are totally worthless.) I have had good luck with a "paddle suit" made for whitewater rafting, made by a kayak company named Phoenix—any good outdoor shop should be able to get them. Best of all is the revolutionary material Gore-Tex, which somehow lets water vapor out but doesn't let rain in. A suit made of this stuff would be ideal for cycling, but it is very, very expensive.

Except in high summer, you'll need something warmer than your jersey and shorts, both for cool days on the bike and evenings in camp. Take a wool shirt or sweater rather than a full-sized jacket; worn under your windbreaker or rain-suit top, this will keep you warm, permit a more versatile range of combinations, and be easier to pack. A light down vest or even a down jacket might be good to have in cold weather, or one of the synthetic equivalents (see the chapter on sleeping bags for a complete discussion of these materials). Incidentally, check out the vests and jackets made for deer hunters, with their shells, or reversible linings, of high-visibility, blaze-orange material, obviously a safety plus when riding on the highway.

If you want a pair of long pants for cool times, light wool ones are better than cotton or corduroy—if it's too warm for wool, you can just stick with shorts, though sweat pants might be a good answer. Avoid denim; as we said earlier, it chafes when wet and takes forever to dry.

Many women say they like to carry one or two pairs of those Winterall panty hose, or even a pair or two of old, ruined panty hose of the regular sort, to wear under their pants when it's chilly. Apparently those light, flimsy-looking things are quite warm, and certainly they can't take up much space in the bags.

A common problem in spring and fall is that you start the day's ride feeling the need for something warm on your arms and legs, but as the sun rises, you have to stop and peel off your shirt or sweater and long pants (to say nothing of panty hose). Then you have to pack all this stuff away before you can ride on, an annoying business at roadside, and just when you're feeling good and don't want to stop. One answer popular with racers is to acquire a set of woolen arm and leg warmers. These are simple knitted tubes which you slip over arms and legs, tucking the upper ends under jersey sleeves and shorts cuffs. This converts your whole outfit into a kind of warmup suit. When you get warm, just roll them off and stuff them into a jersey pocket or your handlebar bag. I've seen well-coordinated racers do this without ever getting off the bike, though I don't recommend trying it! They offer a lot of versatility for very little weight and bulk. Get them from a good cycle shop, or have Grandma knit you a set.

Off of the Bike

    You want to choose your outfit mainly so that you can wear the same clothes for riding as you wear in camp. If you can do this, then you only need a single change. You can wash out one set each night. Other than perhaps an extra pair of socks or a change of underwear (if you're one of those people who wear underwear), don't make the common mistake of loading yourself down with a lot of excess clothing.

    A few cyclists insist on carrying an outfit of ordinary street clothes, because they are afraid they might be ridiculed when they go into a store wearing their traveling gear, or that they might even be refused admittance to various establishments. This may be a problem for a tourist in urban areas, but it has nothing to do with us. Thank God one of the great joys of backcountry bikepacking is getting away from the kind of social attitudes that judge a person by the clothes he or she wears. Yet some people, particularly novices, still assume that they should take along "some regular clothes," and they feel insecure if they don't. I've seen "check lists for bicycle camping" that listed all sorts of useless junk. (Some people apparently even feel that a woman should carry along a *skirt*. My aching ischial tuberosities.)

    Forget it. You'll add useless bulk and weight to your load. The bears and raccoons don't care what you wear anyway, just another example of the superiority of bears and raccoons to people.

    There *are* some additional items well worth having, though. A hat or cap should be carried, particularly in desert country. If you dismount to walk around or take a break and there's no shade, you might want something on your head, and on a chilly evening in camp, a cap will help to keep you warm. Personal taste and packability are the only real limits here; there is even a certain unofficial competition among many bike people to have the most striking "character hat." Berets, knitted watch caps, and long-billed railroad caps are the usual favorites. Or you might like one of those Army jungle-warfare hats that folds up to pocket size. By the way, a knitted watch cap under your helmet is a good idea on cold mornings.

    If your plans include any serious hiking, you'll have to carry some hiking boots or rock shoes. These are very heavy and bulky, so don't take them unless you know for sure you'll need them. Some people feel the need of boots for antisnake protection, but really, snakebite is a very overrated danger in most places.

A pair of moccasins weigh little and take up little space, and are very nice to wear around camp in the evenings.

A bandanna handkerchief is a fine thing to have, on or off the bike. Around your neck, it prevents chapping and is handy for wiping sweat. It can also serve as a headband, potholder, towel, bandage, distress signal, tourniquet, and a zillion other things. Carry two.

Glasses might be considered an item of clothing. If you wear them, be sure to carry a spare pair, well protected. (On really distant trips, take a copy of your prescription as well.) Sunglasses are needed in any case. Sun glare on the highway is not only painful but very dangerous. Glasses wearers may prefer clip-on shades, or prescription sunglasses. The latter, however, are a constant hassle except in sunny, open country, because you have to keep switching back and forth.

My own solution is to have a set of prescription lenses in the new Sun Sensor tinting, which changes all by itself to adjust to changes in light conditions. I suggest, too, a strap or cord to keep your glasses from being blown off by the wind from, say, a passing truck.

Well, we've had us a long day here. Let's see about going to bed.

I'd rather wake up in the middle of nowhere than in any city on earth.

—Steve McQueen

CHAPTER **3**

Backcountry Bikies'
_____ Bedroom Basics

Few experiences can rival that of waking up out in wild country after a good night's sleep. If you've chosen your spot well and slept warm and comfortable and were spared such bummers as hailstorms and marauding bears, you awake feeling marvelously alive all over. You might be sore, perhaps, from the previous day's efforts, but you know that a few stiff muscles are a cheap price to pay for being out amid all this cleanness and beauty. Down inside the womblike warmth and security of your good sleeping bag, cushioned from the ground by your pad or air mattress, with sunshine on your face and the jackhammer knocking of a woodpecker the loudest sound around, you feel ready for anything the day may bring. You feel a great reluctance to leave this comfortable bed, and yet at the same time you feel a paradoxical eagerness to get on with the day's affairs.

In a totally different sense, few experiences can rival—for sheer loathsomeness, that is—waking up after a *bad* night outdoors. Provided you ever managed to get any sleep at all, let us add. Cold and stiff, more tired than when you turned in, you creak to your clumsy feet (which seem to belong to somebody else—somebody unusually stupid) and lurch around making a breakfast you can't taste, which is just as well, since you make a mess of it anyway. It's only five o'clock, but you weren't sleeping and at least this way you can get some circulation back in your toes. You wonder if this is how Lazarus felt when he rose from the dead. More likely it's how he felt when he died. You pack sloppily, losing three or four small but absolutely vital items that cannot be replaced anywhere in a five-state area, and load everything onto the bike so badly that you have to fight for control all day. And for the rest of the day, which goes on and on and never seems to end, you make stupid mistakes, take wrong turns, miss gear shifts, grouse at people, and quite possibly manage to have at least one nasty and totally unnecessary crash, all because you didn't get enough sleep.

If you are not too far from home or have a car somewhere nearby, you may well succumb to the urging of the inner voice telling you that only a fool would endure such misery. You may go home early, or spend the rest of the trip and all of your savings staying in motels and eating in restaurants. Then, for the rest of your life, you'll go around saying, "Man, I tried that camping out, and it's just not for me."

It is very likely that most of the people who say they dislike camping could trace their prejudice back to this problem. So let's be clear about this: If you've got any limits at all on the money you can spend on this stuff, *make sure you get an adequate sleeping outfit as your very first priority* in camping gear. A good bag is far more important than any tent made, let alone such fancy foofaraw as spun-aluminum pots or Tibetan yak-fur parkas.

Heretical though this idea may be, *I'm not even sure it isn't more important than the bike.* Yes, that's what I said. Sure, if you're going a long way or over the mountains, you need a first-class bike. And if you're one to whom cycling is the point of the thing and camping out just something you do in the evenings along the road, your instinct will be to put your money on the bike and skimp on everything else. But on the whole, if you're on a budget, it might not be a bad thing at all if you'd settle for a less sophisticated machine—straight-gauge tubing, no-status components, and so on, something along the lines of a Schwinn LeTour or a Raleigh Grand Prix or even something cheaper—if that's what it takes to make the nut on a decent sleeping bag.

In fact, I think—hell, I *know*—I would personally rather go for a week's tour in the hills with an old three-speed clunker, or even a coaster-brake, balloon-tire job with some improved brakes, and an adequate bag and pad, than to ride a custom touring job and have to sleep in a junk bag on the bare ground. Better to spend an hour or so pushing a heavy bike up hills than to put in eight hours of misery each night. If you get a good night's sleep, you'll have more energy to pedal, whatever you're riding; if you don't, then your deteriorating physical state will destroy any advantage you might gain from a fancier bike. Besides, a good bag weighs less than a cheap one or a blanket roll, so to some extent this compensates for the heavier or less efficient bike. I'm not saying to *have* to go this route—only you know your own situation—but think about it.

If I seem to be beating this point to death, it is because so many people, especially young men, seem to feel it is a point of manliness to be able to sleep anywhere with any sort of inadequate covering. They have the mistaken idea that in providing for a warm, comfortable bed, they are somehow being weaklings or sissies. Or they simply kid themselves into thinking, "I'm pretty tough, so I don't need to get all that stuff." Hah. The Plains Indians constructed elaborate beds of willow wands and buffalo robes inside those teepees, and nobody's ever called them a bunch of sissies. Even if you are one who lives only to ride your bike and begrudges every cent spent on anything else, look at it this way—if you don't get your sleep, you won't enjoy the cycling.

But note that I said an "adequate" bag, a while back. For most U.S. cycle campers, bikepacking is essentially a moderate-weather activity. Few do it in subfreezing weather; the need for additional clothing and high-calorie food in such conditions creates some serious logistical problems, and it's hard to cycle in snow and ice. Many confine their cycle camping to weather so warm that almost anything will do at night. It is certainly not necessary to have a super-expensive, super-sophisticated down bag meant for winter camping: In fact, such a bag is a bad choice for mild weather, since it may be unpleasantly hot.

If you are absolutely certain that there will be no cold nights where and when you will be camping (and remember, deserts get almighty cold at night), it is sometimes possible to do without a sleeping bag or much of anything else. During that dreadful hot, dry summer of 1980, I spent two weeks down on the lower White River in Arkansas, and the nights never got even comfortably cool. The only bedding I took along was a light cotton wrap from Thailand, originally a Buddhist monk's robe, and I did fine. Under somewhat less extreme circumstances you might get by with a light Army wool blanket. (But such weather makes it awfully hot to ride bike.)

Most people prefer to be less limited. Spring and autumn are wonderful times for cycle camping, far better than summer, in fact. There are fewer tourists driving around the roads, the air is cooler for cycling, and the changing leaves of autumn or blooming flowers of spring are a constant joy. For these seasons you definitely need a sleeping bag, and in most places even summer nights occasionally turn chilly.

So what you want is what is called a "three-season" bag by outfitters. This type of bag falls between the extremes of nearly-nothing summer bags and the expedition-grade stuff made for Arctic conditions: adequate down to around 30° to 40°F., but not oppressively hot and heavy in warmer air. Because you have to carry it on a bike, you want it to be light and compact. (Not necessarily in that order—a bulky load, by increasing air resistance, may be harder on your legs than a heavy one.)

Well, let's have a look at the possibilities.

Cheap Bags

Super-cheap sleeping bags are widely sold in discount stores, often at absurdly low "loss leader" prices to get you into the store. Usually these are virtual clones of the same basic design: uncomprisingly rectangular shape, nameless "polyester" fill (often mill-floor sweepings), sewn-through seams, bright, shiny nylon shell, and overall shoddy materials and workmanship.

These wretched efforts should be confined strictly to children's slumber parties or vagabond friends who show up wanting to sleep on your couch. They will not make it for any kind of real camping. They don't keep you warm on even moderately cool nights, they lack durability, and they are impossibly heavy and bulky for the little insulation they provide. In fact, it is almost impossible to cinch one of these things down to a size and shape that can be carried on a bike at all. They are entirely unacceptable for cycle camping. It is true, they will provide enough warmth for mild-weather conditions, but so will a blanket—indeed, an ordinary blanket bag, made by pinning a couple of G.I. blankets together, will provide just as much warmth (if not more) and be lighter, more compact, and probably cheaper. If the budget simply will not stretch to cover a decent sleeping bag, I suggest you stick with blankets.

A variant is the heavy, rectangular bag made for car camping, usually with cotton-duck shell, kapok fill, and flannel lining. Often warm and very sturdy, these bags are far too heavy and bulky for cycling use.

Good Bags: Design and Construction

If at all possible, the bag you take bikepacking ought to be the "mummy" type. No other style really makes sense for the cyclist, simply because nothing else provides the same ratio of warmth to weight and bulk. Cyclists have to watch every tiny bit of weight, more than any other class of camper except perhaps mountain climbers, and we are by far the most bulk conscious of all. Why should you carry around a lot of bag material to warm empty space? The sleeping bag, like the bicycle or the kayak, is something you *wear*. And the drawstring top and fitted hood of the mummy bag will go far to keep your head warm and prevent cold air from blowing in around your shoulders.

Most people who try mummies eventually develop a kind of Freudian relationship with them; there is a unique feeling of womblike security. (Children invariably love mummy bags, even though their squirmy habits make the design somewhat impractical.) A few extreme claustrophobes really can't get used to the mummy, and certainly there's no use in buying something that makes you so nervous you can't sleep in it, whatever its theoretical advantages.

For these people, there are "barrel" bags, somewhat of a compromise between the mummy and the rectangle. They aren't too bad if you simply can't sleep in a mummy or can't afford one. But even a close-fitting barrel bag still allows a lot of air to sneak in around the shoulders and adds much weight and bulk to your load.

Don't be too hasty if you don't care for the first mummy you try. There are mummies and, as King Tut said to Nefertiti, there are mummies. They vary from the extremely close-fitting Alpine designs that you pull on like a sock to rather roomy affairs that almost overlap with the barrel. Check out several different mummies before making your decision. Do not let yourself be rushed by pushy sales people or "helpful" friends. The bag is going to be your most expensive purchase after the bike; it will be the biggest, heaviest single thing in your cargo in all probability; you will be spending your nights in it and your days pedaling up hills and into headwinds with it squatting there behind you, dragging you back. You owe it to yourself to make sure you get what you want, or as close to it as you can afford.

As for the old-fashioned rectangular bag, this should be used only if money is a big problem. Lots of luck loading one onto the bike. Most rectangular bags, even very expensive ones, make up into bundles with all the compact balance of two weeks' worth of dirty laundry.

But—if your money is truly tight, you're probably better off sticking with rectangular bags or perhaps the simpler barrels. Beware of cheap mummy bags. Reasonably adequate rectangular bags, with two or three pounds of the better synthetic fill (usually

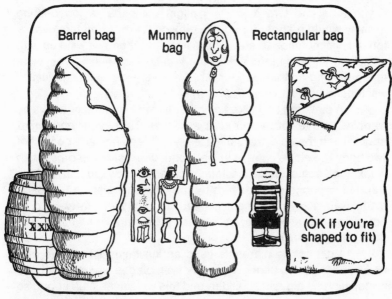

Barrel bag   Mummy bag   Rectangular bag

(OK if you're shaped to fit)

Styles of sleeping bags.

Hollofil II—we'll get to fills in a minute), are sold at discount stores for pretty low prices. Nowadays you can get something fairly decent for around $30 to $40 if you can find a clearance sale, though it will probably be higher by the time this book comes out. One of these should be your choice if finances are low. Mummy bags require very careful cutting, fitting, and sewing, and some of the critical operations are not suited to mass production with unskilled labor; cheap mummy bags are very failure prone. (I've got one I sometimes use—I had to restitch nearly all the seams. Forget it.)

As a general principle in buying *any* outdoor gear, if money is short, stick with designs that are simple and honest, and beware of sophisticated-looking bargains.

If you do get a mummy bag, make sure it's long enough for you. Tall people have to watch this, for a mummy made for somebody shorter than you will cause you to spend the whole night feeling longitudinally compressed. A real drag, this; most good mummy bags come in a tall size, for a few more bucks, and if you need one, be sure to get it. This is another point about inexpensive mummies—they usually come only in a rather short size. Barrels and rectangular bags fit everybody, as much as they fit anybody.

One more thing—consider your own usual sleeping habits. If you toss and turn a lot, you might think that a loose-fitting mummy would be best for you, but it won't. When you turn over, a loose mummy tends to stay where it is, and then you wind up with your face buried in the back of the hood, which makes you wake up screaming and fighting for air. But a very close-fitting mummy will tend to turn with you. Failing this, get a barrel bag.

A sleeping bag, like any other form of insulation, works by trapping a layer of dead air as a barrier. Thus, your body heat stays in and the cold stays out. Nearly all sleeping bags consist of two body-envelope bags of some fabric, one inside the other, with a layer of some loose insulating material between. Air is thus trapped in pockets and layers by the fill. (There are a few bags made with a layer of foam instead, but they are very hard to compress into a compact bundle and hence are of no interest to the cycle camper.)

Most of the materials used as insulating fill tend to drift and wander about, especially away from places where your body rests, such as hip and shoulder, and this will cause cold spots; so there must be some provision for stabilizing the fill. This is usually done by dividing the fill space into separate compartments or tubes by some means, and here is where we get into things that run up the price of the bag.

The simplest, cheapest way to stabilize the fill is simply to run a line of stitching through the whole works—to sew the inner and outer envelopes together in a series of seams and trap the fill in between, like a quilt. Well-adapted to mass production and commonly found in cheap bags, this system is known as the "sewn-through" method of stabilization.

A sewn-through bag isn't too bad for summer use, but basically it's a poor design. No matter how good the fill or the rest of the materials, you've got a lot of lines of stitching where there simply isn't anything at all, and thus you have cold spots. So don't get a sewn-through bag, and check for this construction when you're buying your outfit. Some sneaky types have devised various ways to mask the sewn-through seam. The best way to check is to put one hand inside the bag, one outside, and feel. If you keep finding places where your hands meet along a line with nothing but nylon between them, put the bag back on the rack and move on.

Better bags use a "double-quilted" system (double offset layers). That is, you have, in effect, *two* layers of insulation; they are sewn-through, but they are offset so that each seam is covered by a layer of insulation. (One company did come out with a bag in which there were two layers but the seams lined up—nobody ever knew what they were thinking—but I think this bag is off the market now.) This is what you get with most medium-priced, three-season bags. On the outside, a double-quilted bag may look like a sewn-through bag—both have those seams running all over—but perform the two-hands trick again. Follow the stitching inside and out with your fingers, and if the inner and outer lines of stitching are offset and don't match up, you're okay.

Very good (and expensive) sleeping bags use various systems of internal baffles and partitions, of which the best known is the "slant-box" style. This makes for a truly fine bag, but you bust your wazoo paying for it, and very few cycle campers are going to need it.

It might be added that the bag can be made so that the tubes or pockets of fill run in various ways—crosswise, longitudinally, even in a "chevron" pattern—and each manufacturer will swear on his mother's grave that his system is the best and show you figures to prove it. I wouldn't lie awake worrying about it.

Various other design and construction features should be considered, zippers for one. A sleeping bag zipper has to be

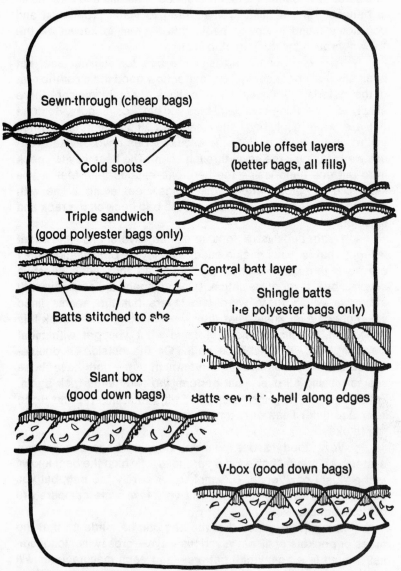

Six stabilization systems for sleeping bags.

reliable and smooth-working under all conditions. This is especially true with mummy bags; with a barrel or rectangle, it's fairly easy just to squirm in and out through the open end, but in a mummy, you're trapped until you get the zipper unstuck. Since you don't have much room to move your arms, you can't get much of a yank on the damned thing. This is when your kidneys decide you absolutely have to relieve the pressure within the next three seconds or they won't be responsible for the consequences. So you flop and hop around fighting the zipper, expressing yourself in such vivid terms that the raccoons cover their ears. It is probably this situation that gave rise to the expression, "The Mummy's Curse."

So when you look at bags, check the zippers out with the scrutiny you would give the fine print on a deed to a piece of Florida real estate. The teeth should be big lug types that won't jam on every loose thread, and the pull should be something good sized that you can find easily and on which you can get a good grip. In a bag with a full-length zipper, it is better to have the option of unzipping either end. Then in hot weather you can open up the foot for ventilation. Most good mummies, however, have a zipper that only goes down to the waist or so.

Any bag with any pretensions of quality should have a "draft tube," also known as a "zipper baffle." This is simply a long, stuffed tube that runs inside next to the zipper. Its function is to keep the cold air from sneaking in through the zipper teeth. It should be stuffed *full* of insulating fill, because if it is slack at all, the loose material will find its way into the zipper teeth, with consequences similar to those described above.

Check the foot area well. Sometimes there is a sewn-through seam there, even though the rest of the bag is made otherwise. With a mummy, there should be a flared, or lengthened, area so that your feet can wiggle a bit.

Take a look at the stitching. Eight to ten stitches per inch is about right. Too few stitches and you've got a weak seam; too many can weaken the fabric itself. Don't be shy about bringing along a little magnifier and a pocket ruler and actually counting stitches in a few sample spots. Feel the bag to see if the insulation is distributed fairly evenly with no thick or thin spots.

I am assuming that you are buying your bag in a store where you can examine all these things, and where the management stands behind the stuff they sell. Most outdoor shops are run by decent people, certainly, but there are a few sleazy flimflam men running around out there, and it is definitely possible to get ripped off. Even basically honest salespeople sometimes tend to hustle you a bit. Take your time and look at things with great care. Whatever you get, you'll have to live with it and depend on it to keep you warm and comfortable for one-third of your time outdoors, and, again, it will probably be your most expensive piece of equipment except for the bike. This gives you the right—the *duty*—to be fussy.

Buy by mail only if the bag is of a recognized brand—North Face, Snow Lion, and so on—or if it's the house brand of a truly reputable company, such as L. L. Bean or Eastern Mountain Sports. This is true of all equipment.

Down

Back to the insides of the bag. Waterfowl down has long been recognized as the ultimate in light, minimum-bulk insulation. No other substance yet discovered can match top-grade down, when used correctly, for pure warmth per ounce (and don't think there aren't some very smart people spending lots of money trying to find substitutes). For the cyclist, down has a special attraction: Down-filled bags and clothing can be compressed into incredibly tiny bundles, greatly reducing the wind-catching and balance-disturbing bulk of the load.

Now for the bad news, as if you hadn't heard: Down is expensive. God, is it expensive. Nor is there any hope for a major breakthrough to bring down production costs. Down can only be produced by live ducks and geese, who have been operating at an unchanged level of efficiency since the Ice Age. (Much debate has centered around the relative merits of goose down versus duck down, and manufacturers seem to agree that a label reading "100% Northern Goose Down Fill" entitles them to charge more for the bag. That there is any practical difference, detectable by the average person or significant to anyone but an Everest climber, is for someone other than the author of this book to believe. I mean what the hell *is* a goose but a kind of Fascist duck?)

Nor does the cost problem stop with the down itself. That's just the beginning. The very qualities that make down a wonderful fill—lightness and compressibility—also make it very demanding stuff to work with. The little plumules of down seem to have a life of their own when it comes to trying to stabilize the fill. Some system of baffling is vital, and it has to be designed and sewn very carefully or the down makes lumps and gaps. Moreover, down will work its way through any seam that is not perfectly stitched with almost a malevolent intelligence. (If you've owned a down vest or jacket, you've probably had the slightly disconcerting experience of finding little down plumules poking out here and there.) If a seam actually rips or comes undone, down pours out like a blizzard and is hell to get back in. All in all, down is highly intolerant of sloppy workmanship or poor materials. Only very careful, skilled work—which costs a lot of money in this country—will get the job done.

So if you want a down bag, be prepared to go first class or don't bother. Cheap down bags are beneath consideration. Like poets, down bags tend to be either magnificent or wretched. Some sleazy types have even been guilty of adulterating the down with such things as chicken feathers.

If you can handle the whopping price tag, there are some truly beautiful down bags around, and a good one is undoubtedly the ideal choice for bicycle camping in most conditions. The North Face Blue Kazoo weighs only a couple of pounds and will keep you warm down to 20°F.; it can be packed into a 16″ × 6″ stuff sack, which is not much bulkier than a good, heavy wool shirt. At the time of this writing, a Blue Kazoo sells for about $165—$170 for the tall-guy model. This is a very, very popular bag—justly so—with hikers, climbers, and cyclists. The construction is absolutely first-rate. There are several other good bags in this category; Snow Lion is one make I think very highly of, and their bags are very light indeed.

One interesting possibility for warm-weather use is a down *liner* bag. These are simple, light bags intended to fit inside a regular bag for very cold weather. But you can use one by itself in mild weather, and the weight and bulk are very low. You might like to start with one of these down inner bags for summer use and then later on get a three-season bag for more demanding conditions. Then, if you wanted to go out in real winter (unlikely on a bike, but you might want to try ski touring or snowshoeing too), you could use the innie and the outie together. A lot of people do this. One very good innie is the EMS Inner Sebago.

Now, before you sell your children to finance a down bag, there are a couple of other angles you ought to know about. You see, down has one tremendous problem—it becomes utterly worthless when it gets wet. You wouldn't think it would do that—I mean, it comes off of birds that routinely swim around in freezing water—but once it's off the bird (which has oil glands to protect the feathers), down has got to be kept dry, dry, *dry.* A waterlogged down bag has all of the fine insulating properties of a sack of dead mackerel. And if you handle it roughly before it dries, the internal baffles can rip right out, thus ruining it.

Certainly this isn't nearly as crucial for the cyclist as for the whitewater rafter or canoeist, or even for the rainforest-walking backpacker. Under normal conditions, there is no real reason a bikepacker should ever get his or her bag wet. A plastic garbage bag or two inside the stuff sack will keep your bag dry even if you ride in a rainstorm, especially if you do as many of us, and wrap your tarp or tent fly around the stuffed bag.

Life is not always perfect, however. Plastic bags develop unsuspected rips and let in the rain. Tents evolve leaks or develop condensation-drip problems; and in some very humid climates, a bag can simply absorb moisture right out of the air—especially inside a tent, with your body and breath giving off water by the bucketful all night. Even when this is not enough to harm the insulating qualities of your bag, it does make the bag heavier. Down also takes a long time to dry and is susceptible to damage when damp.

Besides, are you sure your only outdoor interest is in bikepacking? Isn't it possible that you might want to do some canoe touring or the like one of these days? (You can have a lot of extra fun on a cycle trip, by the way, by renting a canoe for a day or two as a change of pace.) If so, you'll hardly want to need to have another bag for the purpose—in these inflationary days, most of us want maximum versatility out of something as expensive as a sleeping bag.

Also, down bags require very careful maintenance. You can't just wash them any old way; you have to go through a whole business of using cold water, stopping the machine frequently to reach in and gently push trapped air out of the bag (otherwise seams can be ripped), and then drying at a low heat setting. Or, if you do it in the bathtub (which is what most people do), you have to be very, very careful of how you handle the wet bag; if you grab one end and hoist it suddenly out of the tub, it is possible—egregiously so—that the internal baffles and seams will be ripped out, leaving you with an extraordinarily expensive bed for your dog.

Now, none of this is meant to say that you shouldn't get a down bag. On balance, I think a good down bag is still the best choice for cycle camping, except in very wet weather. But if the cost is bothering you, and/or you don't like to have to treat outdoor equipment with a great deal of care, you may want to consider the alternatives.

The Modern Synthetics ─────────

If you've been reading anything authoritative that's more than a decade old—or more recent things of a conservative or unimaginative sort—you will have been told that down is the only real fill for a serious bag, and that synthetic-fill sleeping bags are bulky, heavy, and inefficient. Early polyester fills were indeed all of these things, and the cheap ones still are. The image has clung to synthetic fills like road dirt to an oily chain. And the widespread faith in the total superiority of down has been greatly bolstered by the influence of Western backpackers, who operate mostly in an area of humongous mountains and little rain, where nothing but down makes much real sense.

But the modern polyester fills, Polarguard and Hollofil II, are not cheap makeshifts. High-performance bags with these fills have been tested in such brutal climates as Alaska and the Chilean glacier country. The military, for obvious reasons, do some super-severe testing of every possible insulating fill that comes along, and they have proved that these two substances are first-class fills. Whitewater runners have, for the most part, gone over to synthetics, because polyester has some great advantages over down—it will keep you warm even when soaking wet, it dries very rapidly, and it doesn't much matter how you handle it in the process.

For our purposes, polyester has another big plus—it costs one hell of a lot less than down, isn't affected by fluctuations in supply, and lends itself much better to low-cost, mass-production techniques. The elaborate stabilizing systems used with down are not necessary, though some fine synthetic bags do use them. Since polyester comes in batts and doesn't drift about as badly as down, it can be stabilized quite effectively with very simple systems. For all but very cold weather bags, it is possible to stabilize a polyester batt adequately by simply running a single seam around the borders—what is called "edge-stabilizing," which is not much more costly than the sewn-through process.

Also, while shoddy workmanship is certainly never to be tolerated, it's still worth remembering that polyester is a lot more forgiving than down. If a seam gets a little loose, down will come wiggling out immediately, whereas polyester stays put. Even if the seam is ripped wide open, or the material tears, it's easy enough to cram the polyester back in and sew the tear back up. When you're dealing with lower price ranges, this is worth remembering.

The big drawback, and it is a big one for bikepackers is that polyester fills, even the best ones, are heavier and bulkier than down. According to published figures, all else being equal, it takes about 6 ounces more polyester fill to equal a pound of down fill in insulating value. The actual difference in efficiency of the materials themselves may be misleading. Down is theoretically 40% more efficient than polyester, but the added stabilization required by down runs the weight of the finished bag up somewhat. Much depends on other aspects of construction and shape. In general, a good polyester mummy bag will probably weigh from 1 to 2 pounds more than a down bag with the same temperature rating.

Compressibility of polyester is considerably less than down. The backpacker doesn't much care about this, but we on our wind-fighting machines certainly do. Overall compression in a stuff bag or with straps works out to about 1 inch more diameter (of the stuffed and rolled bag) per pound of fill; but, again, this is very theoretical and general.

What does all this work out to in concrete terms? Look back at the figures on the North Face Blue Kazoo. Now, a roughly similar synthetic bag, with about the same temperature rating, is sold by L. L. Bean for around $80. It weighs 3 pounds 11 ounces in the regular size, and packs to a size of 11″ × 20″. Comparing this with the down Blue Kazoo, we see that we've acquired not quite a couple of pounds and a good many square inches of air-catching area in order to save about $85.

Is this a good deal? Only you can decide. But if money is a problem, I think you should consider it. That extra $85 would make most of the nut on a good, light pair of alloy-rimmed wheels to replace your steel ones, and I guarantee that will do a lot more for your comfort and performance. Or you could get a touring crankset or a wide-range derailleur and cluster, to give you lower gears than your present ones, and that would help more on the hills than knocking a couple of pounds off of your bag weight.

On the other hand, if your bike is in good shape and you've got a good stove and so on, and you're just trying to save a few bucks to get a fancier tent or some other nonessential item, I'd say go ahead and get the down bag. But it's your choice.

The two synthetics, Polarguard and Hollofil II, do not seem to differ much in actual performance. The U.S. Armed Forces tested both in Alaska and could not come up with any meaningful difference. (There are major differences between the fibers, but these are of interest to manufacturers only.) Certainly the specific make of fiber is far less important than the construction of the bag itself. There is a legend that Polarguard holds its loft better over the years, but my own experience has, if anything, indicated the opposite.

Eastman Kodak has something called Kodel, but it has not shown up on the market in any leading maker's bags, so I know nothing about it. 3M is supposedly working on a bag-grade version of their Thinsulate fiber, but so far no word; you might check around. By the time you read this, it is very possible that some totally new material may be on the scene.

DuPont also makes a cheaper fiber, Hollofil 808, which is okay for parkas but not much good for bags. Hollofil II, if I've got this right, is apparently the same stuff that was called "Fiberfill II" but not the same as the lower-case-f "fiberfill" found in cheap bags.

For some reason, Hollofil tends to turn up in bargain bags, while Polarguard bags cost a bit more. I can only assume that this is due to some problem in manufacturing or perhaps a marketing matter—it's certainly not performance.

There are a lot of good polyester bags on the market, and there isn't any point in going into specific recommendations. L. L. Bean and Eastern Mountain Sports both make and sell first-rate synthetic mummy and barrel bags. A good synthetic-fill bag suitable for cycling usually will run about half the price of an equivalent down bag.

Other Possibilities

From time to time, other insulating materials appear. Foam was highly touted some years ago. It was indeed sturdy, cheap, and effective, but nobody ever solved the problem of the enormous bulk of even the most tightly rolled foam bag, and except for whitewater runners, nobody much uses foam bags. As mentioned earlier, I don't think they make the grade for cycling.

There are budget-priced bags out that contain a blend of down and feathers. Ignore them. They lose enough performance to put them into the same class as the better polyester bags, yet they still cost more and are worthless when wet. If you can't get 100% prime down in a first-line bag, go to Polarguard or Hollofil II and save your money.

Wool and kapok, once very common as sleeping-bag fills, are long gone from the scene, unmourned by anyone I've ever met.

If you cannot afford a sleeping bag, or don't want to carry one, and if the night temperatures are fairly certain to stay no lower than the mid-50s F., you may be able to get by with blankets. To some extent, this depends on your tolerance for cold. Certainly an awful lot of people have spent an awful lot of cold nights outdoors wrapped in blankets. I'd hate to tell anybody that he or she would have to stay stuck in the city because they couldn't afford a sleeping bag. Better to get out there and do it with marginal equipment than not to do it at all.

Army blankets are the usual choice. They aren't really ideal, since they're very close-woven and lack "nap," but they can be found in surplus and secondhand stores pretty cheap, and they are certainly very strong. But if you can get hold of a couple of regular wool blankets with a bit more fluffiness to them, you'll do better. Whatever blankets you use, fix them into some kind of bag, so you don't kick them off at night. The usual means of doing this is safety pins; you want the large kind meant for horse blankets, which you can get at any saddle-goods store. Or if you can scrounge up some Velcro, you ought to be able to make something pretty good. If you can get hold of a piece of light, strong material—nylon or cotton or the like—and make an outer bag to act as cover, you'll sleep a bit warmer and have less trouble with dirty blankets. (Don't make a cover out of *any* waterproof material or coated nylon—you'll drown in your own sweat.)

The Army used to issue a wool liner for its mummy bags, really just a woolen mummy bag itself, and these things often turn up in surplus stores, often at very low prices—I saw one in a thrift store once for three bucks. One of these makes a pretty decent warm-weather bag, and weighs little.

Any of these makeshift alternatives can be helped considerably by a few little tricks. If you use a foam pad underneath you, this will add somewhat to the insulating qualities of anything, bag or blankets. Sleeping in your clothes is basically a bad practice, getting you pretty dirty, but it's better than freezing all night. If you can sleep on top of a good thick layer of pine needles or dead leaves rather than bare ground, this too will be warmer. Also remember that you'll sleep warmer inside a tent or under a tarp or other shelter than you will outside, and that you won't lose as much radiant heat under the trees as you will out in an open space. (In fact, a thick layer of decomposing pine needles will generate quite a bit of heat on its own—so, you can seek out such a place on a cold night if you're making do with blankets but should avoid it on a hot evening.) Eating some high-calorie, high-fat food, such as cheese or sausage, just before turning in will help you keep warm too.

Don't try to make do with one of those plastic "space blanket" things sold in outdoor shops. These light, cheap devices, which are silver on the inside to reflect body heat back at you, are purely for emergency use, and very good for that purpose. (In fact, it is a good idea to carry one on long trips, when you aren't expecting to camp out but may be forced to spend a night by the roadside.) But they are no good at all for real camping. The plastic material retains moisture as well as heat, and you sweat like a hog and smell like one too. They are incredibly uncomfortable—the only use they have is when the alternative is freezing to death. Besides, being emergency gear, most of them aren't meant to last very long, and they tear if you look hard at them.

Perhaps I should mention the various sleeping bag covers and liners so popular in some quarters. These usually consist of a light sack of cotton or nylon; the liners are sometimes made of light flannel. The idea is to add a bit of warmth, which at times may be a good idea, and to keep the bag clean. The inner lining keeps you from getting the bag dirty with your own grubby bod, sweat, and other grossnesses, while the cover is just to keep off general dirt. One reason for the popularity of such devices is that down bags are such a chore to wash—anything to delay the day you have to do it—but this seems less relevant in the case of synthetic bags, which you can simply toss in the washer at the first laundromat. Some people also find the slick feeling of a nylon bag unpleasant and like something comfy like flannel against their skin.

To me, this just gives you something else to haul around, and any cyclist ought to need no more of that. If I wanted something between me and the bag, I'd just carry something to wear to bed—a sweat suit or even, for Heaven's sake, *pajamas*— which would weigh less. Liners, in any case, tend to get wrapped and tangled around you when you turn over. As for the covers, a ground/sheet or floored tent will keep the bag clean underneath, and a little care on your part will do the same on top.

There is one time you might want a liner. In warm weather, you often encounter nights when it is too hot to get into the bag but cool enough to need something. A light cotton liner is nice then; you can lie on top of the bag in just the liner, and nights when you do get into the bag, cotton is more pleasant against the skin if you're a little sweaty. But under such conditions, I just carry my old Thai monk's robe and a light woolen airline blanket. Try it yourself, if you know any Buddhist monks.

Underneath

Besides the sleeping bag or other cover, you'll need something under you. In fact, this is sometimes even more important than the bag—as we said, there are warm nights when you need no covering to speak of, but the ground doesn't get any softer at any time of year.

If you try to sleep lying directly on the ground, you'll awaken—if you sleep at all—moving like a terminal arthritic. Your sleeping bag will lose most of its value, no matter how much you paid for it. Your weight compresses the fill under you, and the earth is an enormous heat sink, so body heat gets drained off very rapidly. (It will therefore be seen that under some conditions, a person in a couple of blankets, sleeping on a foam pad of average thickness, might well sleep warmer than another person in a down bag who tries to sleep on the bare ground! Think that over.)

So you definitely need some sort of buffer between you and the planet. The cyclist needs it more than most. Cycle camping very often involves staying at public or other "developed" campgrounds—in some areas this is mandatory, and in any case, this is often the only available place to stay along the highways on a long trip. These places tend to be set up with the vehicle-borne "camper" in mind, with his trailer or van. You may be required to pitch your tent or make your bed on a rectangular pad of packed-down earth or gravel meant for parking wheels rather than bodies. In the forest, the hiker can at least bed down on a heap of leaves or pine needles, or, along the river, make a comfortable bed of soft sand. But on one of those public-site pads, you'd better have some really good upholstering along or it's going to be a long, long night. Anyway, it's enough that your butt and back had to put up with being pounded by that hard saddle all day long—you want more of the same at night too?

The two types of bed padding in general use are the air mattress and the foam pad. Both come in several forms. Each has its fanatical adherents. Each has its advantages and its drawbacks. The perfect camping bed is still waiting to be invented.

Air mattresses have been around a long time and for years were the standard choice. They certainly make a comfortable bed if you get the inflation pressure right, and they are nice and compact when deflated, a big point for the cyclist.

The older air mattresses, with their rubber-and-cotton material and weak, vulcanized seams, were also pretty unreliable, besides being quite heavy. There are a lot of cheap modern ones, and some not so cheap, of which these criticisms are still true. Unfortunately, many people had or have their first experience with one of these inferior air mattresses, and so there is a widespread belief, often stated even by expert outdoors people, that all air mattresses are inherently unreliable and heavy.

This is simply untrue. Air mattresses have undergone some remarkable developments in recent years. You can now get very light, nylon-and-rubber air mattresses that weigh no more than foam pads, take up hardly any room, and are about as reliable as any other item of your equipment. (Your bike's tires operate on the same principle, and you trust your life to them.)

It is utterly absurd to state, as many have, that "all air mattresses, even the best, eventually leak or fail." This is true only in the sense that all man-made objects, even the Great Pyramid of Cheops, eventually "fail" or wear out—if you extend the word "eventually" far enough. I have had quite a few air mattresses of different makes, some quite inexpensive and most of very light construction—I do a lot of whitewater rafting, and since I have to carry an air pump on the boat anyway, I figure I may as well get some use out of it in the evenings. I have used them under very brutal conditions, camping on rocky gravel bars and the like, by foot, paddle, and pedal, and I have had exactly *one* of them go flat. That happened when I stupidly dropped a fish knife point-down onto it. (I had it patched and reinflated for bedtime that night and used it for another couple of years before Trailways managed to lose it.)

Of course, only good air mattresses are worth considering. Those cheap vinyl jobs you see in time stores are strictly poolside toys. I have seen them fail to make it through even a single night. There's no point in bothering to carry the thing and blow it up and then end up on the ground anyway—and I know of few things as loathsome as waking up at three in the morning with a flat air mattress.

My own hands-down choice is a lightweight, hip-length air mattress. I don't see any need for a full-length type; or rather, I think you can put up with the slight loss of comfort in order to save the weight. You can put some clothing under your legs if you feel you need padding in that area, something like a folded-up rain suit.

My own air mattress was bought from L. L. Bean. (Readers may by now have guessed it—I have a pretty high opinion of L. L. Bean's outdoor gear, even if their clothes are the chic thing with a lot of tiresome people.) It cost me $16, weighs a whopping 8 ounces, and takes up less room than a spare shirt. It has six separate air chambers, each of which inflates to the correct pressure with one easy lungful, so if one did go flat for some reason I would still be able to get through the night.

Fragile? That little coated-nylon mattress has been slept on in some awfully rugged places. Last fall I used it on a month-long hike in the Ozarks through country so rocky that I ruined a brand-new pair of Army combat boots, and never had anything between the mattress and the ground but a sheet of Visqueen plastic—and, because it had been a dry year and there was a fire hazard, I camped out in open, rocky ground rather than the softer forest floor. *It has never gone flat or otherwise failed—* and incidentally, I weigh 200 pounds.

One common reason for air-mattress failure is overinflation. It is silly to blow up an air mattress hard; the whole point is to have something soft to sleep on. If it is correctly inflated, it will seem very limp and flabby until you lie on it. It should contain just barely enough air to keep your hips and shoulders from touching the ground when you lie down. If it is blown up hard enough so that you can sit up on it and not feel the earth under your behind, it's too hard for sleeping—if you use it as a seat in camp, let some air out before going to bed. Of course, you ought to have a ground-sheet or poncho or something under it, if you aren't sleeping in a floored-in tent—more of that later on.

Foam pads are currently the fashion among outdoor people in this country. To a certain extent, this reflects the evil reputation gained by the older air mattresses, as noted above. It also reflects a good deal of faddishness, contemporary wilderness types being as given to following fashions and trends as any disco crowd, no matter how hotly they deny this.

Foam does have its advantages, there's no denying it. You can totally forget about punctures and any other kind of damage—you can even whip out your knife and whack off a chunk of foam to pad your handlebars or use it as a target to play darts with your spare spokes, without any harm at all to its function. It is very light; a foam pad weighs much less than the standard, full-length, large-chamber air mattress, though not significantly less than a modern hip-length lightweight. And foam has one important edge over air. It makes a great insulator. An air mattress lets heat escape through air convection within the chambers, a bad thing in cold weather or with a marginal sleeping bag (though nice on a hot night). A medium-thickness foam pad does quite a bit to improve the performance of a blanket bed and doesn't cost much, so the hard-up bikepacker should consider foam as the obvious way to go. On top of all that, some people actually claim to be able to get halfway comfortable on the things.

This is very hard for me to believe. I have tried foam many times; until I got my superlight air mattress, I wanted desperately to use foam for its lightness. I've never been able to get more than five degrees above miserable on any foam pad I've ever tried, except for some open-cell stuff that was far too bulky for any cycling use. In fact, on foam I can just barely tell I'm not sleeping on the bare ground—a couple of times I've actually stuck my hand out of the bag and felt around to make sure I didn't forget to put the pad down. As insulation, foam is wonderful—on cold-weather trips, I often carry a thin foam pad to use in addition to the little air mattress since after all, they don't weigh that much put together—but as something to sleep on, it is just about on a level with hanging upside down from a tree limb like a bat.

Yet, in all fairness, many people find a foam pad very comfortable indeed, or so they say. Perhaps weight and body build comes into it here. As I confessed a while back, I do weigh a couple of hundred pounds. Somebody with less body weight to compress the foam and a bit more subcutaneous fat might like a foam pad just fine—my 12-year-old daughter loves to sleep on foam and refuses to use an air mattress at all. (But why does my 90-pound wife find foam unbearably hard, and why do so many women, with their layer of padding, feel the same way? Truly a mystery all around.)

I hate to sound as if I'm whipping on foam, because I'm not—if you can get comfortable sleeping on it, it's an economical and trouble-free bed, and I wish you well. Yet I've got to drag up another point here, an important one. Foam pads may be fine for backpackers, who can just roll them up and tie them on top of their packs, but bikies, as we keep remembering, have to fight the atmosphere all the time. Indeed, there are published studies that show what a huge amount of the work of pedaling a bicycle is due to air resistance. That's just speaking of the normal resistance of still air. If there's a headwind—and there always, *always* is (see Bikepacker's Law #2 in Appendix A)—the problem is even worse.

A foam pad is hard to pack in any way that does not add a great deal of frontal area to your load. However, this can be minimized by wrapping the pad around your stuffed sleeping bag before lashing the whole thing atop your carrier. As noted, I sometimes carry a thin pad in cold weather. Also, because of some problems with my knees, I often carry a small piece of foam (about 2 feet square) to put under them at night. That is how I carry a pad—wrapped around my bag—and it seems to add little air resistance and probably protects the bag as well.

Foam comes in various thicknesses. Half-inch is the usual choice; anything thinner is awfully hard to sleep on, and anything thicker is bulky and awkward to pack. You can get pads in hip-length or full-length sizes, but since the full-length kind weighs little more, you might as well have full-length comfort. (Full-length for *you*—there's no sense in a 5-foot person carrying a 6-foot pad; take a knife and cut it to fit.) Ensolite seems to be the most common material, but some of the others, notably Volarfoam, are cheaper and are said to be better in some ways. All foam feels alike to me, so I can't say. Some of the more brittle, blue foams seem to be prone to leaving little chunks lying on the ground, a particularly odious form of litter—if you use them, be sure to clean up after yourself.

Open-cell foam pads are far too bulky for cycling use. The kind with a waterproof nylon cover gets around the tendency of open-cell foam to soak up water, but at the cost of considerable added weight. You can pack a featherweight air mattress and a 6-ounce foam pad for less weight and bulk than one of these, and have the advantages of both systems.

There exist *air pillows.* I intend to get one; I think the idea is admirable, and the weight is very little, as is the price. Since I am still at the stage of failing to get around to obtaining one, my information on brands and designs is zilch. If you do not have one, simply roll up some clothing. (One fellow I met said he took his spare tubes—he was carrying two, and on that road he needed them—pumped in a little air, folded them a couple of times, and wrapped the whole works in his windbreaker. Said it was comfortable, and it sounds reasonable enough.)

Hammocks seem appealing in many ways, and a string-net hammock is virtually weightless. You would certainly be free of the need for a groundsheet or even a level place to bed down, and in wet, boggy country you'd be up above the muck. I suspect you would find it difficult to stay warm except in summer, and I wonder if you can sleep comfortably in a hammock unless you are a Jivaro Indian or an old-time sailor.

After I raised the question in *Bicycling* magazine, one correspondent pointed out that one can easily damage trees by slinging a hammock improperly. Obviously only the most utter lout would drive hooks or bolts into a living tree (though, if you'll check around any popular campground, you'll find that the lout count is far from negligible), but apparently wrapping nylon cord or rope around certain trees also can chew through the bark, which can allow certain parasites, particularly boring insects, to attack the trees.

Do not cut boughs or tips from living trees to make a bed. I think this practice has been pretty well eliminated, but there are still a few old-time "woodcraft" guidebooks floating around, and people who trained under scoutmasters of the old school, so I want to make sure we get the word out. There are places in the Far North or the jungle, perhaps, where human traffic is light enough to tolerate this sort of thing, but you are unlikely to reach them by bicycle. Don't cut *any* living tree or shrub, for *any* reason—if you don't understand why, you shouldn't be in the woods to begin with. Anyway, the old-time bough beds takes just about a full day to make.

Sleep well.

*People who have tried it, tell me
that a clear conscience makes you very
happy and contented; but a full stomach
does the business quite as well, and
is cheaper, and more easily obtained.*

—Jerome K. Jerome

CHAPTER 4

___ The Well-Equipped Chef

Almost everyone seems to get a kick out of preparing and eating food in the outdoors Many an old-fashioned male who would be scandalized at the thought of helping his wife in the kitchen at home takes great pride in his "camp cookin'"—and many a modern-day "liberated" woman who views kitchen work as loathsome drudgery and a gas range as a tool of medieval slavery will go into open ecstasies over a white-gas pressure stove, a set of nesting pots, and a selection of freeze-dried food. Odd. But then, if archaeologists are right, we were cooking and eating around outdoor fires long before we were much more than sport-model chimps, so it's only natural that something deep within us responds to the idea.

Not that cooking in any form is always a necessity for the cycle camper. For shorter trips, especially in warm weather, some people elect to dispense with cookery altogether. Instead, they eat foods that need no preparation: bread, sausage, cheese, dried or fresh fruits, peanuts, and so on. In this way they are able to get rid of a considerable amount of weight and bulk in the form of pots and pans, eating and cooking utensils, and stove. They feel that this more than compensates for any hardship in the meal department. (It might seem that there is also a saving in money, especially in the stove and its fuel, but no-cook foods generally cost quite a lot, so over any appreciable time this saving is illusory. Also, people on no-cook diets are much more likely to succumb to the temptation to visit a roadside cafe or truckstop for a hot meal, which really runs the tab up.)

This no-cook alternative is not to be dismissed altogether; in fact, for overnight or even weekend trips, it's worth trying now and then—especially in hot weather, when most of us don't have much enthusiasm for hot food anyway, and every ounce saved is a gallon or two less sweat. There are plenty of nourishing no-cook foods around, if you use your imagination. If you are a vegetarian or into health foods and don't want to eat salami, chocolate, or whatever, I'm sure there are things you can get at a health-food store that would be satisfactory. (You also probably like fresh fruits and raw vegetables, perhaps, which can often be obtained from farmers and the like.) Bearing in mind the limitations of the individual items (for example, greasy sausage or salty cheese is really going to run up your water consumption and your body's heat production, which is rough in the summer, though worth bearing in mind in cold weather), you should have no problem eating properly.

There is also a slightly modified no-cook approach, which might be called the hardly-any-cook system. If all you want is an occasional cup of coffee or other hot drink, and perhaps the odd hot meal for variety, you can heat water directly in a steel, Sierra-type cup and warm a can of stew or soup (bought at a roadside grocery shortly before making camp) in its own can. For this kind of minimal "cooking" it is usually all right to make a tiny little twig fire, if you carefully obliterate the traces afterward. Or you can carry a can of Sterno and learn to develop your patience while waiting for that first bubble.

The no-cook approach is obviously a very limited one. It is feasible only in relatively settled areas, and it requires a stop at a fairly well-stocked store just about every day. This is because no-cook foods tend to be so heavy and bulky—with few exceptions, they contain a lot of water—and in many cases they're highly perishable as well. Bread is a constant bother, being bulky and crumbly, though less so in the case of hard rolls and crackerlike breads such as Ry-Krisp. Cheese stinks up your whole outfit in hot weather, and not all sausages are safe without refrigeration. Stores often sell such foods in prepackaged quantities that leave you with more than you can eat before it goes bad, which causes waste. (If there is such a thing as sin in the 1980s, wasting food has got to be a mortal one.) Finally, in cold or rainy weather, hot foods and drinks can be comforting and even necessary to basic health.

In any case, outdoor cooking is in itself one of the joys of the whole business. For most people, it isn't really "camping out" without a meal cooked in camp. So you'll almost certainly want your outfit to include the means for doing this, even though the cooking in most cases will consist of nothing more complicated than boiling water.

Fires

In Greek mythology, the gods got seriously annoyed with a fellow named Prometheus because he gave people the secret of fire. Ever since then, there's been ongoing tension between people who make fires and authority figures who wish they wouldn't. With good reason. Fire may be man's oldest friend, but people have managed to do more damage to their world with various forms of fire than with any other human invention except agriculture.

Nowhere is this controversy more vigorous, even bitter at times, than in the campfires-versus-stoves debate. Those opposed to fires hurl charges of ecological irresponsibility and general messiness at their opponents; the campfire builders respond with countercharges of elitism and oversimplification. To some extent, the campfire question has become one of those symbolic issues, like gun control or vegetarianism, in which one's position can be taken as standing for a whole set of attitudes and values of dubious relevancy. This is really too bad, because in this case both groups are largely made up of people with a genuine love and respect for the land, and valid arguments can be advanced for either side.

On balance, I think, there are more situations in which a fire is not justified than in which it is. It's not that fires in themselves are basically bad—fire is a natural force, and fires from lightning are actually part of the ecological cycle in most areas. A careful camper can obliterate all signs of having built a fire, especially the small, clean-burning fires that such a person will always build. (Ask those frontier scouts who tried to track

Indian renegades—renegades being, as Ed Abbey reminds us, Indians unwilling to camp in Officially Designated Campsites.) The real problem is the steady pressure of outlandish numbers of people.

In the old days, it was fine to build fires, cut boughs for beds, ditch tents, and the like because people were few and the wilderness was huge. The odds were that nobody would pass that way for another 50 years; the land could absorb any reasonable impact. But people kept coming in greater and greater numbers, and most of them treated the land in such a way as to produce a very unreasonable impact indeed. So nowadays we've got very little real wild country left. Since camping in such country is a very popular activity and not all the people doing it know what they're doing or are even willing to try to learn, it is vital that we bend over backwards to make sure that our own impact is as minimal as possible.

It is therefore almost never justifiable to build an open fire in an area of heavy human impact. In popular recreation areas, such as much of the Appalachian Trail (many parts of which can be reached by bike), or the more accessible parts of the Sierras, it is not only wrong to build a fire, you should even make a point of cleaning up and scattering the remains of fires that others have made.

Now, those of us who have been banging around the outdoors for many years tend to regard much of this as irrelevant to ourselves because we usually have places we know about where hardly anyone ever goes, and we can relax a bit and have a fire now and then. But very few such places can be reached on a bicycle. Generally, if you can get to a place by bike, other people can get there—and do—by things like jeeps and horses. Certainly, you can get away from the real heavy-use areas and should try to do so. The fact remains, though, that any place accessible by bike has already suffered some impact in the form of a road or trail. This means that bikepackers have to be extra-conscientious about such things as building open fires.

It might be added here that you don't always have a choice. On many public lands, open fires are forbidden entirely; you'd better check such regulations, because the penalties can be quite severe. Also, private landowners, corporate or individual, often will let you camp on their land only on the condition that you build no fires. (Many times I have persuaded a wavering landowner to let me in by whipping out my stove and saying, "You can see I won't have to build any fires for you to worry about.")

What are the argument against fires? They use up organic material that needs to return to the often worn-out earth; they leave blackened spots if inexpert campers fail to clean up; they pose a serious threat of forest fires if not carefully built and constantly watched, and afterwards meticulously extinguished; they interfere with the pleasure of other campers who smell the smoke or see the flame, since they must worry whether the person building the fire has sense enough to keep it safe. On the subjective level, they smoke and stink if not built right; they're a lot of work to make and clean up after; they're hard to light in the wet (when you need them most); they push back the night and keep wildlife at a distance—admittedly not always a bad thing; they dirty up your pots. In public campgrounds, which have fireplaces and thus are free from most of the usual objections, it's nearly impossible to find firewood anyway, the Winnebago brigade having cleaned it all up to build huge bonfires over which to roast their wienies.

Now having said all that, let's incur the wrath of the purists a bit and submit that there are times when a fire has a lot going for it. It warms your bones on a cool evening—especially if you build it in front of a lean-to tarp shelter, which traps and reflects the heat of even a tiny fire—and it creates a kind of atavistic ambience that many enjoy. In a group, the campfire is traditionally the social center, and to a solo camper, it is a cheerful friend to help break the loneliness. You can cook things with a fire, or rather its coals, that are impossible with a stove. The smoke, while annoying, can be minimized by careful wood selection and, at any rate, helps keep mosquitoes away. Finally, if you want to split environmental hairs, there's nothing all that ecologically pure about a stove that burns fossil fuels, let alone one that uses throw-away metal canisters.

Despite the statements of various hardliners, with whose philosophy I basically agree, there is nothing so bad about building a *small, controlled* fire, if—

1. the situation is such that there is no forest-fire hazard, such as strong winds, thick undergrowth or inflammable ground cover, or dry conditions;

2. human traffic is light enough, and/or the fuel supply plentiful enough that no harm will be done by gathering and burning a few sticks;

3. wood can be obtained without cutting any standing tree; and

4. it will be possible to obliterate all traces of the fire (as well as other signs of your visit) before leaving, except of course when using fireplaces in public campgrounds.

For example, in the area where I usually operate, the Ozark and Ouachita Mountains of Arkansas, Missouri, and Oklahoma, there is currently an unusual problem: we are overrun with beavers. Lacking natural enemies and no longer trapped in any numbers, the damned things are an actual pest and destroy trees with almost the same enthusiasm as that of the paper companies. So one can walk along anywhere near a wild stream and pick up armloads of sun-dried billets from which the beavers have carefully stripped the bark. The beaver-cut brush is so heavy in some areas, even places of quite heavy human traffic (such as the Buffalo River basin), that it poses an actual fire hazard. In these places, I routinely build fires unless there is a bad forest-fire hazard in effect (at which times I try to stay out of the woods anyway), even though the beavers' favorite, willow, isn't really prime firewood.

You may run into a parallel situation. Along the West Coast, especially the Northwest, the beaches are frequently littered with driftwood and logging debris. In public parks and campgrounds, the rangers occasionally pile up firewood from trees they have had to cut down for some purpose such as disease control; you might as well use it. A severe storm may have blown down a great deal of dead stuff, and so on; you get the picture. If there is more wood lying around than is needed for the soil-reconstitution cycle, it's okay to burn a little bit of it, all other considerations being clearly understood.

As mentioned before, public-campground fireplaces eliminate many of the hazards of fire, and since the sites are already there, you aren't responsible for their ugliness. But you've got your bike, so ride off up the road a few miles to gather your fuel; don't pick it up around the perimeter of the campground, even if you can find any (it's unlikely).

Sometimes you will find a blackened fire ring and some piled-up wood that somebody left behind. It may be best to go ahead and use the ring and burn up the wood, if there isn't too much of it or if the area isn't too heavily picked over. Then in the morning, scatter the rocks, black side down of course, mix the ashes into the dirt, cover the site with ground cover, such as leaves, and otherwise try to obliterate it. When I do something like that, I feel that my cleaning-up-after-others efforts have earned me the right to one fire of my own. (Indeed, the only possible justification for camping in a heavy-use area is if you will clean up after others and leave every campsite cleaner and better than you found it.)

As for the actual business of building the fire, I don't want to go into that in any great detail, because a person who still has to learn such things from books is probably not qualified to judge whether or not a fire should be built at all. I feel strongly that novice woods people should stick with stoves, *period.* They should get their open-fire training under experienced supervision. But perhaps a few basics are in order.

Before building any fire, unless you are using a fireplace, clear away the ground cover right down to mineral-soil level—this usually means some digging. Remember, most forest topsoil is rich in organic matter and will smolder and burn. Get it clear for a good wide radius around the fire, so sparks can't jump. Pile the scraped-back cover where you can easily replace it next morning. If you're building a fire on sand or natural gravel, then dig down a little way past the top layer so that you can cover the blackened part afterwards. The usual "fire ring" is unnecessary if you do everything else right and make a very small, concentrated fire, but you'll probably want a few rocks to make a rest for your pots; don't get them from a stream or they may explode when hot. Remember, next day before you leave, all this stuff has to be put back as it was, including turning the blackened rocks face down and breaking up any unnatural patterns, such as circles.

The key to getting a fire going is to get enough kindling. Gather a lot of little twigs, no bigger than pencil size and at least half smaller than that; get about twice as much of this stuff as you think you'll need. Make sure it's all good dry wood, but not rotten. Pile it in such a way that air can get in; start with a small amount and add the rest as it catches fire. Then you can add the bigger stuff.

"Bigger" usually means up to broomstick thickness and no more than a couple of feet long. You want wood that will burn up completely and not leave blackened butts that ugly up the area or conceal a burning spark. By lifting a stick, you should be able to feel if it's good and dry—the fast-burning dry wood will feel much lighter—and a whack against a tree will reveal the rotten stuff that won't burn cleanly. If it's good wood, you can break it into lengths with hand and foot; if it won't break cleanly, it's too green. You don't need an axe or saw.

Keep your fire very small and concentrated, and keep poking the sticks inward and turning them so that they burn up completely and cleanly. Make it burn itself out; this makes it much easier to make sure it's completely out. Don't make a great big pile of wood you can't possibly use. Experience will show you these things.

Some paper will help get a fire started—I often use the little instruction sheet from 35mm. film boxes, or food wrappers—as will a candle stub, if it's damp weather. If you're experienced enough to get a campfire going in the rain, you don't need me to tell you how to do it.

If I seem to have gone on and on about fires, it's mostly because I want to make you think awfully hard about whether you wouldn't just as soon forget the whole laborious business. Except for oddball situations (since the beavers went crazy in the Ozarks, I think I've built fires more often than I've used stoves), I think the average cycle camper is much better served by using a lightweight stove, and certainly ought to own one if at all possible.

Stoves

Having, no doubt, managed to enrage everyone on both sides of the fires-versus-stoves question, let's look at the stove picture.

The development of small, compact, lightweight, single-burner stoves has been a great blessing to outdoor cooks on the grounds of labor and hassle alone. Rather than spending an hour rustling up firewood and another hour getting it to burn, or staggering around in the morning fooling with a fire before breakfast, you can have almost the same convenience as you do in your kitchen at home. Stoves don't blacken pots badly, burn fiercely even in the rain, can be operated inside a tent (with great care and precautions), and don't blow smoke in your eyes. The price may be high, but fuel costs are reasonable enough, and a good stove will last for years. As I already mentioned, there are some very nice areas where you won't even be permitted to use anything else—the fine for an unauthorized fire is a lot heftier than the price of even the most expensive stove. There are several different types of stoves on the market, each with its good and bad points and its vocal adherents, so we'd better see what's going on here.

Lightweight camp stoves are primarily classified according to the type of fuel used. This will dictate not only performance, but the shape and construction of the stove. With one remarkable exception, and that a partial one, each make of stove burns only one type of fuel. The most popular camp-stove fuels at the present are so-called "white gasoline," and pressurized gas, usually butane or propane.

White-gasoline pressure stoves have been around a long time now and are a very popular item with backpackers, ski tourers, and mountain climbers. The name is a misnomer; the correct fuel is Coleman or a similar liquid intended for these stoves, though, to be sure, such fuels are essentially white gasoline. The point here is that automotive gasoline, white or otherwise, should not be used except perhaps in emergencies; the additives will gradually clog up the orifice and the fumes are extremely dangerous, especially lead. But the name is common and handy, so we'll use it anyway.

The most popular of the imported pressure stoves is the Swedish SVEA, with its vaselike shape and fitted brass windscreen. The various Optimus stoves, made by the same company, are also well liked, though most are heavier. The American Coleman Peak 1 is currently catching on very well; with the usual Coleman sturdiness and quality, it is indeed a fine product, and its considerable size is partly cancelled by its rather awesome fuel capacity.

All these stoves operate on the same basic principle: the heat of the flame keeps the fuel vaporized and therefore under pressure, once the stove is going. Getting it going is something else. The Coleman, and some of the bigger imports, such as the Phoebus, the Optimus 111, or the good old Baby Enders, have little built-in pressure pumps with which you pump up inside pressure before starting. The SVEA and some of the various Optimi lack pumps, and there is a whole arcane body of knowledge involving various tricks to get them started. Most of these tricks involve mucking about with little drips and drops of loose gasoline in the priming cup, a built-in element of added hazard there, to say nothing of the hassle if your hands are cold. There is a little "mini-pump" you can get that screws into the filler cap of an SVEA or pumpless Optimus. It weighs 3 ounces, costs a few bucks, and adds so much convenience that I cannot understand why anyone would own one of these stoves without it.

Which of these stoves is best for cycling? They're all well made and serviceable. (Or rather, the European and American stoves are. Certain Oriental copies of the Swedish stoves exist that are so dreadfully bad, it hurts to think about them. They're unreliable, crudely made, and about as safe as an exploding Pinto.) The only real question is that of weight and bulk. The old standby, the Optimus 111, is too big and heavy for cycling use. Its little cousin, the Optimus 8R, is considerably handier, and its shape packs nicely into a pannier bag, but it's still a bit heavier than other offerings (though not prohibitively so—I own and use one). Most people will arrive at a choice between the SVEA and

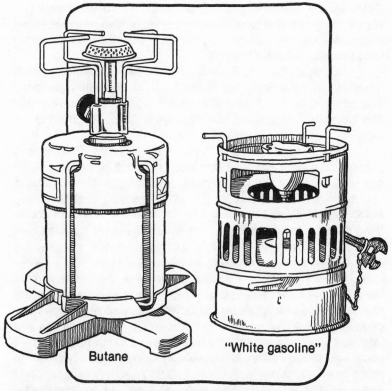

Butane

"White gasoline"

Types of stoves: "white gasoline" SVEA 123 (right), butane Bleuet S-200 (left).

the Coleman Peak 1, simply because these are the most widely available makes in this country at present.

I mentioned earlier that the Coleman is a good deal heavier and bigger (1 pound 15 ounces to 1 pound 2 ounces for the SVEA—both empty—and the Coleman is also 1½ inches taller), but most of this is fuel tank. On a longer trip, you'll have to carry a can of additional fuel, so this greater capacity cancels out the weight difference. But on an overnight trip, you may not need the capacity of the Coleman. My own experience also indicates that the Coleman is much easier to get started—this may be in part a matter of practice—and performs better in the wind. It is by far the hottest of all the light stoves, producing a hellish big flame, which is still easy to regulate at low levels. Prices of the two stoves are roughly similar, but you'll have to buy the SVEA's pump separately, whereas the Coleman already comes with one, so the Coleman works out to be marginally cheaper. As you may have guessed, I've used both, am currently rather taken with the Coleman, but feel that you would not go wrong whichever you chose. (For what it's worth, my guess is that inexperienced people will find the Coleman easier to operate, but such people tend to prefer butane anyway.)

If you do get the SVEA, get the fitted windscreen, which greatly improves efficiency and safety. (It comes with a perfectly silly little pot that has no use worth mentioning, but never mind.) The Coleman has a weird but effective built-in windshield of its own.

You'll need to carry fuel on longer trips. This means acquiring a proper gasoline container; this stuff is far too volatile and explosive to carry just any old way. Special little containers are made for the specific purpose of carrying fuel for camp stoves, and nothing else should be considered. You need something *solid,* because on a bike, you always have the possibility of a fall or crash or even being hit by a vehicle, and a flimsy gasoline container will turn your bike into a bomb.

Sigg cylindrical aluminum bottles are the usual choice. Many bikepackers carry one of these in an ordinary water-bottle clip, sometimes slung *under* the down tube, and this is a rather good idea. (In a bad crash, this bottle would probably fly out and land well clear of everybody, which is an added safety factor—I don't mind telling you, *all* stove fuels make me very edgy when I'm riding down a highway with a lot of traffic.) Another excellent fuel can is the flat, easily packed, stainless-steel container made by

Donner Mountain Corporation. They are not cheap, but they come with well-designed pouring spouts and built-in filters. This last is a good feature, and if you use a filterless can, be sure to get one of those filler funnels with the mesh filter. It will save you spilled fuel, clogged burners, and maybe something worse. Also be sure to get one of those special filler caps with the little plastic pouring spout. Without one, you'll slop gasoline all over the place, which is dangerous and expensive.

Still, that Coleman burns 3½ hours at full blast on a tank of gas, and takes less than three minutes to boil a quart of water. Most of the dried stuff favored by campers only has to be boiled for a few minutes, or if longer, simmered, which uses less gas. You ought to be able to hack it for quite a few days on a full Peak 1 tank, especially if you eat no-cook lunches. So the above information on gas tanks may not relate to you.

Butane is the convenience fuel that comes in little steel canisters, already pressurized. With a butane stove, you just turn the knob and stick a match to the gas, just like your kitchen stove. (There are even models with electric ignition, but this does seem a little effete.) The better butane stoves, of which the most popular is the French Bleuet, are totally reliable and do not have to be fiddled with in any way. Refilling is simply a matter of installing another canister. This is why inexperienced campers, or campers who are put off by the occasional hassles of liquid-fuel stoves or are a bit afraid of gasoline, usually choose butane.

Butane stoves are a little bit heavier than white-gas models of comparable capacity and efficiency, though the bulk is about the same. Extra canisters of butane do add weight and take up a lot of room. The heating efficiency of butane is somewhat less than that of white gas, but in mild weather, this is nothing to worry about. Butane doesn't work well at freezing temperatures, but few people go cycle camping under such conditions. While a butane stove may take a bit longer to bring water to a boil, this may be canceled out by the extra time needed to get the white-gas stove going in the first place, something that you never see figured into those neat little charts.

One real drawback of butane: Its efficiency drops off drastically as the last contents of the canister are burned. In fact, at the end there is a point when the stove will not generate enough heat to boil water, yet the canister still contains too much gas to throw away or even to remove safely. This is a serious handicap; it seems that you always reach this point just when you really need the stove, such as at the end of a very long, cold, wet day, and it is very unpleasant to have to sit and watch the stove sputter and flicker its way out before you can have your hot cocoa. Indeed, this is probably the single factor most often responsible for people abandoning butane as a camp-stove fuel.

The canisters must be discarded in a proper way, not thrown into the woods. Cyclists usually have no problems with this—and anybody stupid and insensitive enough to throw a Bleuet canister on the ground would find something else to make a mess with anyway. Still, the whole concept of a one-shot, disposable, nonrecyclable container is rather alien to the modern ethic—I've certainly had my twinges about it.

You cannot tell, except by rough guess, whether a butane canister is nearly full or nearly empty, and there is no way to fill a partially empty one before leaving home, which can be inconvenient. A few butane stoves have a provision for removing and replacing partially full canisters, but the Bleuet does not. Once it's on, it must be totally empty before removal. Besides being the most widely popular stove on the market, the Bleuet is also the only one whose cartridges are readily available in most cities.

In spite of all of these criticisms, I think butane has a place; I use my own Bleuet very often. In wet weather, when I may have to cook inside the tent, I always take the Bleuet—cooking inside the tent is dangerous enough without the added hazard of a possible gasoline spill. Anyone just starting out in the outdoors might be better off with butane at first; it's easier to use, and that's one less thing to have to get the hang of. While butane itself is in the long run a more expensive fuel, the Bleuet is quite a bit cheaper than any white-gas stove, about half the price of the Coleman or SVEA. This last point may be the decisive one for may people.

I'd better mention here that there are some very tiny butane and LP-gas stoves made for mountain climbers and the like; the Bleuet Globetrotter is a half-capacity version of the bigger S-200, for example. These little stoves might seem like good choices for the cyclist, but beware of the limited fuel capacity and the above-mentioned properties of butane as you exhaust the canister. Butane is even less efficient when broken down into several small containers, and since you'll have to carry more canisters, the little stove winds up being heavier than the big one. It may be good for overnighters, but who can afford to buy a stove for nothing but overnighters, or possibly as an auxiliary to a mainly no-cook trip? Certainly these are not serious stoves for extended bicycle camping.

The very light, compact, and efficient Hank Roberts Mini Stove has great potential for cycle camping. It is in many ways better designed than the Bleuet, and it's lighter and more compact. Fuel for it, however, has not been widely available in the U.S. compared to the availability of Bleuet's Gaz cartridges. Recently, however, a few discount and sporting-goods stores have begun to carry the Hank Roberts Mini, so it is possible that this may become a really worthwhile alternative. Let's hope so, anyway.

Propane gas is widely available in the familiar, long, heavy cartridges. Heavy, heavy, heavy. Remember that word. Too bad; the best propane stoves, notably the Primus Grasshopper, burn like inferni even in subfreezing weather, have all the convenience of butane, and do not lose efficiency in the same way. The cartridges are sold at all sorts of rural stores and small-town hardware emporia, too, being universally used in soldering torches. If somebody could invent a lighter canister, propane would be wonderful.

Alcohol is certainly very safe and clean burning, and will no doubt be available when fossil fuels become extinct. (A point worth considering—it is possible that we will see the day when gasoline is far too precious to let us burn it in our little stoves.) If gasoline and butane make you nervous, and they indeed are explosive and should be treated as such, alcohol may steady your nerves. As it may do anyway, but alcohol stoves burn the no-drink kind, which is probably just as well. Alcohol isn't pressurized, so the stoves are very light and simple. In fact, the alcohol mostly just sort of lies there and burns.

Unfortunately, alcohol is an inefficient fuel, and you'll have to carry a lot more of it and wait a lot longer for your meals. It is also hideously expensive, the most expensive of all stove fuels. Very few American bikies and packies use it, though it is popular in Europe, where white gas is virtually unobtainable. (But for all that, given world fuel supplies, alcohol still may be the wave of the future.)

Kerosene is used in many parts of the world and does burn with a very hot flame. Kerosene is quite safe to use, being nonvolatile compared to gasoline, and nonexplosive. It is reasonably efficient, at least comparable to butane. But it is hard to start (you have to carry special primer paste), it's foul smelling, and it gives off a towering column of black, oily smoke that clings to everything—your pots, your tent, your face. All the same, in some countries, such as Mexico, it may be the only fuel you can get. Kerosene stoves tend to be pretty heavy, too, and rather expensive, though kerosene itself, when you can find it for sale at all, is dirt cheap.

Sterno, for all practical purposes, does not work. I would use it only if the alternative were to give up going out at all. It does make a neato fire starter.

There is one more type of stove that should be mentioned. It's rather a make of stove, since only one on the market falls into this category. This is the unique and ingenious Multi-Fuel stove made by Mountain Safety Research, manufacturers of the excellent yellow helmet. This remarkable device will cheerfully burn Coleman, Blazo, Stoddard solvent, diesel fuel, #1 stove oil, JP-4 jet fuel (this probably of marginal relevancy for bicycle campers), kerosene, regular auto gasoline for a couple of hours before the burner clogs up, and, I suspect, though I have not seen any reports, quite possibly gasohol. I'm not certain you couldn't get it to run on beans. For people going to really remote places (such as the amazing Mr. Hibell), the MSR Multi-Fuel is the obvious choice. I would not get one, however, unless I had a real need for its versatility; it is very expensive (more so than it looks—in addition to its whopping price tag, it has no fuel tank, but runs off a Sigg fuel bottle, so you have to buy that too), and its various connections and fittings are very fiddly and delicate. The stove in effect consists of a kind of kit that you have to assemble every time you use it, and this is a great pain, particularly with wet, cold hands—though it starts quite easily and readily once you get it together. It is indeed very light for its heat output. Except for those who need the multi-fuel capability, I don't recommend it. There is a version that burns only regular fuel, but I don't see the point of it at all, unless you have lots of money and simply enjoy tinkering with a lot of little parts all the time. Come to think of it, that does describe a good many bicycle people.

To sum up, then: Gasoline is more efficient, especially in cold weather, and over the long run the fuel is cheaper, though the stove itself isn't; the weight-to-efficiency ratio is also better with gasoline. Butane is much more convenient to start and refill, though there are problems as the cartridge nears emptiness, and it is clean burning and somewhat safer. Propane has many excellent qualities, but the weight makes it marginal for cycling.

Other fuels have drawbacks that make them poor for bikepacking use. On balance, it comes down to a choice between butane and white gas, and the advantages and disadvantages of these fuels are so nearly matched, and in many cases based on such subjective considerations (convenience, for example), that it is really up to the individual to decide.

It is often said that gasoline is more widely obtainable in rural areas, but this is rather misleading. Coleman fuel is indeed sold all over the country, but only in big, heavy, gallon cans—what are you going to do with something like that, tie it on top of your bike? You might just possibly find some people at a campground and persuade them to split the cost of a can among a bunch of you, but I wouldn't hold my breath. Actually, you've got a better chance of finding a Bleuet canister for sale—they've become very popular—than of finding somebody who'll sell you a single liter of Coleman. Realistically, you're going to have to carry your own fuel supplies, so it hardly matters what you choose in this regard. If you're going on a super-longie and fuel replacement is looming ominously in your mind, get an MSR Multi-Fuel, or go to propane and live with the weight.

Other odds and ends of the information just to confuse you further: If the hissing roar of most gasoline stoves put you off, the Coleman Peak 1 is uncannily quiet; I don't know how they did it, but bless them for it. The little German Baby Enders is one hell of a fine stove if you can find a source. Butane canisters get cold as the contents evaporate, so watch out about touching one on a cold morning with your bare hands. If you have sinus trouble, you may not be able to stand to use white gas. (One writer, in an otherwise not-bad book on backpacking, wrote that Coleman fuel was "odorless"; I can only conclude that a bear had bitten his nose off.) Don't let white gas get onto your tires; if it does, wipe it off fast.

Safety

You ought to know the rules about open fires: Don't leave them unattended, even briefly, don't build them at all if it's windy or very dry, drown them and redrown them before leaving. If you have to be told things like that, you don't belong in the woods at all! I understand Smokey the Bear has had it with telling people nicely and is practicing with a .44 Magnum, so you'd better watch it. Make sure other people watch it too. I have on a couple of occasions used the threat of physical violence, when all else failed, to make a careless camper go back and put out a smoldering fire, and I would not condemn anybody else who did the same. (You might not be able to bring this off—I stand 6'3" and weigh 200 and was on one occasion holding a machete—but I toss it in for what it may be worth.) You have every right to do these things, because if some jerk sets the woods on fire, you'll burn up too.

Stoves must be treated with respect. Gasoline is a more powerful explosive than dynamite; butane is nothing to kid around with either. Handle any stove with the same respectful care you would give a live grenade. When you fill your stove, get well away from others, preferably in a clear, sunlit area (where any spilled fuel will quickly evaporate), and *never* fill the stove inside a tent, no matter how hard it's raining. Don't stow your stove inside the tent, or even nearby, if you're using candles; don't smoke (anything) around gasoline. Should you build a fire, remember to put the stove somewhere well clear of the area, and your fuel can as well. If you have to burn auto gas in an emergency, make sure you've got lots of ventilation, and don't sit too close to the stove while it's burning.

In view of several incidents reported in outdoor magazines, I'd better add that your stove is a precision instrument designed by trained engineers. *Do not get cute with it,* by trying to lighten it or improve its performance with home-rolled modifications. A few clever types have managed to blow their stoves to bits—and, on occasion, themselves—with such efforts as home-designed windscreens that caused stoves to overheat.

Butane seems safer, and it is in some ways, but you can definitely blow up a butane stove if you go at it right. The cartridge *must be cool* as it runs. *Never* put a butane stove down among rocks, in a hole in the ground, or in any other arrangement that causes heat to be trapped or reflected down onto the canister. It *must* have free air circulation to keep it cool. If the fuel canister gets overheated, it will go off like a bomb, and a couple of people have wound up in the hospital for long stays by doing this.

Many single-burner stoves are a bit unstable, particularly with a pot on top, so be sure the ground is level when you set up the stove. Read the directions for your stove and follow them to the letter, with the literal-mindedness of a game of Simon Says, and you should be all right. (The Coleman has the directions printed on the fuel tank, and I suggest rereading them each time you use it until you can quote from memory—it might keep you from doing something thick one day.) Don't get creative with stoves. Like any other good friend, your stove deserves to be treated with respect.

Pots and Pans

If you're anybody who is anybody, or want to be perceived as anybody, then you absolutely have to have a ducky little set of spun-aluminum pots from some country where they talk with umlauts, at about 30 or 40 hard-earned bucks. If you just want something to cook in, you can score all sorts of neat, light, aluminum pots in any hardware or grocery store for much, much less. Or, if you're hard up, the local Goodwill and similar stores have pots and pans in all shapes and sizes for nearly nothing— and it's a good cause, too. You can get by with a 1-pound coffee can for quite a bit of cookery, and for that matter, it's very likely you've already got something in your kitchen at home (or your doting mother does) that can be used just as well.

I will hasten to add here that there is one exception to all this reverse snobbery: Though it's far from necessary or even important, if you've got the money, the Sigg Tourister cookset made for the SVEA is very handy for cycle touring. Everything goes together with the stove inside, making a very compact, easily packed setup, and when you get ready to use it, everything is together. I wish Coleman or somebody would make something equivalent for the Peak 1. But this is strictly in the luxury category; forget it unless money is truly unimportant in your choices. (You might try leaving the catalog lying around before Christmas.)

For a solo camper, a 2-quart pot is big enough. A large group will need at least one pot that holds 4 to 6 quarts if communal meals are planned. You can use one pot for everything, but a second pot is well worth having for fixing hot drinks and side dishes. Don't bother with a frying pan unless you'll be fishing or building fires—it's very hard to fry effectively over a one-burner stove anyway. Each pot should have a lid to fit.

A light plastic bowl is more useful than a plate; if alone you may even prefer to eat straight out of the pot. Carry two fair-size spoons, one for eating and one for stirring. A fork isn't necessary, and you'll have a knife for other purposes anyway.

Each person will need a cup. The stainless-steel Sierra cup is a very nice item, very rugged (you can even heat it over a fire to warm a cooled cup of coffee, for instance) and hard to tip over. However, I also like the little plastic Palco cup, which is graduated for measurement. Any light, unbreakable cup will do all right.

You can get neat little hot-pot grippers for lifting pots off the stove or fire. Most cyclists prefer to have a pair of pliers for this purpose, though since these also have many uses in working on the bike.

A can opener should be carried, unless you have a knife with one; try carrying a tiny G.I. P-38 in your wallet. Carry an extra—they're easy to lose. Don't be too quick to assume you'll never need a can opener; a can from a rural store may contain your only possible food one evening.

Waterproof match holders are very nice, no doubt, but these days I just carry a few of those cheap butane cigarette lighters. They light in any sort of rain, they don't break or fall from your hand when your fingers are cold the way matches do, and the spark alone will ignite your stove.

You will also want some sort of water container besides your bike's bottle(s)—a 1-quart poly bottle at least, so you don't have to spend the evening trotting back and forth with water. The best answer is one of those soft, roll-up Igloo water jugs; they hold about a gallon or more, and when empty, they weigh very little and can be rolled and tied behind your saddle. They even have a clever little spigot; I don't know what we did without them.

This whole business of utensils for cooking and eating has been blown all out of proportion by hardware snobs and self-serving outfitters. I have made very lengthy wilderness journeys with no kitchen gear except a cheap plastic cup, a large empty coffee can, and a big spoon, and I never noticed that the food tasted any worse.

> *Hunger is the best of all possible*
> *sauces.*
>
> *—Vilhjalmur Stefansson*

CHAPTER **5**

_____ Fuel

People seem fascinated with their stomachs. A book on diet is a sure-fire moneymaker, especially if the author has a degree after his or her name. Vast reams of published material have been produced on diet, ranging from excellent scientific studies to the worst sort of cynical rubbish, and the worst charlatans can sound the most convincing.

Many writers on outdoor sports—cycling in particular, God knows why—have unaccountably felt called upon to get involved in these controversies and to drag their views into discussions of entirely separate matters. My own feeling is that if anyone wants to know the arguments for or against eating meat, processed foods, sugar, or whatever, there are many, many books available on these questions already.

For anyone who really has to know, I myself am not a vegetarian, nor do I follow any sort of "organic" or "natural" diet; I do try to pay attention when my body seems to be making a request for a specific item, but then it quite frequently puts in demands for things like black coffee, Ding-Dongs, and gin. . . . I eat what is available, and I eat a lot of it, except for an allergy to tomatoes. The nearest thing I've got to a personal philosophy of diet is the observation that the most intelligent and successful animal species—chimps, raccoons, bears, and pigs—are naturally omnivorous; they will eat anything and not infrequently take your arm off to get it. Since there are no doubt people who could advance all sorts of impressive arguments to demolish this view, I do not present this even as a worked-out theory.

I have, it is true, worked mostly from standard U.S. eating patterns in this chapter. It's what I know best. Anyway, vegetarians and health-food devotees surely know more about their own wants and needs than I do. The health-food stores I have visited certainly had lots of items that appeared to be eminently suited to lightweight, minimum-bulk travel—dry cereals, herbal teas, and the like. Indeed, even people who are not normally concerned with such matters might do well to look over the selection available at larger health-food stores. Some of the cereals, in particular, look very useful indeed—the bulgur wheat hot cereal favored by many natural-food types is excellent for lightweight camping and hard to get anywhere else.

Just one cautionary note: A lot of these health-food items are not readily available except at specialized stores, which are usually found in the cities. Therefore, if this is what you eat, and it is important enough to you that you do not feel you should vary it even for a trip of a week or so, then you will need to figure on carrying a lot of your food along. This will affect things like your choice of racks and bags, bike gearing, and many other matters. Otherwise you'll have to make some arrangements for resupply, such as the common practice of mailing packages to yourself care of General Delivery at post offices along the way.

This brings us to the matter of logistics. As I remarked in the introduction to this book, one of the greatest joys of cycle camping is the food-supply situation. The backpacker, who has to carry it all on an aching back, or the canoeist, who may be off in a lonely river gorge for weeks, can only envy the bikie in this respect; it's a rare, back-of-beyond bike trip that doesn't pass some sort of store in a couple of days. Even when the route is basically through unpopulated country, detours for food resupply are simple enough. During hikes, I've had to write off a whole day to walk into some nearby town for groceries, when I could have covered the same distance on a bike in an hour without hurrying.

Consequently, your only real limitations in the fuel category will be what the stores have, what your kitchen setup is capable of preparing, and what you like or feel you should have.

Within any reason at all, weight and bulk should not be too much of a problem, especially if you can make your food-supply stop in the afternoon, not long before you make camp. (If you pass the last store early in the morning and there are giant mountains or a serious desert coming up before supper, that's something else again; but common sense ought to tell you when to watch it.)

Now, before you begin wallowing in fantasies of gourmet meals, let's back up and look at those first two limitations again, because they are more severe than you might think.

"Store" is a word that can cover a wide range of business concerns, and those found in rural areas or small settlements tend to be very small and have little variety in their stock. Rural people tend to grow much of their food, make weekly or monthly drives into the nearest sizeable town to buy various staples in bulk quantities, and use the local store mostly as a place to pick up minor items that come up unexpectedly and don't justify a drive into town. Indeed, with modern roads and cars making it easy for people to get into town and the low prices at city supermarkets, the rural grocer tends to have a pretty thin time of it. This is why you see so many closed-down country stores.

I have encountered some truly strange scenes in these roadside establishments. There was one memorable, almost Gothic place that stocked nothing whatever except canned corned beef hash, canned green beans, Kellogg's All-Bran, lime Jell-O, and vanilla wafers, all in mammoth quantities. I've lain awake nights thinking about it.

This is not necessarily the only possible picture. In areas where outdoor people frequently visit—near a famous hiking trail or canoe stream, for instance, or a lake noted for its fishing—the stores will have much better selections of the kind of foods you'll want, as well as things like stove fuel and flashlight batteries. True, the locals often adjust prices in keeping with the ancient tradition of skin-the-city-dude, but not always. Upon occasion I have run into some real bargains out in the country.

Fresh fruits can be especially hard to get, and meat and dairy items as well. Most small rural stores lack extensive refrigeration facilities. Staples such as sugar or coffee may be put up in quantities too big for your needs.

So if you're counting on acquiring supper at that dot on the map up ahead, don't ride along thinking about something you've absolutely got to have, or you may be disappointed. They may not have it; in fact, the store there may have gone out of business, so you'll need some reserve food in your bags. This element of chance can be part of the fun if you look at it right, but be prepared. This is particularly important if you have certain things you don't believe in eating, or certain allergies or special needs.

(I can't resist telling this story, though I'm not sure what it proves. One day last fall I came out of the woods near a tiny crossroads community after a truly brutal hike over some of the roughest country in the Ozarks, most of it without trails and nearly all of it either straight up or straight down. Anyway, it felt that way. I hadn't been near a store, or even had any human contact, for a couple of weeks. As I grunted up the highway, I found myself locked into a growing craving for junk pastries—Twinkies, Honey Buns, Ho-Hos, Zingers, Little Debbies, Moon Pies—it's a wonder my teeth didn't fall out just thinking about it. I wasn't hungry, and I even had quite a bit of food left in my pack; I was just on a munchies trip. I nearly ran the last half-mile or so—and then discovered that the grocery store there had gone out of business. In its place, the only store for miles, was a hard-core health-food place that didn't sell anything remotely close to what my lusts ravened for. I believe I rather frightened the nice young man behind the counter as I stomped, growled, and cursed my way out. Health-food devotees may feel free to find this tale hilarious or infuriating, as it strikes you; my point is, watch out that you don't get caught in this type of situation, whatever your particular hungers.)

As for the limitations of your cooking setup, what it comes down to is that you're pretty much restricted to boiling or simple warming. There's no way to do anything decent with a steak or chicken over a one-burner camp stove; the heat is too concentrated to fry anything properly, and of course, broiling is impossible. Just browning the vermicelli for Rice-a-Roni without burning the pot is a good trick. There's a little folding oven that sits on top of an Optimus stove and supposedly can be used to make biscuits, muffins, and the like, but while I have never owned one, it does not look like anything you'd want to pack around on your bike. All of which reduces the range of meal possibilities. If you're going to be able to build fires, that is another matter; in fact, one attraction of a fire is the delicious meals you can make with coals. But this is pretty rare. (On a few occasions, spending a night at a public park or campground, I've cycled into town and picked up some steaks and a bag of charcoal and had a cookout, but this only works with large groups, unless you feel like throwing away most of a sack of charcoal.)

So as a practical thing, your meals will tend to be based on boilable items, such as rice, noodles, potatoes, spaghetti, and so on. This isn't as monotonous as it sounds; with a bit of imagination, you can go quite some time without repeating yourself. Occasional fresh fruits or no-cook items will break the monotony. Foods of this general type are relatively light, compact, and inexpensive—and very filling besides.

Food Requirements

Nutritionists mostly agree (insofar as they agree on anything) that a precisely balanced or scientifically correct diet is not essential over the short periods typical of bike-camping trips, provided you're in good health and are eating correctly before you go. Except for people with special medical problems, it takes about a month to develop serious vitamin deficiencies, and longer than that to run into mineral problems, if you eat halfway reasonably at all. Protein needs over short periods are relatively low, too, and easily met by any normal diet.

What you need on a trip is *fuel*—food your body can convert into energy. You need carbohydrates and fats in a readily digestible form, enough to provide the staggering number of calories you'll burn up during extended, hard cycling. Never mind those little tables—the people who tell you cycling uses up 110 calories an hour have in mind some joker fooling around on a flat road at about ten miles an hour with an unloaded bike.

A racing cyclist in training burns 4,000 to 5,000 calories per day. A camper cycling through mountain country with a 30-pound outfit may not need quite that much, but shouldn't be too far behind. The Army figures 4,400 calories per man per day (one of their favorite terms) for "hard work." So I'd guess 4,000 calories a day would not be a greatly excessive estimate.

This is not to say you ought to get out your calculator and your tables and start figuring out what you need to eat to get 4,000 calories a day, in the most weight-efficient way—though such an approach might well be instructive. I just want to point out that our orientation here is mainly toward energy production rather than other dietary needs.

Carbohydrates and fats both produce energy calories but are used in different ways. Carbohydrates are burned rapidly and easily and so are good for quick boosts and energy snacks, but by themselves they do not "stick to the ribs"—give a long-lasting feeling of fullness. Fats (and proteins) are harder for the body to digest, and the process requires more water and gives off more heat, but the effects last longer. Thus, fats are better suited for evening meals, when they will help you stay warm through the night, than for lunches on warm days, especially if water is in short supply. (Thus, it's obvious that the ordinary practice of using cheese and sausage for lunches is a poor idea, especially in the summer; better to save such items for evening snacks.)

Your body, given a chance, will prefer to stash fats away—usually in embarrassing places—and burn carbohydrates for immediate energy needs. This, incidentally, is why cycling to lose weight is often a futile business; before the body will start to burn up stored fats, you have to cycle long enough to exhaust carbohydrates and free fats in the blood, and few casual cyclists ride that much. (Sleeping outdoors on cool nights will help considerably—you'll probably find yourself looking trimmer after a long bikepacking trip.)

Not all carbohydrates and fats behave alike. Sugar gives a fast rush of energy and an equally fast burnout, making it largely useless for real energy needs. It's rather as if you threw a half a cup of gasoline into a fireplace; you'd get a big, bright whoomp and blow off your eyebrows, but you probably wouldn't raise the temperature of the room a single degree. Starches burn more evenly and are more useful for our purposes. (I am being deliberately imprecise here. I lack professional credentials to go into the chemistry of all this, which in any case is not fully understood even by experts. If you want to know more, do your own research.)

What all this means is that the cycle camper needs to eat mostly starchy foods—rice, cerals, potatoes, beans, pasta—and, at the right times of day, some fats as well, in a digestible form, such as margarine or cheese. Many dishes are rich in both—macaroni and cheese is an obvious example.

Now, please note that such foods are also ideally suited to lightweight camping, since they are light, compact, nonperishable, and readily prepared over single-burner camp stoves or small campfires, with simple utensils. One might be tempted to speculate that God intended us to be hikers and bikepackers; it is certainly uncanny how human nutritional needs for such efforts seem to coincide with the limitations imposed by physics and technology on what food we can carry and prepare. Major philoso-

phies and successful religious cults have been built on less.
Let's not forget economics. Most of this stuff is *cheap.*

Main Meals

Because you don't want to eat very heavily when there's
cycling left to be done, the biggest, most important meal will be
the one at the end of the day (known, depending on your regional
origins, as "dinner" or "suppah").

Based on the requirements just outlined, lightweight
campers of various persuasions have over the years developed a
basic pattern of the typical evening meal and its main dish. It is
usually some form of dry, rather starchy food, rich in carbohydrates and often a good deal of vegetable protein as well, which
must be prepared with boiling water: a cereal grain, such as rice
or bulgur wheat, a pasta such as macaroni or noodles, or potato
powder, with dried beans or peas an occasional substitute. (You
have probably figured it out already: Theoretically wonderful due
to their excellent nutritional content and packability, dried beans
and peas are very rarely carried by modern campers because of
their very slow cooking time—which can be reduced with freeze-
dried varieties—and their gas-forming tendencies, which are, of
course, the subject of much Rabelaisian humor.)

Such foods alone tend to lack palatability, so usually
some kind of sauce or other flavoring is included. There is also
some kind of fat in most of these dishes. There are several
reasons for this, beyond simple taste (enough butter and you can
eat anything, somebody said), in that fats, as we noted, take
longer to digest, and burn more slowly. Since this meal is usually
eaten with night coming on, and night tends to be considerably
cooler, this is a good time to run up the calorie intake with
high-calorie, heat-producing fats that your body can work on while
you're asleep, when it doesn't have anything else to do. Also, fats
move more slowly through the digestive system, while foods with
little or no fat content exit the stomach rather rapidly, leaving you
with a hungry feeling if you aren't used to it. (Incidentally, this is
why Westerners who eat Chinese food, which contains few fats,
say they feel hungry again an hour later.) Foods with more fat
content tend to "stick to the ribs," in the old expression.

The most common and easily packed form of fat, compatible with many of the food bases mentioned above, is margarine.
Enormously rich in calories, and much more digestible than regu-

lar butter (and less likely to go rancid), margarine serves a double function in that it also acts as a flavoring sauce, either on its own or mixed with various condiments. Cheese is another fat-rich substance with high flavoring value. Some carry it in powdered form and mix it with margarine.

Animal fats are rather less easy to digest, and in any case, it is difficult to carry such things as bacon, except in dried form—in which case the fat content is less—but a small can of boned chicken, for example, isn't monumentally heavy and adds quite a bit to the meal if you like meat. Many Americans are used to having meat in some form every day and may feel unhappy without it. If a person has a genuine psychological need for meat, there's no point in giving him a harangue on the finer points of nutritional analysis. So the classic one-pot Glopola of the cyclist/backpacker/kayaker frequently contains some small bits of meat or fish, or something else made to resemble it. Due to problems of weight and perishability, the meat component is rarely a significant part of the actual food content. It is primarily a kind of condiment, used to give the otherwise bland, starchy dish a "meaty" flavor.

You may have seen those textured-soybean, imitation bacon crumbles on supermarket shelves. Imperishable, feather-light, and acceptable even to vegetarians, they ought to be ideal. But I've tried them, and while they're delicious, they make me belch endlessly—huge, evil-tasting belches that go on all night. Might be just me; you could experiment.

Dried vegetables—freeze-dried or ordinary dehydrated—and dried fruit can be added to the mixture sometimes for added food value and more interesting flavors. You can get very creative in this kind of cooking, if you like.

Meals of the above sort can be bought in complete or semicomplete form, with various components already measured and perhaps mixed. Obvious examples are the numerous freeze-dried dinners sold by outdoor suppliers, Lipton's Lite Lunch, and Rice-A-Roni. Or you can buy the basics and assemble your own equally valid meal units. This doesn't really save you much money, but it does add a bit of variety and is certainly more gratifying to the ego. For example, my own favorite home-rolled Glopola is a chicken curry that I make with instant rice, margarine, powdered milk, an envelope of chicken gravy mix or cream of chicken instant soup, some onion flakes and garlic powder, and a little can of boned chicken. (You might prefer to substitute freeze-dried chicken to save weight.) Toss in a handful of raisins and dried apricots.

This brings up what is often a rather sore point: freeze-dried foods. Freeze-dried foods are unquestionably a valuable and admirable modern invention. (Modern invention, hell; the Incas were doing it with potatoes, by simply exposing them on freezing nights at extremely high altitudes and then grinding up the resulting dehydrated potatoes into a flour that they could store indefinitely, before Pizarro and the other predators showed up. Well, a modern rediscovery, then.) By this unique and clever process, it is possible to produce very light, compact meals that contain what would otherwise be very perishable foods—even steaks—or impossibly heavy ones, and as a bonus, the cooking time is greatly shortened, bringing some items such as beans into the range of the practicable. True, the resulting food usually has all the flavor of expanded polystyrene, but a few easy-to-carry condiments will help that.

Freeze-dried foods are expensive, however, grotesquely, outrageously expensive. Not only are prices high for the packaged meal units themselves, but you also have to buy two or three times as many of these units as you'd think from the serving information. You've undoubtedly noticed already that ordinary supermarket groceries carry some pretty farfetched claims of this sort—"Serves Three" usually turns out to mean "serves three infant hamsters if nobody wants seconds." The companies that put out freeze-dried foods for backpackers are in a class by themselves; virtually any healthy adult, after a day of hard cycling or walking, can put away two or three of those supposedly full meals and ask for more. This is not meant to turn you off freeze-dried foods altogether, but if you use them, get some samples and fix them at home. Eat them after you've had a pretty strenuous day, jogging or whatever, and find out what you need. If you accept on blind faith the serving information on the package, you're in for some lean, lean times.

Just to fan the flames a little, there is some reason to believe that some of these "freeze-dried" foods actually contain ordinary, dehydrated items. Really, freeze drying isn't necessary in the case of things like macaroni, which you can get at the supermarket much more cheaply.

Which is what I've been building up to. For the most part, I think cycle campers can do better passing up the freeze-dried specialties. (After all, a backpacker or mountain climber has different needs.) If you are going off into the real boonies, where you may spend days and even weeks with little or no chance to make grocery stops, then freeze-dried food clearly represents your best means for carrying food supplies—maybe your only chance of carrying enough without overloading your bike. In cold weather, when you have to pack extra clothing, or on desert crossings, when the weight of water reserves is a big item, then the need to pare away every ounce and gram you can might make freeze-dried food your logical choice. For what it's worth, though, I frequently backpack in extremely rugged country with a starting load of up to two weeks' worth of food, because I sometimes like to get completely away from people for a while. On occasion, combining hiking and whitewater running, I pack along 20 pounds of inflatable canoe and accessories as well. In a situation like that, you watch your ounces. Yet I never carry anything but regular supermarket foods, and I eat *big*.

Some of the fancier freeze-dried items, such as steak or pork chops, might seem tempting, but you'd be surprised how seldom most people feel any real desire for things like that. Most backcountry food fantasies tend to involve junk food (as in my earlier tale), fresh fruit, or booze—usually cold beer—but rarely meat. In 30-some-odd years of bushwhacking, I don't think I've ever developed a serious case of the hots for a steak or other meat dish, except in frustration after missing an easy shot or letting a fish get away. And I am highly carnivorous in town.

As for the great number of freeze-dried selections I've seen, they seem to consist mostly of stews and the like, based on rice, beans, or something similar. Equivalent dishes that weigh only a trifle more—a trifle in terms of the two or three main meals that are all the average cycle camper ever carries at a time—and are nutritionally similar, can be bought at any supermarket for a fraction of the price.

Some freeze-dried items do have potential used in combination with cheaper stuff. There are freeze-dried meatballs, for example, or chicken that could be combined with, say, Minute Rice or noodles for a total price considerably below that of the fully freeze-dried selection. You might like to carry some freeze-dried vegetables for similar use.

I suppose some readers will think I tend to go on and on about the cost of things; no doubt many people don't have to worry about such matters, within reason. It could be pointed out that a fancy, custom touring bike is cheaper than a car or truck, a fine down bag is cheaper than a water bed, a freeze-dried dinner is cheaper than dinner at a good restaurant, and so on—and rightly so. But I am tired of seeing outdoor sports, such as cycle camping and backpacking, turned into exclusive clubs in which the affluent can vie for status with their high-priced toys. I'd like to make sure that people with average and even below-average incomes realize that they too can get out there and have fun. Because they are not blinded and distracted by status games and tricky technology, they may well have a superior experience.

The shelves of any supermarket offer numerous possibilities. The macaroni-and-cheese dinners already mentioned are extremely rich in energy content and are very cheap, and there are some good egg-noodle dishes along the same lines. Some supermarkets even stock things like bulgur wheat and kasha. Envelopes of various gravies are good for flavoring, as are some of the powdered soups. (Lipton's cream of chicken makes a good base for curry sauce.) Bigger stores also have the better dried soups, such as Knorr's excellent products.

Unless you'll definitely be building fires, check the cooking time before you buy, or you'll go through your fuel supplies too fast. Rice-a-Roni (an otherwise outstanding energy dish), scalloped potatoes, and dried beans all have to be boiled so long that they aren't really very practical over a camp stove, unless you're towing a trailer loaded with cans of white gas.

Look for instant or quick-cook items; they cost a trifle more, but the saving in fuel consumption more than compensates. Many products call for nothing but bringing water to a boil and then mixing and letting the pot sit for a few minutes; the retained heat "cooks" the meal without further boiling. Most freeze-dried foods have this feature, but so do plenty of common supermarket items. Lipton Lite Lunches, while a bit more expensive than other supermarket foods (about 80-some-odd cents a box, two envelopes to a box; generally it takes four envelopes or two boxes to fill me up), are fast and easy to fix—I've even pulled it off with Sterno—and come in several good flavors, which, incidentally, can be mixed together if you feel creative. Ramen noodles (you can get them by the block from any Oriental grocer, who will also have yummies like dried shrimp) don't take long to cook. Minute Rice certainly lacks the flavor and texture of regular rice, but the saving in fuel used is so great that I never use anything else.

Mashed-potato flakes are popular, and they do fill you up well and give excellent energy for their weight, especially if fixed with plenty of margarine. The cheap, light, flaky kind don't have much taste, or food value either. The only ones I will use are French's; they are far and away the best, the only ones that taste like mashed potatoes rather than recycled cobwebs. Fix them by pouring boiling water over them; they'll cook rapidly. A packet of powdered gravy goes very well with this dish. In fact, a big pot of mashed potatoes with plenty of butter and gravy is just about a meal by itself in my book.

Vegetarians and health-fooders have their own sources of supply, of course. However, vegetarians needn't worry too much about the "chicken" and "beef" element in some of the packaged foods just described. In most cases, the alleged meat is really textured vegetable protein, such as soybeans, and there is only a tiny trace of animal matter to keep the Federal authorities pacified.

Naturally, there will be times when you won't have to be concerned with all this dried-and-desiccated stuff. If you can get to a grocery in the last hour or two before making camp, you might prefer simply to buy a can or two of beef stew or the like and heat it up for chow, figuring that you can live with the weight for such a short distance.

This is part of what I mean about the fun of cycle camping. Indeed, most of the preceding discussion of freeze-dried and dehydrated foods was intended as guidance in selecting the backup supplies most of us like to take along. Given the mortality rate of rural business concerns and the chance of failing to make a schedule due to some accident or malfunction, only a very bold cyclist would depend entirely on along-the-way supply sources. When you do go off into the less settled country, you'll have to take your own.

On a trip through lightly settled country—no real towns, but a few small communities and crossroads stores—I generally try to carry along enough dried foods for two days, three if the weather looks as if I might get stuck somewhere for a rainy day. Then I do my best to avoid using these supplies if I can get anything else, and when I do use them, I try to replace them as soon as possible. Even small rural grocery stores usually have things like potato flakes and macaroni dinners.

I would tell you about my own favorite pickup item—Sweet

Sue canned chicken and dumplings—but I can't stand to see a grown vegetarian cry.

Breakfast

This is pretty simple; breakfast foods tend to come in easy-to-fix forms anyway, because nobody wants to fool with fancy cooking in the morning, at home as well as in camp. Many people just eat dried cold cereals, such as Granola or the Swiss Familia, with some powdered milk. If you want something hot, and most of us probably do if it's a chilly morning, try Quaker's Instant Oatmeal, or instant grits, or Cream of Wheat. (Be warned: Things like grits, Cream of Wheat, and farina are hell to clean out of your pots.) I used to eat regular, yellow corn meal when I was a kid, boiling it as mush, and it went down well.

A few people feel the need for pancakes, fried eggs and bacon, or other such civilized mahoohah. Lots of luck. You cannot make decent pancakes on anything you'd want to carry on a bike, especially with a camp stove. The same is almost true of eggs and bacon, though you can fry them in a light aluminum skillet over the very lowest setting of a Coleman Peak 1 if you have a really steady hand and perfect timing. Eggs and bacon are impractical to transport, anyway, though if a store is near the campsite, a group of cyclists might buy eggs the evening before. Freeze-dried eggs and bacon exist, about which all of the related comments I made in the preceding subsection are valid.

To tell you the truth, everything tastes alike to me in the morning anyway; the only thing I care about is getting my coffee. This makes me a poor authority on breakfasts. The whole subject is a matter mostly of personal habits, I think. A person who wakes up slowly and wants to putter around awhile before breaking camp is likely to want things like pancakes. The get-up-and-haul-it type barely will be willing to pause for a cup of instant oatmeal; in fact, I know a lot of people who prefer just to munch up a Granola bar or the like while breaking camp to get an early start, and then stop down the road at around nine or so for a leisurely breakfast. This last is quite a good idea in hot weather, incidentally, so that you can make some mileage before the sun gets high.

It's all a question of individual tastes. Remember, still, that the longer you take breaking camp, the harder you're going to have to pedal during the day to get anywhere before dark.

Lunch _____

Except in cold weather, in which hot food is needed, few cycle campers care to bother with a cooked midday meal. Lunch tends to be merely an expanded snack. In fact, there are cyclists who never eat lunch per se, but just munch steadily all day at intervals of an hour or so. If you can get used to this, it could make considerable physiological sense.

As we saw earlier, the old favorites, sausage and cheese, are poor choices for lunch, especially in hot weather. (Unless, of course, you've finished your cycling for the day—there will be days, perhaps, when you intend to cycle only till noon and then lie around camp for the rest of the day.) Fruit is good, though some kinds tend to increase thirst. Bananas are an old favorite of cyclists. A lot depends on the weather and your water-supply situation; peanut butter isn't a very good idea in the desert.

Bread and crackers provide considerable energy value and fill you up, if you can carry them. Granola bars are an excellent item, except when water is scarce. Dried fruit is another popular choice, but beware of its laxative effect if you eat too much.

Lunch is really rather open-ended and subjective. You can approach it pretty much as you please or as the situation seems to dictate. This is one meal that is very commonly supplied from rural stores and even from private farmhouses, where in season it is often possible to buy fresh-grown fruits.

My own lunchtime habits are so atypical that I hesitate to mention them. I nearly always fix myself something hot, usually soup, occasionally Lite Lunch. I seem to feel more of a "recharged" effect when I do this, but I suspect this is really psychological. I am one of those pathological hurry-up types who has to go hard all day, and it is difficult for me to make myself take a proper break for lunch. If I have to get out the stove or build a twig fire, cook up some soup, and then wait for it to cool, I get some rest that I probably would not get otherwise. Then, when I start up again, I'm more energized. If you, too, are a compulsive hurrier, you might like to try this. Lipton Cup-A-Soup takes just about the right amount of time to prepare, it doesn't upset the stomach in hot weather, and the fuel expenditure is minimal.

Gorp, Munchies, and Others _____

Whatever you do about lunch, be sure to have some snacks for munching on the road. Cycling is a rather peculiar form of exercise in terms of food consumption and energy needs; it is important that you try to eat a little something *every hour.* It doesn't have to be much, but eat *something.* You may prefer to eat while riding, or you might want to stop and rest for a few minutes while you eat. Either is valid—you aren't in a race.

"Gorp" is a cyclists' and hikers' term for various mixtures of peanuts, raisins, chocolate or carob chips, dried fruits, and other munchies that people mix up and carry along for road food. There's no peeling or wrapper to fool with; you just grab a handful out of the bag and chomp away. The word "gorp" is either an acronym derived from "Good Old Raisins and Peanuts" or else, depending on whom you believe, "Godawful Old" and so on. Gorp recipes are a favorite topic of conversation and correspondence among touring cyclists, marathon runners, rock climbers, and hikers. Given the popularity of these activities nowadays, you should have no trouble finding an infinite variety of recipes if you're interested. On the few occasions I've used it, my own gorp has consisted of raisins, peanuts, and plain M & M's. But raisins give me gas, as do peanuts, so I mostly leave gorp alone.

Fruit—bananas, oranges, apples—is great if you can get it. There was at one time a belief that bananas increased the incidence of cramps, but this seems to have been a false alarm. Granola bars, the regular kind, that is, are good if your teeth can cope. The new Granola clusters with the sugary, soft center are so excruciatingly sweet that they make my gums itch. Candy of any kind is less helpful than you might think. Sugar burns too fast in the body to be a serious fuel, though a Hershey bar might get you going long enough to make that last hill. (Chocolate does contain some useful fats, whereas other candies are mostly sugar. So, if you must have a candy bar, get chocolate.)

Some of us, as observed earlier, develop cravings for sweet pastries, such as Twinkies, but this has to be considered more in the category of indulging a minor vice (like my pipe) than anything to do with real food. Not that I'm putting Twinkies down; all I mean is that you can't count those Twinkies from the gas station as any real contribution toward your daily, or even hourly, calorie needs.

While we're ruining our teeth, we might note that most people will want something for dessert after the main meal, at least now and then. Instant puddings are what I carry, mixed with powdered milk—you can make them with plain water in a pinch. Or you might prefer dried fruit; apricots are especially good, and dried fruit after supper will help relieve the constipation that occasionally affects people on camping trips.

Staples and Condiments _____

Powdered milk is pretty much a necessity in preparing most of the usual dried foods, and it contains a fair amount of food value itself. If you get it in those envelopes, double-bag it with some Baggies. The original envelopes are very flimsy, and the stuff leaks out through the tiniest hole. A very handy way to carry milk powder is to use a plastic baby bottle without the nipple. I don't know about other people, but I never seem to carry enough milk powder; it just goes and goes, and I keep running out. Take more than you think you need, since you can always drink the excess.

Margarine is best carried in liquid form. You can get it in 16-ounce plastic bottles at the supermarket, and it won't go off in warm weather. (But it will separate out—shake well before using, as they say.) Stick margarine is a royal pain to pack; if you exhaust your liquid and have to replace it with stick—rural grocers never seem to have liquid—you can melt it down over a gentle flame and pour it into the bottle you just emptied. Since margarine is a monster calorie source and a major component of such things as macaroni and cheese, as well as a necessity in rendering powdered potatoes fit to eat, don't stint here. By the way, if you're worried about cholesterol, don't; hard cycling burns the stuff off like a blast furnace. I have to watch cholesterol levels a little myself, due to a minor gallbladder problem, and I gobble margarine greedily on the road or trail without a twinge. Anyway, liquid margarine is very low in cholesterol, nothing like butter.

Seasonings of various kinds can be carried in those little 35mm. film containers. Take a good selection, according to taste; such things make a lot of difference in an essentially bland diet, and boost morale. Curry powder is useful, as are garlic and onion flakes or powders, and the usual things like salt and pepper. Label everything carefully, or you're in for some possibly unpleasant surprises. If you put a lot of sugar in your cereal, coffee, or whatever, you'll need either a larger container or Ziploc bags, doubled.

Drinks _____

Beverages are a personal matter, since few have any real effect on calorie totals anyway, cocoa being one possible exception. In wet or cold weather, it is advisable to have some sort of hot drink along—coffee, tea, cocoa, or herb tea—to ward off the chill. Cold drinks, such as lemonade made from crystals, usually call for so much sugar that they're impractical for cycling. Sugar slows the absorption process of the stomach lining, so it's not good in hot weather. (Gatorade and similar replacement drinks are fine, but often contain sugar; Gatorade will do you more good if cut 50-50 with water.) Sugar is heavy and bulky anyway.

You may be surprised at how your tastes change in the woods. In town, I am strictly a coffee drinker—black, strong, lots of chicory. Yet in the backcountry, I find myself preferring tea, very sweet, or cocoa. Swiss Miss Instant Cocoa with those teeny little marshmallows—I could drink a gallon some mornings. My wife won't drink hot drinks at all in town, loves them on the river. So it goes.

Alcohol is unnecessary and usually inappropriate, much as it grieves me to say so. You'd be crazy to cycle under the influence, both from the safety angle and that of your own comfort—a couple of beers at midday can induce awful nausea and cramps an hour or so down the road on a hot day. You'd be even crazier to fool with a gasoline stove after a drink or two; and anyone caught building an outdoor fire under the influence of alcohol ought to be given a year at hard labor. So that leaves you with only the possibility of a drink in the evening after everything else is done. It's pleasant sometimes, but not worth going to a lot of trouble and expense. A hot cup of tea will probably relax you just as well.

Anyway, there's no good way to carry booze in useful quantities. Beer is certainly far too bulky and heavy—in most of the U.S. you can't buy single cans—and wine bottles are heavy and fragile. I carried a *bota,* a Spanish wineskin, on a few trips and wasn't totally pleased with the results; something about the acidity of the wine did not seem to sit well. I've seen some pretty interesting-looking little metal flasks, but they appear to hold only a jigger or two, hardly worth fooling with.

Of course, the basic drink is water. While you don't have to buy it—at least not yet—water can pose some problems. It's not just the obvious one of water supply in desert country; I mean getting water that is fit to drink. There are, sadly, very few places left in this country where you can drink free-running water safely. It is almost always necessary to carry some means to purify drinking water. Boiling is a great bore and wastes fuel; there are little tablets you can buy, based on chlorine or iodine chemistry—theory now is swinging toward iodine, but don't use it if you have goiter or thyroid problems. Or you can do what I do: Carry a little bottle of drugstore tincture of iodine and add it to the water, eight drops to the quart. Double the drops if the water is really dubious. A few people say tincture of iodine gives water an unpalatable taste. Bull. It tastes *good;* I even put it in my water at home sometimes if I've got a sore throat.

Some makers offer filtering systems, said to be very effective; I've never used one. The only one I know about weighs a pound, which is enough to stop me cold.

Filtering of another kind may be necessary at some public campgrounds, where old iron pumps sometimes turn the water unpleasantly rusty. I don't suppose it really hurts you, but it tastes and looks awful. If you're going to stay at public campgrounds, you might like to pick up a pad of filter papers—those little things you used in high school chemistry class—and use them when you fill your water jug or bottles.

Remember, in "civilized" areas, *nothing* will remove or neutralize chemical poisons—and this problem is far from unknown. If you see a free-running stream that seems unnaturally clear, still, and lifeless—no fish, crawdads, frogs, bugs, birds, nothing—don't touch that water. Some of the most dangerously polluted water looks quite clean. (Whereas a swamp or bayou, with its black water teeming with bugs, reptiles, and fish, for all of its evil aspect may be quite safe to drink.) Be cautious about streams in commercial farm country; pesticides from crops may be washed into the streams by rain and irrigation systems. The same is true in forest land owned by large corporations that may be spraying with various chemicals. You might check with your own local environmentalist groups about the situation in the areas you plan to visit.

Don't even look with more than one eyeball at a time at water running past *any* factory, no matter how loudly the company's PR flacks protest their purity and innocence. Many of the most dangerous substances cannot be detected except by experts using scientific equipment that you can't carry on your bike. What's worse, some of these substances might not show up in your system until after a long, too-late time.

CHAPTER **6**

Housing
and Housekeeping

Novice campers—cycling or otherwise—tend to assume that they'll have to have a tent as part of the basic outfit. If they consult the usual "authorities" or seek guidance at the average outdoor shop, they are immediately given to understand that just any tent will not do—they mustn't even *think* of spending a night outdoors in anything less than three digits' worth of overengineered, ripstop nylon in the latest configuration. "Over here, sir, this is one of our more popular models. . . ."

At the other end of the spectrum, plenty of quite experienced campers actively dislike tents and don't use them if they can help it. The good Mr. Richard Ballantine, an author of strong views on most subjects, says, "For myself I see no point in hieing to the Great Outdoors and then sleeping in a dark hole." Colin Fletcher, who stands in relation to the modern U.S. backpacking movement as did St. Augustine to Christianity, says, "Under most conditions, the best roof for your bedroom is the sky." Such people prefer to sleep out under the sky, enjoying the fresh air and the feeling of freedom, as well as saving weight and bother. If

121

it rains, they rig a simple tarp or poncho shelter and live with it.

You don't *have* to have a tent at all. If money has to be watched, put a tent a long way down your list of priorities. Don't consider getting one until you've got a suitable bike with the necessary accessories (including carriers, bags, and tools), proper clothing, an adequate sleeping bag with pad or mattress, a good stove, and funds for food and other expenses. Such things are essential; tents are basically luxuries. Before you go into debt to a Mafia loan shark in order to finance the latest ripstop igloo or taffeta teepee, consider the following possibilities.

Nontents

The simplest type of shelter in common use is the *tarp,* a rectangle or square of waterproof material that can be rigged to keep rain and/or wind off of the occupant. Far from being a makeshift for impoverished novices, the tarp is the number one choice of many experts, most of whom own one or more of the finest tents made. With a little imagination and some practice, you can make the tarp a very versatile and effective shelter; an exprienced tarp camper can rig a surprising variety of "houses" for various conditions with this deceptively simple device.

Tarps are available in coated nylon and fitted with loops and grommets. Nylon tarps are cheaper and lighter than tents, yet provide similar protection and privacy in most situations. But a cheaper and increasingly popular alternative is a plastic tarp, usually a rectangle of the thick, shiny, translucent plastic called Visqueen that is commonly seen around construction sites. Don't be misled by the flimsy sandwich-bag look of it; Visqueen is tough stuff indeed. I have waited out a full-sized hailstorm—marble-sized stones—under an already badly worn Visqueen tarp, and it held. Try cutting it to size, and you'll find you actually have to cut it, using a sharp knife or stout shears; it doesn't tear worth a damn.

The main drawback with Visqueen for some situations is its translucency. It provides no privacy at all, a problem in groups or public campgrounds, and it does nothing very useful to keep off the sun. The look and feel of the stuff is also rather offensive to some on aesthetic grounds—though others enjoy the all-round full view; you get a lot of the feeling of sleeping out under the sky while still having the added protection. On the whole, if you're in a tight-money situation, a Visqueen tarp is the best bargain around when it comes to shelter.

Guy lines can be attached to Visqueen with clever little ball-and-clip devices sold in outdoor shops. Some people have also devised means of using little rubber balls from the toy counter with those figure-8-shaped curtain rings. But you can fasten lines anywhere you like without any of these gadgets. Just get a marble-sized rock—a big acorn will work—and fold the Visqueen around it where you want your line. Then tie the cord around the resulting protuberance.

Tarp size will depend in part on the user's own body dimensions. Some short people rig capacious shelters with 8′ × 12′ tarps, but a tall man or a couple will want something bigger. A 12′ × 10′ tarp provides quite a bit more room for not much more weight. Don't be too stingy with tarp area. If it sets in to rain all day, you'll be a lot less miserable if you've got a tarp big enough to let you rig yourself some headroom, cook, play solitaire, and so on. As a matter of fact, this is another plus of tarps—a light tarp can be arranged to provide quite a bit more space and headroom than you could get with any tent except for a relatively large, heavy one. A tent does provide security in a hard storm, but with a day-long drizzle, it can get pretty claustrophobic in there.

The usual method is to rig a rope or cord between two trees. The tarp is hung over this and staked out in some way to create the shelter form. Usually this is either a kind of pup-tent roof or an open-sided lean-to shelter, the latter being by far the most popular arrangement. If the back of the lean-to is toward the wind, the occupant will stay warm and dry, yet have excellent ventilation and vision. (If you misjudge the wind or it shifts during the night, your shelter will try to fly away—and may well succeed—so a good eye for weather is essential to successful tarps-personship.)

There is one problem here. Trees have a distressing tendency to grow everywhere except where you need them. In particular, they do not like to grow in neat pairs, spaced exactly the right distance apart, aligned at right angles to the prevailing evening winds, and with the ground between them level and clear of stumps, boulders, thorn bushes, or colonies of fanatically fierce red ants.

Hikers get around this problem by using their staffs as supporting poles; cyclists sometimes use their bikes in a similar fashion. I've seen some undeniably clever arrangements using bikes to support tarp shelters, and it does make it a bit harder for somebody to steal your bike while you sleep. (Harder, not impossible.) But I wonder how stable the setup is; bikes tend to fall over even when just standing there, so I wonder how well they hold up a tarp in a strong wind. Anyway, it takes your bike out of action, and I like to be able to work on the bike or even ride around the area after setting up camp. But it's a possibility worth keeping in mind if you find yourself lacking a cooperative second tree.

A variation on the tarp concept is the *tube tent*. These are popular, but wrongly so. I've used them enough to come to hate them. You've got a simple tube of Visqueen-type plastic or, occasionally, nylon. You run a rope lengthwise through it and tie the ends to trees or whatever, and there you are; you can stake the ends down or just let your weight hold the floor in place.

The tube tent has only one thing going for it—it is very fast and easy to rig. (Which is why it is popular in survival kits, where it may well have a function—an injured man might find it simpler to put up.) It is far less versatile than the tarp. You can't set it up to let you sit up and move around, or have a flap over your cooking area, or bring a lot of stuff in with you, all of which are easy to do with a tarp. The ventilation is nonexistent, unless you rig it so that the wind blows straight through it. Water vapor from your body, therefore, condenses on the inside of the plastic, and since this is only inches away and usually touches your bag in places, you can get wetter than if you'd just slept out in the rain. The side against

A tarp set up as a lean-to.

the ground gets abraded in time, so if you don't rig it with the same side down every time, you'll end up with a very leaky tent. They're trash and garbage. I wouldn't even have mentioned the wretched things if they weren't so popular.

You should carry some regular tent stakes, even for a nontent. In theory, you can tie guy lines to little bushes and the like, but in practice, such things are even less cooperative than trees. If your camping will be done in a public-use area—and sooner or later it probably will be—you'd better make sure your stakes are rigid, sharp, and tough. The ground in such places is always packed hard, and stakes will have to be driven in with a rock or with your crescent wrench. Cheap plastic stakes break, and aluminum stakes bend. Thin steel stakes weigh more but are worth it. Half a dozen should suffice for most tarp architecture.

Most tarp campers carry a groundsheet to keep things dry and organized and to keep the sleeping bag clean. A groundsheet is also supposed to discourage creeping fauna, though the mental picture of a tick slipping and breaking his legs while trying to crawl across a plastic groundsheet is probably not scientifically defensible. Any rectangular piece of waterproof material will do; a cheap plastic poncho is a common ad hoc groundsheet. A few improverished types have been seen using old shower curtains. (And what a *good* idea, when you think of it—getting one more bit of use out of a nonrecyclable article.) I must admit that I have never used a groundsheet of any kind. I just carry a tarp long enough to let me fold part of it under to form a kind of floor to my shelter area. If you do this, be sure to use the same part of the tarp for this each time, or you'll get leaks—mark it in some way, such as with a piece of duct tape. Pretty soon you'll be able to tell just by looking.

Some people rig up emergency shelters with ponchos, usually on the basic lean-to pattern. But a poncho is a poor raincoat for cycling, as I explained earlier, so I don't know why you'd be carrying one. A Visqueen tarp costs no more and is much roomier.

Tarps won't keep off insects, so, in mosquito season, carry a small rectangle of cheesecloth or mosquito netting and hang it over your face when you go to bed—you can fix up something with string, no doubt.

Remember to carry plenty of nylon parachute cord if you use a tarp. In fact, carry a generous hank of this handy stuff anyway; it has a million uses.

Another type of shelter that might be called a nontent is the famous *jungle hammock*. This contrivance, invented for tropical warfare, consists of a fabric hammock over which is sewn a neat little tent with bug-mesh walls. Once inside, the individual can laugh at mosquitoes, monsoons, and cobras. At least, this is the idea. The jungle hammock weighs little and needs no poles or stakes. It also eliminates the need for a mattress or pad. The ground beneath can be rocky, muddy, or uneven with no effect on the comfort of the occupant.

Before you go haring off to buy one, note that the jungle hammock is not without drawbacks. It is, in fact, a very limited form of shelter. You can't sit up, cook, or move around in its disturbingly coffinlike confines. It's strictly for sleeping (and that alone, which may be a characteristic of importance to affectionate couples). All of these things can be most frustrating, and let's remember the remarks in a preceding chapter on possible tree damage due to careless hammock-slinging. Still, in swamp country or heavy bush—neither of which is very accessible by bicycle, but I have to remember Ian Hibell slogging through the Panama jungle—a jungle hammock could be a good thing.

In recent years, many superlight campers have taken to using a device called a *bivvy sack*. This is simply a waterproof cover that fits over a sleeping bag, with a raised section to cover your head and shoulders, and with little screened openings and flaps at the upper end. The covering would create a soggy sweat bath from condensation but for the use of Gore-Tex, an astonishing material that keeps rain out but lets water vapor escape.

Bivvy sacks are light and compact, and some cyclists use them, but they are very confining, worse even than jungle hammocks. All you can do is crawl inside and go to sleep, or, if you aren't sleepy, listen to the rain and the mosquitoes. Count Dracula had better accommodations. The damned things also cost as much as good tents, or more. Forget it. A tarp or a tent is better.

Tents

With all the above enthusiasm for tarps, I've got to say it: Tents *are* pretty nice things to have on cycling trips if you can manage it. I find that I use my own tents more than I use a tarp, especially with the bike. The big drawback of tarps is that there is no real protection against insects. This is really serious in some areas and seasons. Bugs are one of those problems, like sunburn and poison ivy, that people often treat as funny or trivial, when actually they can ruin the whole trip and even pose a serious health hazard. It's not just that the little bastards whine around at night and keep you awake—bad enough, it you consider the remarks earlier in this book about the consequences of a sleepless night—but quite a few of them carry dangerous diseases as well.

(A few philosophical types have rather sanctimoniously suggested that one should accept insect attacks as part of the natural experience of the wilds and extend a Gandhian forbearance. They imply that to seek shelter or employ chemical warfare, let alone be so brutal as to swat something, is somehow a sign of the alienation of modern man from the natural world. There may be merit in such a view in relatively insect-free areas, but it is clear that these people have never seen a grown bull moose literally driven mad by insect bites, and they've never seen primitive people coating themselves with things like mud and rancid animal fat to keep off the bugs. Nor have these philosophers had any dealings with malaria or spotted fever. Pardon the sermon, but a good deal of misinformation has been spread by people who do their camping in highly specialized, atypical environments, and then lay down their experiences as universal principles.)

Cycle campers have far less of a bug problem than anyone else. We don't wade through tick-infested brush or float down mosquito-patrolled lakes and rivers—we whiz down open roads. But in camp, we're just as vulnerable as anyone else, and a good deal of cycle camping is done at precisely the time of year when the insects are most numnerous and militant. Zipped up in your tent, and having first engaged in the sadistically satisfying ritual of hunting down and squashing the ones that got in when you did, you can lie back and make impudent gestures at the whining hordes outside. This business of the bugs is, in fact, the single best argument for using a simple tent. It is the one area in which the tarp can't compete.

Another point, and this one is peculiar to cyclists, is that of privacy. Backpackers and paddlers don't have to worry about this, unless they do strange and unaccountable things, like traveling in big groups or camping in heavy-use areas. Cyclists are more restricted. While a good rough-stuff rider can find secluded spots where no one is likely to come, if you do much cycle camping at all, you will occasionally have to camp quite close to a public road, and very likely at a public campground as well. For that sort of situation, it may be better to be able to go inside, so to speak, and shut the door, for certain purposes. No doubt the importance of this aspect depends somewhat on your personal attitudes and inhibitions, if any.

If you do get a tent—and most campers eventually do; I mean, the things are simply *fun,* if nothing else—it isn't necessary to spend several hundred bucks for some highly sophisticated model that may have been designed for a set of conditions you are unlikely to encounter. Don't let yourself be unduly swayed by all those spectacular ads, color catalogs, displays in outdoor shops, and the rest of it; all those fantastic-looking domes, cones, parabolas, and mushrooms; self-erecting poles, tunnel entrances, catenary-cut ridgelines, geodesic forms and diagrams with little arrows showing wind-flow patterns; till you wonder how all those poor Arabs and Indians muddled along all those years without the benefit of this body of knowledge. In particular, don't be tempted by the specialized "mountain tent," which is intended strictly for use at high altitudes under conditions of snow and tremendous wind forces. While a marvelous invention for its purpose, the true mountain tent is much more tent than any ordinary cycle camper will ever need. Not only is it too expensive, but it's also too heavy and too complex, and usually rather oppressive in warm weather.

After all, cycle camping is usually a mild-weather sport. Even if the weather should turn gruesome while you're out in the boondocks, the situation gets nowhere near as serious as that of the hiker or paddler, let alone the mountain climber. They may be stuck out of reach of help, and their outfit may be their only hope for survival. But there are, unfortunately, very few places in the lower 48 states where you can go on a bicycle and not be able to cycle out to some sort of human habitation or outpost in a day's time. (Remember, in an emergency, you can cover considerably more than 100 miles in a day's ride—I've done 200 on a day when it never got above 28°F.) Given this escape potential, a cycle camper can live a trifle more dangerously in terms of shelter—though, of course, that is not to say that you should get something that is actually flimsy.

What you need for most bikepacking purposes is a simple, basic, lightweight tent—what is often called a "forest" tent. It should have a minimum of poles and stakes, and none of those long wandlike poles used in some large dome tents. There must be mesh screens that can be closed against insects, and storm flaps to keep out rain and wind, or else it will offer no advantage over a simple tarp. (So shun those Boy Scout or Army pup tents and shelter halves.) It should have an integral floor that is waterproofed and of tough material. The waterproofing should progress well up the sides of the tent, creating what is sometimes called a "bathtub" floor. If you ever spill water inside, you'll say it is aptly named.

Now, in discussing tube tents and rain suits, we have already spoken of how water vapor from the human body condenses on the inside of a fully waterproofed surface. Don't get the idea that we're just talking about a little foggy film, such as you see on the windows of a parked car. A sleeping adult gives off mind-boggling quantities of water in a night; if you've been cycling hard all day, while you sleep, your body will be working to eliminate or neutralize the fatigue poisons, and this process causes it to give off even more water.

So, if you sleep inside a fully waterproofed tent, you could awaken to find all of your things soaking wet—including your sleeping bag, which is very bad if you're using down—an experience to avoid if at all possible. The problem doesn't come up with tarps because the open nature of a tarp tent allows water vapor to drift harmlessly away. For the same reason, vapor doesn't affect

Typical low-priced tent; note the simple design and the separate fly.

big umbrella or Baker tents, but it is a real headache with small, crawl-in pack tents.

Canvas, which breathes, gets around this problem, but canvas is too heavy for cycling. So, the usual answer is to make the upper part of the tent out of nonwaterproof nylon, so that the water vapor can pass out through the tiny spaces between fibers, and then to rig a "fly"—a waterproof sheet, essentially a small tarp—over the outside to keep the rain off. A space between the fly and the tent allows air to circulate and also increases insulation against the cold.

Some cheap tents come with a fully waterproofed roof and no fly. This "single-wall" construction may be adequate in very dry climates—though I don't know why you'd want a tent there anyway—but in most of North America, it is a sure ticket to a wet, wet night. Some of these tents have big ventilation windows that are supposed to provide enough air circulation to carry away moisture, but don't you believe it. Sooner or later the rain will be blowing in, or there'll be a cold draft and you'll have to shut the window flaps, and then it's sauna time.

The "breathability" idea, however, isn't 100% effective either. I've never seen a tent of any construction that wouldn't sweat at least a little under the right conditions, especially cold and wet, with all flaps shut. Ventilation is important if you are to whip condensation completely, and it is also vital to safety and health. So make sure that any tent you buy, breathable or not, has adequate venting, at least a mesh door and a window, and, if at all possible, some vent area along the sides too. When you use a nonbreathable shelter, such as a tarp, make sure there's no way it can get closed off at the ends or down over your face, because you could suffocate. Every year somebody manages to die this way, usually by cooking or burning a lantern inside an unvented tent.

Low-priced, crude, adequate tents are sold in discount stores. Usually of Oriental provenance and described as "2-man backpack tents," they are almost invariably made of blaze-orange ripstop nylon in the familiar wedge shape. Usually you have to buy a fly separately. Some are fully waterproofed, but if you avoid these and stay with the separate-fly style, you can get pretty fair service out of these little cheapies. Certainly they'll keep the bugs out just as well as an expensive one, and screen out the eyes of the curious or prurient, and they don't do a bad job of keeping off the elements, either. Four years ago, I bought a little nylon tent of this type for about $30, with another $10 for the fly; I was in a hurry to leave on a long walk and had to pick up something fast, and I figured it would last a couple of weeks at least. I've still got it, and I use it quite often. It's held up in torrential rains, strong winds, and hailstorms; it's never blown down and never been badly ripped. It's certainly more shelter than a tarp, let alone a tube tent. I don't say you should run out and buy one of these cheap tents—though if you do, you may find yourself, like the author, becoming quite unreasonably attached to it—but if you want something more than a tarp but don't have the bread for anything fancy, it might be worth considering.

If you can afford one, there are better tents around. L. L. Bean has some good ones. Eureka is another good brand, but shun their cheap, single-wall model, for all of its quality construction. Or consider the unique Moss Solus, a very fine little tent for solo use; a mere 4 pounds, it has an odd but efficient shape that should give good headroom for the size. One good feature of the Solus is the upper walls are made of mosquito netting, so that you can have full insect protection and total ventilation at the same time, besides a fine view of the stars. Yet a fly, which comes with the tent, will make it fully waterproof—damned clever. This same net-walls design is found in some other tents, such as the Eureka Mojave.

With these fancier tents, watch out that you don't get something too heavy. It's an odd thing: With most backpack and cycling gear, you pay more to get less weight, but with tents, the costlier ones tend to weigh more. My little Korean doghouse, with poles, pegs, and fly, weighs 3 pounds 11 ounces, of which, I suspect, a few ounces are tracked-in dirt. Why would anyone pay four times as much for a tent that weighs over 7 pounds? Yet many of the most popular "lightweight" tents weigh in this range. I certainly cannot see any sense in a two-person-size tent, meant for use in moderate weather and at low-to-medium altitudes, that weighs more than 5 pounds, yet you see them all over the place.

One recent design that I like is the Sierra Designs Starflight, a light (4 pounds 9 ounces) A-frame tent with remarkably good headroom that is ideal for cycle camping. The reason I like it so much is that the basic shape is very much like a design described by the turn-of-the-century outdoor writer, Horace Kephart, which had been devised by English cycle campers of his day—whom he commended for their pioneering work in developing lightweight equipment! It is nice to know that the cyclists have always been out in front, and Sierra Design's nice little tent seems to me to be a kind of link with that faraway Golden Age of bikepacking. Kephart called the original a "pocket-house" which is pretty appropriate.

Your own "pocket-house" can be improved in a few ways, if you like. With a cheap or simple tent, try sewing some little pockets along the inside of the walls and ends, to hold those small things that get lost at night. Or install some loops here and there for hanging various things up. You might even, as I have myself, find yourself spending a rainy afternoon doing cartoon murals and grafitti on the walls. I think it is important to give your tent some degree of individuality. You'll be crawling into it now and then when things have perhaps not gone well or you're feeling a bit down, and then it helps if it has a feeling of "home" about it. In this connection, don't hesitate to consider color in choosing a tent; it ought to make you feel good, not set your teeth on edge.

Keep your tent clean. Throw the whole thing into a washer after a trip, but remove all lines first. (Otherwise you'll have a hell of a time untangling them after the spin-dry cycle.) At the end of each season, go over it and patch any holes, replace or reinforce worn tabs and loops, and apply some seam sealant to all the seams, which tend to leak. The fly's waterproof coating doesn't have to be in perfect condition in a double-wall setup, but if the fly

Sierra Designs Starflight tent.

has had a rough life, you might spray it with some waterproofing compound, such as silicone.

Take care of your little house; these days it's the only kind a lot of us can hope to own.

Furnishings

The homey gadgetry associated with guided pack trips or white hunters on safari—folding tables and chairs, pressure lamps, and so on—is hardly practical for cycle camping. There are, however, a few things you might want to have.

If you like to read or write in the evenings, and nearly everyone does, you'll want a light. Flashlights burn out fast if used for anything but brief illumination. This is a serious problem, and one with no good answers. A standard Coleman-type pressure lantern is out of the question, because it's bulky and heavy. The big battery-powered jobs are even worse, to say nothing of the trouble and expense of replacing those huge batteries.

The only light source that doesn't weigh a short ton is a candle, but a bare candle inside a tent is a constant hazard, and, outside, the wind blows it out. A candle lantern is the usual answer. Sold in outdoor shops, candle lanterns are, simply, little housings with glass windows that hold a candle safely and shield it from the wind. Most types take about as much room as a small flashlight and weigh 4 to 5 ounces, which is certainly reasonable enough. They do not deliver a really bright light, but usually they produce enough illumination for writing in a notebook or reading a book with good paper and large print. (Strain your eyes over a yellowing paperback at your own peril.)

The most widely sold design employs a spring-loaded feed tube that is alleged to push the candle gradually upward as it burns, so the flame stays in the same place—though actually I cannot think why it is considered particularly important to accomplish this. Some people even manage to make the damned things work. I can't—not properly. Even when I use the special, "no-drip," pink stearine candles, the feed device frequently clogs with wax and has to be dismantled before it will function in its fitful way again. Oh, it worked all right for about a year, but for the last couple of years, it's gone haywire. The hell with it. There is in one of my catalogs a small collapsible candle lantern, just a folding metal box with windows, in which the candle simply squats there and burns itself down as God intended candles to do, and by the

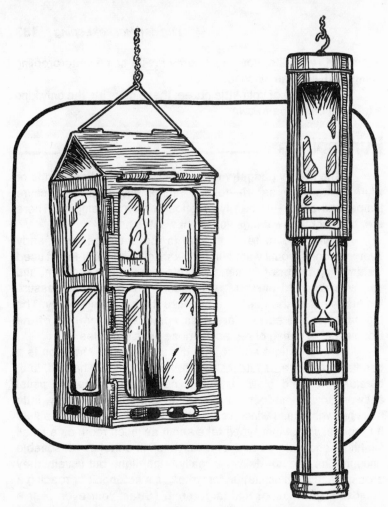

Two types of candle lanterns. While they don't light up the woods, they are better than complete darkness.

time you read this, I am going to have myself one, and I suggest you do the same.*

Carbide lamps are favored by a few; they do give a fantastic light. Too fantastic for me. It's downright painful. You don't want *that* much light if you're going to have any feeling of the outdoors at all. The hard white glare pushes the wild night away and creates a feeling of isolation. Too much light in the wilderness

---

*I got one, I got one. Seven bucks from Indiana Camp Supplies, and I love it. Looks so classy I hang it in my living room between trips.

is worse than too little, and if there are other people camping nearby, it is very inconsiderate.

Anyway, carbide is a hassle to keep dry, though the lamp and fuel are very light and compact. One writer claims to use a carbide headlamp while cycling, but since they blow out in any kind of wind, he must ride at about a walking pace.

You'll need a flashlight in any event. The little Mallory AA kind is very small, light, cheap,—and shines with quite a decent light beam. Stores sometimes sell them for a buck or less as promotional gimmicks. Use Duracell or similar batteries, and carry spares, and a spare bulb. Tape the switch so it doesn't accidentally flick on and burn itself out in your bags during the day.

Other than lighting and the various items of equipment already discussed in previous chapters, your camping kit will be mostly a matter of personal taste and common sense. After all, I shouldn't have to tell you to take toilet paper, or basic items needed for hygiene—use a biodegradiable soap such as Trak— or a first-aid kit (more about this in another chapter). A compact little sewing kit will add little weight and be handy to fix rips in your clothing, tent, or bag; include a small pair of folding scissors (handy for tire patches too). Such things as insect spray and sunburn lotion should be self evident, according to season and region.

Some sort of knife is essential for many purposes; I won't even ride a bike across town without one. You can carry a folding knife for everything, or take a sheath knife for heavier jobs and a small pocketknife for finer work. A Boy Scout–type utility knife is all you really have to have; the can opener and the screwdriver blades are handy, too. (If you've got access to a grinder and know how to do it, you can turn that mumbly-peg blade, also known as leather punch, into a small screwdriver to fit your derailleur adjustment screws.) But you don't even need that—any good-quality pocketknife, such as Schrade-Walden, Ka-bar, or Buck, will be fine.

I do not think much of those elaborate little multi-purpose Swiss Army knives with the umpteen blades and the cuckoo clock in the handle. No doubt some of the little tools are handy, notably the Phillips screwdriver found on some models—some derailleurs use this type of screw head—but how badly do you really need a corkscrew in the woods? (If you could even do a proper job with that dinky corkscrew.) Other tools, such as the saw blade, are too small to be of practical use, or, like the scissors, are clumsy to use due to the bulk of the attached handle. My father always said,

"Watch out for any tool or any man that claims to be able to do too many different jobs."

The Swiss Army knives *are* beautifully made, and this is probably the reason for their very great popularity with people who should know better, despite their blatant impracticality. One widely sold model is called, so help me Ernest Hemingway, the Safari Survival Knife. You'll never get out of the jungle alive, bwana, without that corkscrew and bottle opener. . . .

A sheath knife of reasonable size is a handy item. Some of the current crop of largely self-anointed authorities will cast great scorn on you if you carry one, but there are valid uses for a sheath knife all the same. The main use, and this may surprise you, is in fixing food. There is just no way to keep a folding knife reasonably clean, unless perhaps you want to boil it every time you use it; the hinges and the hollow handle get full of grease, fish scales, and other things too horrible to mention. (And if there's any salt in there, it will rust your knife to hell and gone.) So, while you have no real need for a tool to cut firewood in most cases, nor, like the old mountain men, a weapon for disembowelling grizzlies and the members of aboriginal liberation movements, a small sheath knife does have its less melodramatic uses.

I find I never go anywhere away from town without a sheath knife, usually a sharp, light, handy little thing that Schrade-Walden aptly calls a Sharp Finger. Another good sheath knife, especially for fishing, is the Finnish Rapala, which is the only inexpensive knife I know of that will actually take and hold a good edge. But if you want a knife for fixing food and slicing onions and so on, you could just as easily carry an ordinary kitchen utility knife, perhaps making a simple leather holder for it. You don't actually need to be able to wear it on your belt—in fact, you can't while riding the bike, and you'd look like a fool if you did.

Axes and the like are inappropriate and heavy. If you can't find wood that you can snap over your knee, don't build a fire.

You'd better check state and local laws before carrying any knife at all. Most localities are very reasonable about such things if you're obviously carrying your knife as a camping tool rather than as a weapon, but some states, notably Massachusetts and New York, have laws that are positively grotesque.

Personal items for entertainment or enrichment may be carried, within reasonable weight limits. These might include a small musical instrument, such as a harmonica or recorder, a deck of cards, or a pocket chess set for whiling away long rainy days. Books are terribly heavy, but all of us take them; you might want guidebooks on birds or wild flowers. One of those little plastic star charts with the wheellike finder will provide a lot of interest and enjoyment on clear nights and turn the sky from a rather cold, alien place to a familiar and even friendly pattern.

Made nervous by snakes or spiders? Take along a small paperback on the subject and actively look for species to identify, and force yourself to watch them without prejudice. You'll find that familiarity and knowledge will demolish your foolish fears.

Take *something* to pass the time; sooner or later you'll be struck in a tent or under a tarp for a rainy day, and you'll go kazooties without a means of diversion, especially if you're alone.

If you're really into birds and the like, you might want to pack a pair of those very compact binoculars, though even the smallest pairs add some real weight, and the light ones are very costly. For photos of your trip, a compact 35 mm. will weigh little more than a Pocket 110, and the pictures will turn out better. Cushion camera or binoculars well against road vibration, and don't leave film or a loaded camera in a bike bag while the bike stands directly in the hot sun.

As an alternative to photography, you might try sketching, either with pencil or felt-tip pens. A sketch pad and a set of pencils or markers will weigh less than a camera. Don't be too quick to assume that you have no talent—almost anybody can draw basic landscape shapes with a little attention to proportions and the angles of lines. The value of this is that in making a drawing, or trying to do so, you begin to look at things—to really see the way the light falls on a valley after a rainstorm, or the angle of a wind-felled tree on a riverbank, or the way a country road curves over a hill—and this enhances your whole perception of the world around you. With a camera, all too often we simply point the thing and snap, and let it do the work. If you really get into sketching there are tiny watercolor sets that are ideal for bikepacking use.

Fishing is lots of fun and can vary the diet as well; there are many fine takedown rigs on the market now, as fishing with ultralight tackle has become the latest fashion among fishermen. If you don't want to carry a skillet, carry some aluminum foil and bake your catch in the coals. Or turn it loose and lie about how big it was.

Enough, enough. Let's get all this junk loaded on the bike so we can go somewhere.

> *"I hope you're a good hand at pinning
> and tying strings?"* Tweedledee remarked.
> *"Every one of these things has got to
> go on, somehow or other."*
>
> —Lewis Carroll,
> **Through the Looking Glass**

CHAPTER **7**

Loading Up

Now, I'm afraid, we're back for a moment to the stuff you have to have. If you're going bikepacking, you not only have to have a bike and at least minimal camping gear; there must also be some provision for loading and carrying your camping outfit securely on the bike.

For the benefit of a few misinformed or optimistic souls, let me repeat: *on the bike.* A backpack *will not* work. If you mount a bike carrying any load on your back, you offer a mortal insult to the whole physical principle that enables you to ride it at all; your center of gravity is raised to an absurd height, and you will wreck your bike handling. You will also put added pressure on your behind and probably hurt your back. A small nylon daypack is fine for carrying, say, a loaf of bread from the store, or making a run to the creek for water; anything big enough to hold a full camping kit, or even any significant part of it, is entirely out of the question. Your primary load must be carried on the bike, not on you.

Racks and Carriers

A solidly constructed, well-designed carrier rack, securely fitted to your bike's frame, is an irreducible necessity. You might succeed in getting by without panniers—I've seen some reasonably useful rigs made from a pair of old Boy Scout or G.I. knapsacks, and a few people get by just rolling and lashing things here and there—but there's *got* to be something to fasten the stuff to. A few of the older touring bikes came with adequate carriers already fitted as factory equipment, and a very few modern ones still do, but most cyclists will have to buy their racks separately. The cost is not high—even the most sophisticated racks are cheap compared to most cycling equipment—but the requirements are very stringent.

A rear rack is necessary, while a front one is merely nice to have. That is my opinion, anyway. Some tourists—a distinct minority—carry much or all of the load on front-fork-mounted carriers and claim that this distributes the weight more evenly. It certainly does; that's what's wrong with it. The weight *shouldn't* be evenly distributed, or even nearly so, on a camper's bike; the weight distribution should be very distinctly toward the rear. I'll talk more about this later on, but the basic point is that the bike should be tail-heavy, because otherwise the back wheel tends to skid dangerously on turns and downhills, especially on dirt roads. Traction is improved in mud or loose dirt, too, if the bike is tail-heavy. (I also think a front carrier makes the fork stiffer, increasing the numb-hands problem, but I have no real proof of this.)

Front-fork panniers do have value in cold-weather camping, as they serve well to carry additional clothing, underwear, and the like. But I think they should be used only as auxiliaries to rear-mounted panniers, not as the main carrier system.

Now, with any type of rear carrier, the basic principle is the same. There's a horizontal platform or rack, usually skeletal rather than solid, to which the load is secured. This platform, of course, sits somewhere just above the back wheel. The front end will be anchored to the frame in the general area of the upper seat stays, while some arrangement of supporting members and braces will run from the rack itself down to the rear dropouts. The platform or rack itself may incorporate some system for attaching bags or other items.

That sounds simple enough, and it is. (In fact, any really competent home craftsman ought to be able to design and build an efficient rear rack, given the right tools and materials and a grasp of the requirements.) The difficulty is that while the whole device doesn't have to do very many things, it has to do what it does do very well indeed. There are only a few things that can go wrong, but any one of those things can be catastrophic.

It goes without saying that the rack must be made of very sturdy materials and put together solidly so that nothing will break or come apart even when riding over bumps and holes with a load. It is, perhaps, equally obvious that the system used to attach the carrier to the bike must be extremely solid and foolproof, so that nothing comes adrift. This is not just a question of things falling off or of having to stop and tighten bolts, annoying as that might be. Bear this constantly in mind: *we're talking about a bunch of metalwork next to the back wheel.* If something breaks or works loose, it is very likely to go into the spokes. If it does that while the bike is in motion a crash is almost inevitable, and your back wheel will be destroyed as well. If this should happen on a fast downhill or when riding on a highway with heavy traffic, you could be seriously injured, and it is far from impossible that you could be killed. Therefore, flimsiness is unacceptable, period.

Another source of trouble, though less serious than the preceding, is the means of anchoring the front end of the rack to the frame. If this is not solid, a heavily loaded rack can slip downward and lock up the back brake. This is not very dangerous in most circumstances, but it is certainly irritating and undignified to be brought to a stop in this way. Yet, because the bike-frame tubing is rather thin in this area, the mounting system must not create the possibility of damage to the metal.

The whole rack assembly needs to be reasonably stable and rigid. That is, it mustn't whip and sway severely from side to side when you lean into a turn or hit a rough patch. Once a load starts swaying, it can build up into an uncontrollable oscillation that causes you to lose control of the bike. Even less violent whip and sway will quickly loosen the nuts and bolts that secure the rack to the frame, and weaken the rack itself.

Finally, of course, a suitable rack should be as light as is consistent with strength and rigidity. The very heavy steel racks sometimes seen on old-style utility bikes are far heavier than you need.

The whole technology of bolt-on racks has undergone some very healthy development in the last decade. Earlier, people who used bikes for touring or camping usually bought specially built frames, or else stock touring bikes, like the old Louison Bobet, that came already equipped with racks usually made by the cycle company. It is a relatively new phenomenon for cyclists to buy general-purpose sport bikes and adapt them to various uses by fitting them with different accessories, and it has led to the introduction of some very good products indeed.

The cheapest sort of carrier, the thin steel or alloy rack sometimes seen on low-priced bikes, is usually inadequate for carrying real loads. This is the type that consists merely of a couple of wobbly struts and a skeletal platform of the same coat-hanger-wire-like stock, sometimes with a useless spring-clip fitting. Such racks are meant to provide the casual urban cyclist with a place to put something on the order of a windbreaker, nothing heavier.

Considerably better and still quite inexpensive is the familiar Swiss Pletscher, with its cast-aluminum rack and oddball mousetrap gadget on top. This is undoubtedly the most widely used of all the rear carriers sold in the U.S. today; indeed, at one time it was almost the only decent carrier you could find in bike shops. Despite a lot of propaganda and defamation by various people, the old Pletscher is not such a bad rack; it definitely is adequate for general cycle camping, and a real bargain on today's market. Ian Hibell used a modified Pletscher on his epic Western Hemisphere journey. I am not in that class, but I have certainly used a Pletscher under brutal conditions. It just needs some imagination and understanding, that's all.

The Pletscher's most notorious problem is in the attachment of the front end to the bike frame. This consists of a rather crude metal clamp bar which holds the rack against the seat-stay tubes; and, since the Pletscher has only a single pair of support struts, this fitting has to take a good part of the weight of whatever is loaded onto the carrier. It is simply not up to the job. No amount of tightening, short of crushing the frame tubes—and the clamp metal is too soft for this, fortunately—will cure it of slipping under even moderate loads, and when it slips downward, it clamps the back brake on, dragging and eventually locking the wheel. As a bonus, it also gouges the paint of the frame.

A great deal of fuss has been made about this problem, more than is really justified; inability to cope with clamp slippage indicates either a failure of the imagination, a badly overloaded bike, or both. All the Pletscher really needs in this area is a little additional support to keep it from sliding down. This can be supplied by fitting a stiff, thin metal plate, drilled with three holes, to the brake's center bolt and to the two clamp bolts of the carrier. Such devices are listed in most good cycle-equipment catalogs, but many bike people simply build their own, or get a do-it-yourself friend to make one. All it takes is a bit of stiff, thin metal (I made mine from an old track-racing cleat, and I've seen some pretty good jobs done with Erector-set parts), some careful measuring, and a few minutes' work with an electric drill or hand drill and, perhaps a file and a hacksaw. Some duct tape wrapped around the frame tubes will ease the paint-gouging problem. Nothing to it.

The Pletscher has also been accused of instability and fragility. Some say it will whip and sway when loaded. One author even says flatly that the Pletscher and other single-strut racks should be used for "loads not exceeding 15 pounds" and "light loads on a casual basis." Rubbish. If a Pletscher wobbles and sways, it is overloaded or the load is incorrectly distributed. We'll get into the question of total weights later, but for now, suffice it to say that except for expeditions to truly remote regions or in winter weather, there is no reason for the rear carrier to have to support more than 30 pounds. Even that is really too high unless a lot of food is being carried; 25 pounds is more like it. This should be loaded in such a way that most of the heavy items are down near the axis of the back hub, where the carrier struts are mounted to the frame dropouts, so there is no way that their weight can have much effect on carrier whip. Only very light items, such as the sleeping bag and pad, are loaded on top of the carrier, or in the tops of the pannier bags. Loaded in this way, a Pletscher should not wobble, assuming, of course, that the pannier bags themselves are not of some faulty design that can shift and slip around, which will make any bike carrier wag its tail. As for strength, I've never seen or heard of a Pletscher strut breaking under reasonable loads. (This might be possible with a rack that's bent out of shape in a crash and then straightened; in view of the low cost of racks and the ease with which metal fatigue can be induced, I strongly suggest that you replace any lightweight carrier that gets pretzelled rather than trying to raise the dead.)

Rather than worrying so much about rack designs, many people would do better to go through their outfits and throw out a lot of useless junk that weighs the rack down.

I have defended the Pletscher at some length because there are so many of them around. In fact, my guess is that quite a few readers of this book bought a rack when they got their bikes and that in the majority of cases this was a Pletscher. I do not think a person who owns a Pletscher should be panicked into buying something else unless he or she really wants to and can afford it. But all the same, if you're buying a rack for cycle camping for the first time, there are others around that are really better and don't cost so terribly much more.

Best of the lightweights, I think, is the Blackburn, a very good design and not too high priced. One model of the Blackburn mounts directly onto the rear brake bolt and can be adjusted to level the platform—a very useful feature, since the platform definitely needs to be level before you can get the load arranged right. Like the Pletscher, the other model clamps to the seat stays, but because of its additional support struts, it doesn't slide down under a load. The latter Blackburn model doesn't adjust and will be hard to level with a frame 24″ or larger. There is also a slightly cheaper Japanese copy of the Blackburn, if you don't mind subsidizing a design ripoff to save yourself a few bucks.

There are a couple of very good racks made in England, the Karrimor and the Claude Butler. Made of steel and therefore heavier, both of these excellent racks are extremely sturdy, far more so than any alloy model, and for really rugged conditions, I think steel is better. The Claude Butler, in fact, is my own all-time pick in bikepacking racks. It comes hard to me to tell the already overloaded bikepacker to get a relatively heavy steel carrier, with lovely light things such as Blackburn's brainchild on the market. The fact remains, though, that a steel rack that gets bent out of shape in a fall can be straightened without much risk, but an aluminum alloy one will snap almost invariably. Even if it doesn't, it still must not be trusted, ever again, with any real load.

Eclipse makes a very nice rack at a price not much above the Blackburn. However, it employs a rather complex and fiddly-looking arrangement of plastic tracks and metal channels to accommodate the special Eclipse pannier system. I fail to see any advantage in this—simple buckles and straps have worked adequately for generations of us—and I wonder about its reliability under truly grisly conditions. (That metal channel, in particular, looks to me as if it could be clogged with mud or jammed by a fall.) At the very least, it's something else to fool with, and undoubtedly harder to fix under field conditions if it goes crazy. I may be exercising too much skepticism here, but I have a deep-rooted mistrust of technological cuteness that seems to be mostly for its own sake.

The carrier, whatever the choice, must be anchored to the frame like a veritable barnacle. If you get a custom frame built, be sure to have them braze on fittings so that you can anchor your carrier solidly and forget the little clamps and clips. (Jack Taylor does some lovely custom touring frames with light steel carriers made to fit.)

Remember when we looked at the frame, how we noted the need for those little eyelets on the rear dropouts. If you went ahead and got a bike without them, you're in big trouble now. There is just no way to mount any carrier that even halfway compares to the solidness of those integral eyelets. There are

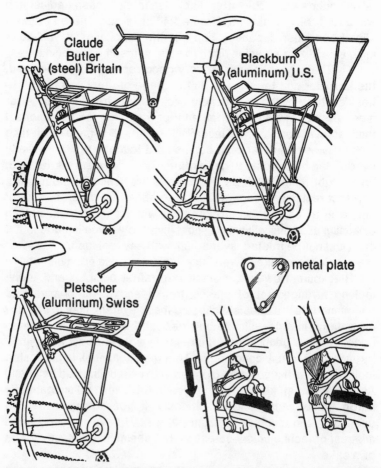

Three models of bicycle racks. Slipping by Pletscher clamps (lower central figure) can be prevented by bolting a metal plate to the clamps and brakes (lower right figure).

little clamps that go around the ends of the seat stays, but these are so ridiculously inadequate that I wouldn't trust them to support a copy of this book. They are really meant for fenders, and they're inadequate even for *them*.

Blackburn makes little metal doohickeys that slip into the cutout holes in Campagnolo racing dropouts and, supposedly, make it possible to anchor rack supports solidly. I must confess that these things fill me with deep and abiding mistrust, yet I think too much of Jim Blackburn's ideas to entirely dismiss them. Certainly they are the only adapters I've seen for this purpose that I'd even consider. But if you've got a frame without dropout eyelets in back, chances are it is a very light, stiff, nervous-handling racing frame, and I wonder if you'll ever succeed in turning it into a satisfactory touring bike.

The bolts that hold your carrier supports to the eyelets must be tight, **tight, TIGHT.** Use lock washers and Loc-Tite or another thread-lock compound, and check the whole setup every single day you ride. In rough country or on bad roads, check the bolts at lunch break too. If you find a loose bolt, fix it *right away*. Imprint on your mind the picture of those whirling spokes and what will happen to you if that strut comes loose and goes into the wheel. This is one area in which you can't be too fussy. Carry extra mounting bolts, washers and nuts, and a small tube of Loc-Tite.

It is sometimes possible to fix a broken strut well enough to get home. What you'll need is a bit of light steel tubing that will fit snugly over the strut. Alloy tubing might be all right, but it's probably best to be extracautious. You'll also need some epoxy, and it's not a bad idea to carry a couple of epoxy tubes anyway, since the stuff has a lot of possible uses in camp or on the bike. (But be careful when you pack those tubes—keep them tightly sealed and separated.)

Coat the broken ends of the strut and slip them into either end of the tubing, forcing them in until they meet. You may have to do some work with a file to get them to go. Usually the tubing only needs to be about 3 inches long. Of course, you aren't likely to find something like this lying around by the roadside; tubing is an item that you have to carry in your repair kit. Scrounge around home, at work, or at hardware stores and see if you can find some scrap tubing of a diameter inside that matches the thickness of your carrier's struts. This is strictly an emergency repair, and the strut or the whole rack should be replaced as soon as possible.

The repair job ought to get you home, anyway. Remember to give the epoxy overnight to dry.

Front carriers, as I mentioned earlier, are less vital, and many of us dispense with them altogether. A set of panniers up front is unnecessary with a well-chosen outfit, though they might be good in the winter to carry extra clothing. A front rack will keep a handlebar bag from dragging on the front tire, however, which can be a real problem with smaller frames. Blackburn's is good. T.A. makes a bag support, not really a carrier, that mounts on the pivot bolts of a centerpull brake, such as Weinmann. I had a T.A. model a long time ago, and it worked fine but was a terrible job to install. (You'd better know how to take the brake completely apart and reassemble it, or have the job done at a bike shop.)

There are various metal brackets, once common and sometimes still seen, that go around the stem and bars for mounting handlebar bags. Since modern handlebar bags now incorporate their own supports (more of this below), such devices are obsolete, as are the bags for which they were designed.

Panniers

The primary means of carrying your outfit will be a pair of panniers—matching bags that hang down on either side of your back wheel. Kids and novices sometimes refer to them as "saddlebags," perhaps due to the influence of cowboy movies. On a bicycle, a saddlebag is an entirely different article, so we call them panniers. Sometimes, under difficult circumstances, we call them other things, many, many other things.

When I began cycling, the only panniers you could get in the U.S. were big, heavy, canvas jobs with leather straps and buckles. They were very strong and serviceable—I carried my tools to a lot of construction jobs in them—but extremely clumsy, heavy, badly shaped, and ugly. Nowadays there is a wide range of modern panniers, many of which by now have had time to prove themselves in heavy use. The new style is made of strong, light nylon, usually brightly colored, fitted out with zippers, webbing straps, Velcro closures, and the like, and often featuring various little auxiliary pockets on the outside. Makes and models proliferate like rock bands. Except for the special systems, such as those from Eclipse, any set of panniers should be compatible with any standard rack.

The primary decision is not what brand to get but how much total capacity you need. You certainly don't want undersized bags, so that you have trouble getting everything in and perhaps strain the material, but you shouldn't have a lot of excess space either. If you are an experienced backpacker, you know that in hiking, it is considered all right to have a pack bigger than your outfit will fill, since it will ride more comfortably on your back. In cycling, the idea is to have just the opposite. The bigger the panniers or other bags, the more wind-sensitive, drag-inducing area you add to the bike's profile—which, even at best, is nothing you'd ever want to enter in the Human-Powered Speed Contest. Also, gear loaded loosely into a set of oversized panniers will tend to shift and shake around, thus greatly increasing any tendency to instability. Also, of course, bigger panniers are correspondingly expensive, and you hardly want to pay for more than you need.

While some impoverished or overoptimistic types may try to go camping with little, undersized bags meant for commuting to campus, the more common error among affluent cyclists is to buy too much bag. Besides the problems just mentioned, this usually has a subtler but even more deleterious effect on their cycle-camping experiences; they tend to succumb to what one canoe camper called the "bottomless pit" effect. That is, just as we've all noted that our expenses seem to expand to take up all of our income, or our clothes at home seem to multiply to fill any increase in closet space, so the camping outfit tends to mysteriously expand to occupy available space in our bags. If you replace a set of bags with larger ones, even though your basic outfit has been giving you good service, watch and see if you don't catch yourself sticking some extra stuff into that tempting additional space, even when you know you shouldn't. So, one way to make sure you hold your outfit to a light, compact minimum is to begin by holding down bag size—if you can't find a way to carry it, the old maxim says, you'll damned well find a way to live without it.

It may be useful to compare the bicycle pannier set to the hiker's frame backpack, with which many readers may be familiar. In both cases, the largest, bulkiest item goes on the outside—the backpacker straps the sleeping bag to the bottom of the pack, just as yours will be lashed to the top of your carrier rack. Also, most of the best lightweight camping gear suitable for bikepacking was originally designed with the backpacker in mind, so the needs of the two groups are in many ways similar.

Now the typical modern frame backpack of the ordinary sort—the kind used by most casual recreational campers, not the "expedition" monsters—has a total capacity of somewhere around 2,700 to 3,000 cubic inches, counting all the little outside pockets. But the backpacker has to carry more stuff. As we've already noted, it's a rare bikepacker who has to carry more than a three days' supply of food at a time. (The bikie has to carry several tools that the average packie couldn't even identify; though they are heavy, these tools do not take up much room, and they're almost always stuck in an auxiliary pocket of the handlebar bag.)

The bikepacker has another place to carry some of the stuff—that big handlebar bag up front. It's true that you can ruin the bike's handling qualities with too much weight here, but it's a good place to put light but bulky objects—I often put my tent in the bottom of my handlebar bag. Most good handlebar bags run to about 500 cubic inches or so in size. Also, long items, such as tent poles or fishing rods, that are usually carried inside a backpack can be strapped along the sides of the sleeping bag atop the bike's carrier.

Figuring all these things into the pattern, a careful bicycle camper, under moderate weather conditions and traveling in areas where food can be obtained at least every two or three days, should be able to manage with a total pannier capacity—both bags—of 1,500 cubic inches. Most people will be a bit more comfortable with 1,700 cubic inches. Much depends on the complexity and bulk of your kit; if you're using a tarp, you can just wrap it around your sleeping bag, but if you take a tent, you'll need somewhere to carry it. My own bags are about 1,500 cubic inches, and I find I use it all! In warm weather, when I'm carrying a minimum of extra clothing and making daily food pickups, I've done some successful cruising with a pair of little commuter bags that barely measured 1,000 cubic inches—so, a lot of this is up to you. If you're going out in cold weather and must take extra clothing, you'll need quite a bit more capacity—you'll want a set of those 2,500-cubic-inch "transcontinental" touring jobs.

A glance through a typical catalog will show you that most of the common pannier sets are somewhat bigger than the sizes recommended above. No problem; 2,000 cubic inches, which is about average, isn't too much, and in fact may be needed by an inexperienced person.

In studying listed figures and trying to pick your set, don't be misled by some of the imaginative math used by various makers. The differences in capacity are seldom as great as they appear. The fact is that except for commuter bags—those little cigar-box-sized things, which *are* too small for camping, except on a front carrier—and a few monsters made for long-range tourists carrying lots of clothes, most regular pannier sets are not all that different in total useful capacity. The dimensions are, after all, dictated basically by the geometry of the bike and of the carrier, which will not vary that much; nearly all standard carriers are very similar in size. The bags will be the same length as the rack and tall enough to reach from the rack to somewhere in the vicinity of the rear hub. Depth may vary a bit, but not much, because panniers can bulge out only so far on either side before they become unmanageable.

The way it works out, the typical medium-capacity pannier set measures about a foot long fore-and-aft, about 12 to 14 inches top to bottom, and about 4 to 5 inches deep. This is not a simple box shape, though; the bottom is tapered or cut back to leave clearance for the rider's heels, and thus cuts into the bags' volume considerably. There may or may not be additional outside

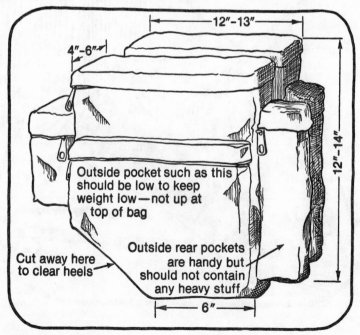

A typical pannier set.

pockets. Any decent-quality bags of these approximate dimensions are fine for cycle camping, so don't worry about it.

Some bags close with zippers, some with straps. Zippers
are more secure and keep contents cleaner; a flap-top with straps
will tolerate a bit more overloading. Yet, this isn't necessarily a
good feature—in fact, since a flap-and-strap top encourages, or
at least permits, overloading, I think it's a bad feature.

A common fault in cheap panniers is that they cause the
rider's heel to hit the lower front of the bag when pedaling. This
could drive you crazy and in time, could wear a hole in the bag. It
is especially bad if you have big feet. It should be considered an
unacceptable characteristic. A well-designed pannier is cut back
at this point far enough to clear your heel, even when the bag is

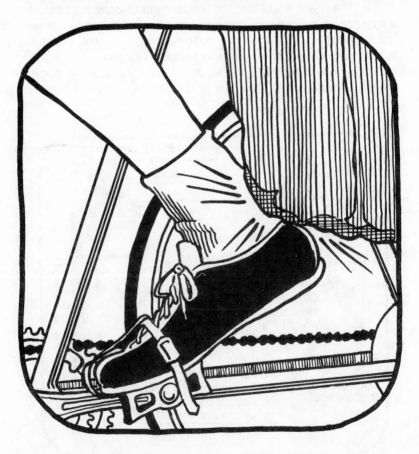

stuffed full. (I've encountered panniers that worked fine this way until filled. In fact, the first ones I ever made turned out that way, and I had to go back and recut and resew.) Just because a pannier is cut back a bit, don't assume that it will clear your heel, for it may not be cut back enough. Be especially cautious if your bike is a relatively short-coupled "club racer" or "sport" bike; the long-wheelbase, long-chainstay design of the true touring bike gives a little more room in this area.

Some very good designs taper the bags symmetrically, so that the weight is concentrated near the hub area. This improves bike handling, though it does cut into the bag capacity.

Examine the way in which the bag is to be attached to the carrier. The usual system involves straps and buckles. Some sets

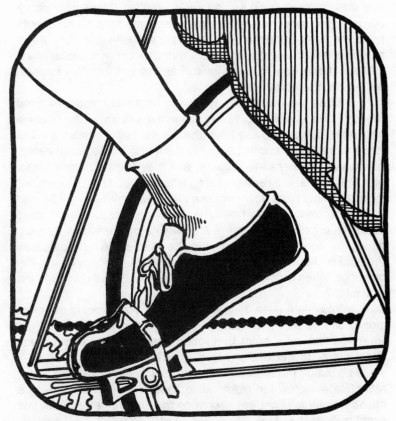

The shape of the bike bag is very important to cycle tourists. The bag on the right offers heel clearance, while the one on the left does not.

are permanently attached via a piece of fabric that sits across the rack like a saddle. If this is the case, you must have some way of getting at the rack in order to fit on the straps or bunji cords that hold the sleeping bag in place. A few modern bags use little hooks, and then there is the unique Eclipse system described earlier. See if the whole arrangement appears to be sturdy and reliable; it must cling to your rack with limpetlike tenacity. Are there any small parts that might be easily damaged? Can the system be operated easily with cold, wet fingers? If it breaks, can it be fixed under field conditions? (You can sew a web strap back in place; other gadgets may be less readily serviced.)

Is there some means of securing the bags at the bottom—not halfway down the inside, but *at the bottom*—so that they don't swing and sway or bounce up and down? Some of the new makers have done some very interesting things with shock cords. Make sure the bags incorporate some form of stiffener to keep the inner surfaces from fouling the spokes. In fact, make sure there isn't *anything* on them that can get into the spokes. (Bikepacker's Law #3: Anything that can get into the spokes, will, and at the worst possible time.)

Does the whole bag appear to be solidly made, of good fabric? (This is, perhaps, rather subjective unless you have some expertise, but try anyway.) Are the seams neat, without a lot of loose thread ends sticking out? Are the fabric edges hot-sheared, not frayed? If there are zippers, are they the big, lug-toothed, plastic kind that will resist jamming when wet or dirty? Remember, those panniers hang down where a lot of road crud can get tossed into the zippers by the wheels, so the zippers have to have good digestive capabilities. If there are outside pockets, are they big enough to be of real value, or are they just some little dinguses the maker used to get your eye and your money? Are the openings, when undone, big enough to let you get things in and out with ease?

You might even think about color. If you're going to spend money on this stuff and ride around with it, you might as well get what you like, or a color that looks good on your bike. Or you might prefer to get red or some other bright color for safety, if you'll be out on the highway. Kirtland makes bags covered with a reflective material for night riding, and if you think there's a chance that you might get caught on the highway after dark, you might well want to look into this—it costs about 20 bucks extra, but how much is your life worth?

You can't go far wrong if you simply purchase a good, medium-capacity pannier set made by a reputable company and sold by a dealer who backs up his merchandise. Cannondale bags, I think, are very good indeed—any experienced camper will recognize the name as a good one—as are Kirtland and Bellwether. While I don't care for the Eclipse system as such, their bags are beautifully designed and made. I must add that I can't speak with real authority on any make currently sold; I make much of my own equipment, and the only panniers I own are strictly home rolled. If you're handy with scissors and a needle, you might try this. Oh, yes—do not get those panniers with the compartment over the top of the rack. That is where your sleeping bag goes.

Handlebar Bags

Some cyclists refuse to ride with any weight on the bars; they say it makes the bike harder to handle. To some degree they're right. Anything hanging up there will affect steering and balance. So whatever handlebar bag you get, it's strictly for the lighter items. With that limitation observed, the handlebar bag is still useful enough to justify its small effect on steering. It's very handy for things you want to get at while riding—snacks, sunburn lotion, maps—and it's where most cycling photographers stow their cameras. And, of course, it is a conspicuous area on which to display your various patches and emblems from bike clubs, rallies, century runs, and the like. (Mustn't forget the really *important* things.)

Because of the need to avoid heavy weights in this bag for reasons of balance, there isn't much point in worrying unduly about stress limits. Just about any decent bag ought to withstand far, far more weight than any cyclist needs to hang on his bars. But you do want to be sure there's a solid, stable means of carrying the thing, because it gets bounced around more than the back end of the bike. If a handlebar bag starts to flop and shift from side to side, it will just about take the bike away from you.

Older model handlebar bags were simply hung on the bars by little straps, which interfered greatly with the hands in some positions. There were also various metal racks meant to hold the bag clear of the bars. But the better modern bags incorporate their own support frames, which get around all of these problems. The usual support consists of a metal rod that loops under the stem extension and over the bars, spreads out to either side rather like a coat hanger, and then slides into built-in sleeves or channels on the upper sides of the bag. This holds the bag away from the bars, so that you can grip any part of the bar; it supports the bag in a neat shape with the top held open; and it adds less weight than a separate carrier. It's altogether a great advance in bike-bag design. The support can be of steel or alloy. Either is strong enough to hold any reasonable load in this area, but steel, as noted earlier, is less easily broken in a crash.

A bag of the older type can be adapted to use this form of supporting frame by sewing in some pockets or channels to accept the metal rods. Nylon web strapping can be used for this purpose. My old canvas T.A. handlebar bag has been with me so long and over so many miles that I couldn't bear to part with it, so I took a length of steel rod and bent myself a support of this type, and now the old bag has the advantage of this new concept. If you own an old-fashioned, strap-to-the-bars bag, you might like to try this—but you'd better learn something about bending metal. (I broke two rods before I got the hang of it!)

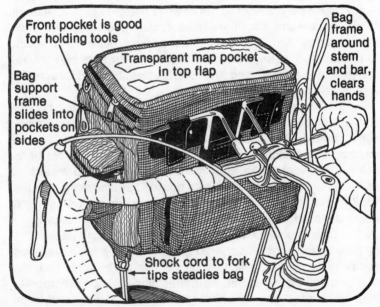

Typical modern handlebar bag.

In addition to the support, there should be some system for anchoring and stabilizing the bag from below. Some bags use a strap or elastic cord around the head tube, while some use long, elastic shock cords that hook to the front fork dropouts. (Make sure that you get these secured so that they can't come loose and get into the spokes—remember Bikepacker's Law #3.)

How big a bag? About 500 cubic inches is right. Get much more and you'll be tempted to overload. If you can't get everything in standard panniers and 500 cubic inches of handlebar bag, then get a front carrier and front panniers, not a bigger handlebar bag. One that's 600 cubic inches is okay if you've got something bulky but light that you want to carry up there.

The top flap should open away from you, so that you can get at things without dismounting. I don't like a zippered flap on a handlebar bag; it's hard to operate while riding. A transparent map case on top is a handy feature, though checking your map while riding calls for flat, straight, deserted roads and a very steady hand on the bars.

Makes? Cannondale's impresses me enormously; the support frame can be supplied for either dropped or upright bars, a very good feature indeed. Kirtland and Eclipse also make good handlebar bags. Eclipse, indeed, pioneered the whole modern support-brace system. Bear in mind the same criteria of quality work and materials that you would bring to bear on any other piece of equipment.

Other Bags

English tourists and a few Anglophile Americans often use a saddlebag. This is simply a roughly cylindrical bag suspended from the back of the saddle. It's fine for holding a change of clothing, but the capacity is much too limited for camping use, and it will get in the way of mounting your sleeping bag. If you are tall and ride a big frame, which puts your saddle well above the strapped-on sleeping bag, you might like to have a small bag back here to hold a few minor items—it's a good way to carry a spare tube and a tire-patch kit. I often tie my rain suit there, though not in a bag.

There are small packs made to fit atop a carrier rack. As I said, that's where your sleeping bag goes. Now, I suppose there could be a pack of this type big enough to hold a light down bag;

I've never seen anything of the sort attempted, but the idea seems to have potential. Some bike-bag manufacturer could do quite well, I suspect, with a well-designed, rack-top bag specifically designed to hold a sleeping bag. (Interested, anyone?)

A type of bag occasionally seen is the one that fits inside of the main triangle of the bike's frame. These are of very limited value; if filled with any useful load, they interfere with pedal action, make the bike sensitive to crosswinds, and also make it difficult to lift the bike in the usual way. I don't recommend them for normal packing use; however, they are handy for carrying a large sketch pad or watercolor block, if you go in for such things.

A few brave souls tow trailers behind bikes. Not me, *bubbe.* How do you stop one of those tractor-trailer rigs on a fast downhill, or corner on dirt and gravel? The jackknife-and-fishtail potential seems to be horrendous. Anyway, I don't see any earthly reason why you can't carry adequate camping gear in the normal pannier-and-handlebar-bag setup.

Some people use a trailer for hauling small children. No doubt this is a better and safer method than the usual rear-mounted infant seats—I had just about all I could stand with those things back in days gone by—but really, I don't think it's a very good idea to subject children of that young an age to the rigors of extended cycle camping. Wait till they get big enough to ride their own bikes.

Bits and Pieces

Besides the load-carrying fittings, there are a few other accessories that go on the bike, and this seems as logical a place to talk about them as any other.

Water bottles are pretty much standard; your bike probably already carries one. If you're buying a new bottle holder, I suggest steel rather than aluminum. Light alloy bottle cages are very popular right now, but they're best reserved for racing. Alloy cages are too given to breaking. If you're getting a custom frame, don't forget to order brazed-on bottle-cage mounts, which eliminate those clamp bands that scar your paint.

Usually the water bottle is clipped to the down tube, low down so as not to disturb the bike's center of gravity. In desert country or hot weather, you might prefer to carry two bottles; you can put a second cage on your seat tube (if you can figure out what to do with the pump) or just stick it into your jersey pocket. As I mentioned earlier, some campers like to mount a water-bottle cage under the down tube to hold a white-gasoline container, though not all frame layouts will accept this.

Handlebar-mounted bottle cages used to be standard—some held two bottles—but they are rare items now. In any case, they interfere with mounting a handlebar bag, and the added weight up there is bad for control.

A *pump* is a distinct necessity, and you'd better have a good one. You can't expect all of your punctures to occur within walking distance of a gas station. The fashion now is to have a plastic Silca pump of the type that fits into the bike's frame, thus eliminating the need for pump brackets. But these plastic pumps are easily cracked and usually fit only Presta valves. Most American cyclists use Schrader valves (the type found on auto tires) and, in addition, frequently use their pumps to repel dog attacks. For both reasons, an aluminum Zefal pump is what I recommend. The Zefal has a solid head that clamps directly onto the tire valve, so you can get it off without losing air. The pumps that employ little hoses are very inferior and make it nearly impossible to get a tire up to a really useful pressure.

Fenders are another of those things that bikies argue about. In England, it's taken for granted that a nonracing bike will have fenders (which they call "mudguards"), but in the U.S., very few cyclists use them, and many hotdog types regard them as strictly turkey equipment.

Fenders do have their appeal; they reduce the spray of water off of the tires on a rainy day and deflect mud and gravel from your legs and bike. A front fender can also provide a place to hang a small headlight.

Fenders add a bit of weight and air resistance, though less than is worth making a real fuss about if you have reasons for wanting them. On dirt roads in wet weather, they get clogged with mud, and you have to stop and clear them. They get in the way of changing a tire, and in time they work loose and begin to rattle, or get bent and drag the tire. With some makes, the front fender tends to hit your toe in a turn. All in all, they're a fair amount of trouble for dubious value.

On the other hand, they serve a social function in groups—if you ride behind another cyclist in the wet, you'll certainly appreciate it if he's got fenders, so you don't get dirty water in your face. This, no doubt, is the reason for the popularity of fenders with affluent international tourists who ride in groups; another may be the grubby stripe that forms up the back of a fenderless rider in the rain, tourists being more concerned with their appearance than we backwoods campers. And there's no denying that fenders make a bike look sharp, especially those white plastic jobs.

I've ridden with and without fenders, and I can see both sides to the question. If I lived in England or the Pacific Northwest, where I either had to ride in the rain or not at all, no doubt I'd use them. Generally, I don't feel the need. (The bike I've got now won't accept them anyway, which may influence my attitude somewhat.) As long as I've got my tent and my stove and some food, I try to avoid riding in the rain at all, and rainy weather is the only earthly reason for using fenders.

If you do want them, Bleumel's fenders are considered best by British tourists, who may be presumed to be the fender experts of the wheeled world. Before you buy fenders, though, make sure that your bike has enough room between tire and frame to accept them. Some very good bikes don't.

Kickstands are similarly controversial. More than one authority has stated flatly in print that no serious cyclist would use one. I do not know about this—I've never met but one cyclist that I thought might be serious, and I got the hell away from him as fast as I could pedal—but I know that most U.S. cyclists won't have them, regarding them as heavy, useless, and unreliable. True in part; kickstands aren't the most reliable things in the world and they add weight, and usually you can find something to lean the bike against. When you've got a lot of camping gear loaded on, though, especially full panniers, it's very difficult to lean the bike against anything or lay it down without messing something up. There are times when you want to stop for a minute and get something out of a pannier, and there simply is nothing to lean the bike against. So a kickstand can be a handy item. I've got one on my bike.

Only a good kickstand is worth considering. The round kind found on cheap U.S. bikes is no good. The alloy kind with the trapezoidal-section leg and the allen-key bolt is what I've got. The trick is to make sure that it holds the bike at the right angle; it can be shortened cautiously with a hacksaw if necessary. If you have the clamp-on type, don't tighten down so hard that you damage the stays.

You'll have to make up your own mind about kickstands; this is very much an individual choice. Don't go buy one because I said I've got one, and if you dislike the one that came on your bike, don't hesitate to remove it. Don't be deterred by a lot of polo-club snobbery, either, if you do feel you want a kickstand.

Other stuff. Lights are important, but will be discussed in another chapter. A little cyclometer is handy for keeping track of miles, if you can stand that tick, tick, tick. (Solo riders like them because the sound is like having company. People in groups hate them because invariably some joker rides up alongside and asks, "Hey, what's that noise coming from your front wheel?") Flags might be good eye-grabbers in urban traffic, but they get caught by overhanging limbs on forest roads; and out on an open highway, any overtaking driver can see you perfectly well with or without your flag, even though they often swear in court they didn't. They just didn't give a damn.

Getting It On

Having acquired all this good stuff (and yes, my poor friend, we are at last coming to the end of Things To Buy), we don't just toss it all onto the bike any old way and ride off into the sunset. It does no good to own a fine bike, carrier set, and camping outfit if you don't put it together properly. In fact, a badly loaded bike can end your trip the first day out.

We will assume for now that you've got the bike set up to fit you, with your body weight correctly distributed, *unloaded.* You *have* to to this before you can distribute any additional weight and bulk. After all, your body is the biggest item the bike has to carry and weighs more than the bike and the camping stuff combined. Besides, it's very hard to adjust your saddle, and so on, with a lot of bags and racks in the way. So if you don't have this worked out yet, check the next chapter for guidance; if you're really lost, try some books from the reading list in back.

Taking it, then, that the bare bike is correctly set up, the next step is to consider your outfit in terms of weight and bulk. Mentally, on paper, or even with the stuff laid out on the floor, classify everything according to weight and bulk. Sleeping bags and tents are more bulky than heavy. Books and filled stoves are heavy but not bulky. Some items such as the tire-patch kit and certain tools are neither bulky nor very heavy, but must be packed where they can be reached easily; put them aside for now. (If something is both heavy *and* bulky, don't take it!)

The basic principle in loading a bike is the opposite of backpacking practice; it is more like loading a canoe. The heavy things on a bike go down low, with the light things on top, to keep the center of gravity as low as possible for better balance.

Weight must also be distributed fore and aft, something many cyclists neglect. As you may know, a bare bike is set up so that the rider's weight is 55% on the back wheel and 45% on the front. However, with the usual rear-pannier setup and a typical camping outfit on board, there's no way you'll come anywhere near this. Most campers wind up with about 30% of the total weight on the front wheel when fully loaded.

This is okay; in fact, it's good. Weight on the back wheel holds it down. There is a tendency, particularly on downhills, for the back wheel to break loose from the road and "float" and skid, and on a gravel or dirt road this is even more pronounced. Yet, don't overload the back wheel to the point of straining it—at a minimum, 20% of the total weight should be on the front wheel, and 30% is better. This weight business is so important that you ought to keep a bathroom scale handy to find out how much weight is on each wheel. It may sound picky, but it's that kind of pickiness that makes for smooth rides.

If your rack and panniers have any adjustment controls at all, get the rack dead level, or as level as you can, and position the panniers as far forward as possible without allowing it to foul your heels.

Now, when you go to load the panniers, keep the heaviest items at the bottom *and toward the front*. These will usually consist of things like the stove, books, heavier food items (margarine bottle, etc.), and tent pegs. It is important to keep the weight in the panniers toward the front because this centers the weight over the back hub and, therefore, above the point at which the wheel touches the road. Any considerable weight in the far rear corners of large pannier bags will tend to make the bike fishtail and skid. The shape of most panniers will resist your efforts to keep the weight forward in the bottoms, because they are cut away to clear your heels. So, despite the basic principle of heavy-stuff-at-the-bottom, you may find it helpful to stuff the rear bottom corners with, say, socks to keep the heavier things up toward the vertical plane of the axle. (The tapered-bottom design of the Eclipse panniers helps in this respect, though it reduces total volume.)

The upper part of the panniers will then contain things like toilet paper, clothing, and lighter food items, such as milk powder. The tent may go here if you have a small one. My own tent generally goes up in my handlebar bag, where it serves admirably to cushion my little Olympus camera. If your tent won't go inside one of your bags, I'd say you're trying to carry too big a tent; those complicated three-man domes with all the poles really aren't well suited to cycle camping, and your present packing problems are what you get for letting that bearded guy at the outdoor shop sell you one.

In the outer pockets of the panniers, if you have any, put things like your first-aid kit and other small items you need to be able to get at easily. This is also a good place to put little things that are easily lost, such as a spare bulb for your flashlight. If the handlebar bag has multiple pockets, and most do, your tools and spare parts may be distributed about in these. Incidentally, 35mm. film containers are excellent for holding little nuts and bolts, a bit of axle grease, bearing balls, and the like.

It has perhaps been stated with sufficient frequency that your sleeping bag goes on top of the rack. There are two ways to do this. The way I do it—the method used by most of the back-road bikepackers I respect—is to lay the sleeping bag in its stuff sack lengthwise along the rack, with the forward end jammed tight against the bike frame. This is secure and neat, reduces wind resistance (an important point, and one too often overlooked by cycle tourists, who could learn much from racers), and does not get in the way when you have to walk along with the bike. The tarp or tent fly can be wrapped around the bag, as can a foam pad if you use one; this adds little area or weight and helps to protect the bag.

A great many cyclists—possibly even a majority, and certainly most of those I see depicted in bike books and magazines—fix the sleeping-bag bundle *across* the forward end of the rack, with the ends sticking out on either side. Somehow the idea has gotten about that this is the correct way to carry the bag. I do not know why; perhaps Americans have been confused by English tourists, who carry saddlebags in this way (but a saddlebag is an entirely different affair), or perhaps it is the Western heritage: That is how Hoppy, Gene, and Roy lashed their bedrolls aboard their faithful horsies.

Bicycles aren't horses. I do not see any reason to carry the bag in this way, and there are several reasons against it. For one, if you have to walk the bike along for any reason, and most of us have to do this now and then, it is in the way—the protruding ends of the bedroll keep bumping your legs. For another, the bag sticks out and gets hit by brush and mud and everything else. Also, being essentially soft, it tends to sag at the ends and droop down so that it gets covered with road dirt and gets in the way if you have to adjust the back brake. It adds instability, since it's virtually impossible to get the weight really centered, and it's very hard to get it really secure. Worse than everything else put together, it increases drag. It's not just a question of frontal area, but of shape; on account of airflow patterns, a long cylinder

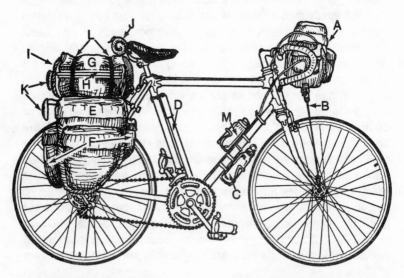

A—Handlebar bag—light items only!

B—Shock cords to steady bag

C—Gasoline bottle

D—Pump

E—Main panniers—keep weight low and forward

F—Outer pockets hold small, often-needed items

G—Tent fly or tarp wrapped around sleeping bag

H—Tent poles

I—Sleeping bag

J—Rolled rainsuit (lashed to saddle)

K—Reflectors

L—Nylon straps

M—Water bottle

Loaded for the road.

passing endwise through the air creates far less resistance than the same cylinder moving sideways, which is about as grossly inefficient an aerodynamic shape as you could devise. As far as I'm concerned, it's enough work pedaling all this stuff around without needlessly adding *any* kind of drag—and in flat, open country, such as the desert or the Midwest, headwinds can be strong enough to stop you in your tracks. In fact, most experienced cyclists agree that a headwind is a far more brutal antagonist than any hill.

It is claimed that this crosswise arrangement brings the weight forward, and so it does, and this is to the good. A sleeping bag, however, weighs only from 3 to 5 pounds, of which at least half is forward of the vertical plane of the rear hub with either setup, so all you're talking about is maybe a couple of pounds. I don't think this is enough to cancel out the other problems. If we can visit scenic downtown Subjective City again, I've tried it both ways, and there's simply no comparison.

The advantage of the crosswise arrangement for many people, I suspect, is that they can then engage in the even more obscene practice of lashing a big, fat, 6-pound tent across the rack behind the bag (which plays hell with the weight-distribution theory), and a rolled-up foam pad, often the full-size variety, and not infrequently a super-bulky, open-cell model, on top of the whole mess. Overtaking such a rider, all you can see is this huge mound of stuff with a head or helmet sticking out above and a bit of wheel at the bottom. (People who load this way nearly always have flags on their bikes, too. They need the kind that reads WIDE LOAD.)

The tent ought to be stowable inside one of your bags, fore or aft. If it won't go, your best answer, in my opinion, is to get a lighter tent or else just use a tarp, or get rid of some extra junk to make room in your panniers (if you're a typical bike tourist, odds are you're carrying more clothing than you really need), or possibly get bigger panniers. Under normal conditions—barring a situation like a cold-weather or remote-country run, which might force you to carry extra gear—I can't see any need to have the tent up on top of your rack. With tent and bag both up there, you're putting about 10 pounds in the worst possible place. Who needs it?

As for the pad, if you use one, a closed-cell pad of adequate size can, as I already said, be wrapped around the bag. So much for that.

I don't want to seem doctrinaire; there are skilled and experienced bike people who have used the crosswise setup for years, and you might find you like it too. But I remain unconvinced and unregenerate.

This person paid $800 for the bike because it weighed 2 pounds less than the $200 model . . . you will also note that he is not wearing a helmet. He will tell you he can't stand to wear a helmet. Too heavy.

Whichever way you fasten things on, you'll need some nylon straps with secure buckles. Elastic bunji cords don't really make it; no matter how you tighten them, there is always a bit of play, and if a bunji snaps, it can get into the spokes. The hooks at the ends also make the bunji heavier than the strap. I do carry one bunji, which I use to secure my rolled-up rain suit behind the saddle.

Bunjis, incidentally, are not as innocuous as they look. Don't get yourself in a position—bent over trying to get a taut bunji hooked, say—in which a breaking or suddenly released bunji can lash its hook into your eyes. There are reports of just such accidents. So if you're hooking up a bunji, keep your face well back out of range.

It is impossible to be specific about some of these things because there are so many different bag and rack designs on the market. You'll have to use these ideas to develop your own loading system. Do work on it. Once you have evolved a good loading plan, you'll find it easier to locate things, and it will take much less time to get packed and rolling in the mornings.

One more thing: Be sure to wrap everything against wetness and road dirt. Even if it doesn't rain, splashes from a puddle could cause trouble if water should get into your bags. Cycling is basically one of the dirtier branches of outdoor travel, in that roads tend to be rather messy places, and your tires are forever throwing crud all over the place. Don't depend on the watertight integrity of any pannier or handlebar bag, and certainly not of a stuff sack. A double layer of ordinary garbage bags inside the stuff sack will protect your sleeping bag—get those Hefty or similar heavy duty-type bags—and I strongly advise you to use smaller plastic bags, preferably the handy Ziploc type, to hold individual items inside your panniers. This isn't just to keep things dry; it makes it simpler to pack and unpack if things are separated. You don't get annoyances like rice in your socks or honey in your shorts. Many people like to have small nylon bags for this purpose, though plastic is more waterproof. You can get several good nylon bags from the sleeves of a worn-out windbreaker, and old nylon stretch socks are fine for such functions as holding your spare tube. But *don't ever* put anything damp inside plastic or other waterproof, airtight bags, especially in the dark! The smell when you take it out will about knock you down. If you've got a pair of wet socks or the like, tie them under your sleeping-bag straps and let the wind dry them.

Let's go for a ride.

CHAPTER **8**

Bike Driving

This *isn't* going to be a primer on how to ride a bicycle. Bicycle camping is in the nature of a high-school subject, not kindergarten. (Racing, if my own bygone experience is any indication, might be compared to reform school.) I don't mean to seem elitist about this, but you've got to consider your own safety; if you're still having trouble remembering how to shift gears or use the brakes just riding around where you live, you're not going to have much fun trying to do these things with a fully loaded bike in rough country. So it is assumed that you are reasonably proficient at operating a bicycle of the type you're going to be using—that you can shift the gears smoothly most of the time (every now and then we all miss it), ride a straight line, corner properly, operate the brakes, and otherwise control the machine. If not, I strongly suggest that you get a bit more practice in ordinary recreational riding before you try to go bikepacking.

Even if you are quite a skilled bare-bike cyclist, you'll find that riding a loaded bike, especially in hilly country, is trickier than it looks, and very different from riding an unloaded machine. I took up cycle camping after retiring from a five-year racing career, and I was absolutely amazed at the difference; it was almost like learning to ride all over again. Several other ex-racers have remarked on similar experiences.

Riding a loaded bicycle for respectable distances over varied terrain and under varying road and weather conditions demands a body of skills and techniques that must be practiced and mastered. They can be mastered by anyone with the physical fitness and coordination to learn to ride a bicycle at all, and it should not take long nor involve a lot of hard work. Becoming a skilled touring cyclist is nowhere near as hard as becoming even a marginal novice racer.

In this chapter, then, we will consider various aspects of bike riding technique as required in touring with a loaded bike. More general or basic information may be found in some of the books in the reading list in the back.

Position

The bike, to begin with, must be set up so that the rider is correctly positioned. A good deal of research has gone into this matter, but unfortunately most of it has been directed toward racing cyclists, whose needs are in many respects different. In determining the optimum position for any rider on any bicycle, the basic goals are to (1) provide control, balance, and stability; (2) permit the rider to use his or her strength to best advantage; (3) establish a reasonable level of physical comfort, including free breathing; and (4) reduce frontal air resistance. These factors are listed arbitrarily rather than in any order of importance.

Obviously, there are some inherent conflicts of interest here. An extreme head-down position, as adopted by the track sprinter, is certainly the most aerodynamically efficient and employs the rider's muscles at their most effective angles, but it would be hopelessly uncomfortable and dangerous on the open road. (We might add to the above requirements that the rider does have to be able to see where he or she is going.)

On the other hand, the upright posture created by the conventional flat-bar, mattress-saddle, three-speed bike is extremely comfortable for short rides, but wears down the rider very rapidly because it is so inefficient and produces so much air resistance. And so on; the conflicts have to be resolved according to what the individual cyclist is trying to accomplish.

Tourists and campers have more problems than most, and the compromises are more complex—and not just because we have to share the bike frame with a lot of equipment. The rider who must be on the bike for hours each day, often over bumpy roads, will have to assume a pretty efficient position and will hardly want to fight any unnecessary air resistance. He or she may not be interested in speed, but nobody wants to have to work extra hard. Yet most bikepackers will want to be at least fairly comfortable, and certainly few will accept the Spartan discomfort that a racer considers normal. So some middle ground must be reached.

There are a couple of factors peculiar to bikepackers. For one, most of us are out there primarily to look at the scenery and observe wildlife and the like, and it is very difficult to do this from a pronounced, down-in-the-hooks crouch. (A kid I used to race with once remarked, "You know, I've ridden this thing over some of the most fantastic country around and never really got a look at it.") You'll want the bike set up so that you can sit up and look around without losing control. Also, bikepackers frequently have occasion to ride on very rough or loose surfaces, such as gravel or dirt, which make special demands.

Remember, most of all, the first of the above points. The loaded bike requires absolutely solid control and stable weight distribution, especially in the mountains and on wet or loose surfaces. In fact, owing to the added weights we have to hang on our long-suffering machines, this has to be considered the primary requirement in setting up the bike; we may have to make sacrifices in comfort and efficiency, but never in stability or control. The possible consequences of a loss of control are just too great.

Saddle height is the basic adjustment; on this will depend all others. Many formulae and tables and diagrams have been published, and many studies done, on this business of saddle height. Most such studies have been done with the racer in mind, but others sometimes adopt these ideas. Usually a racer will want a slightly higher saddle than the camper; most racers tend to extend the foot a bit more at the bottom of the stroke. This isn't a fixed rule, and in any case, the basic starting point won't be too different.

Some studies have indicated that the saddle should be set so that the distance from the pedal spindle at its lowest point to the top of the saddle equals 109% of the rider's inseam measurement (crotch to floor). I think this is a bit too high as a starting point for a nonracer; 104% may put you in the ball park.

A rough rule used by many: The rider should be able to sit on the saddle and just barely put his heel on the pedal at its lowest point, with his leg fully extended. (I keep saying "his" in part because I'm not at all sure that these things work out exactly the same for women; I think more work needs to be done in this field.) With this as a starting point, finer adjustments are made according to trial and error and general experience.

While it might sound crude, this approach is not so bad. At least it works directly from the individual's body right from the start, rather than getting you locked into somebody's theories. A lot of harm has been done by trying to force people, in their infinite variability, to fit paper patterns, when it should go the other way. If you are willing to take the time, while being *very* cautious, you can get a good position on the bike from this seemingly primitive technique.

You have to make all adjustments very gradually, just a fraction of an inch at a time, unless something is obviously totally wrong. A sudden huge change in saddle height can hurt your knees, even though it results in a "correct" position. A handy accessory is a Campagnolo quick-release seatpost bolt, which enables you to make adjustments rapidly without chewing up your paint or stripping the threads.

Take note of body signals. If you find that your pelvis rocks from side to side as you pedal and you have to actually "reach" for the pedals at the bottom of the stroke, your saddle is much too high; besides knee pains, you'll get saddle sores in short order. If your knees and ankles feel sore and tight and your muscles sort of cramped as you pedal, as if your leg wants to straighten out a bit more and can't, your saddle may be too low. Ride around and think about it, and you'll see what I mean.

It should be pointed out that this adjustment will definitely be affected by the shoes you wear. There will be a considerable difference involved between cleated racing shoes and Batas or joggers, so if you switch, be prepared to readjust your saddle— and everything else. This is one reason why, if at all possible, your shoes should be purchased when you get your bike.

Saddle angle ought to be pretty straightforward, but isn't for some. Basically the top of the saddle should be level. Some women like the saddle nose a bit lower than this, but I suspect this means they need a saddle designed for women. A few men do better with the saddle nose raised a degree or two. If you've been used to doing your riding mostly in the racer's full-dropped crouch, when you go over to bikepacking you'll probably find that your saddle nose needs to come up a trifle to compensate for the more upright position. Even more than with saddle height, this adjustment is a *very* fine one, and a micro-adjusting seatpost is needed if there is any real problem. Basically, the saddle ought to be horizontal, and any variation from this should be extremely minute. A carpenter's level should be used to get it right.

One occasionally sees riders who have the saddle tilted severely nose up or nose down, and such people invariably defend this aberration vigorously as being a great improvement— or at least, they say, "It works for me!" or "I've been riding this way for years!" This merely proves that human bodies and bicycles are capable of withstanding incredible amounts of abuse. If the saddle nose is much below neutral, your weight is forced forward onto your shoulders, arms, and hands, causing numb fingers, poor control, and improper weight distribution. If the saddle is tipped too far back, you're in for lower back pains as well as a loss of balance.

The saddle can also be moved forward and backward. Generally, a vertical line from the nose of the saddle will fall about 2 inches behind the center of the crank axle; use a small weight on a string to check this. This measurement will vary a bit according to the size and angles of the frame, the rider's build, and the use for which the bike is intended. Racers often set the saddle forward, while dirt-road riders may want it farther back.

Sliding the saddle backwards or forwards obviously has a major effect on the bike's weight-distribution pattern, so use a bathroom scale (or two, if you can borrow an extra) and check this. Remember, the bare-bike formula is 55% of total weight on the back wheel and 45% in front. For nonracing setups, this should be regarded as a maximum forward distribution—that is, if there is any deviation, it should definitely be in the direction of more weight over the back wheel. Because you're going to load a bunch of equipment back there, you don't want to start out with a bike that is excessively tail heavy. So try to keep pretty close to this proportion.

This fore-and-aft adjustment is also used to get optimum leverage for the legs. This is a concept with which few American cyclists are really familiar, but it is well worth your attention. Still got that weighted thread you used a moment ago to check the saddle nose/bottom bracket relationship? Take it and sit on your bike in normal riding position, braced, perhaps, against a wall or door. With the crank arm horizontal and your feet in place—get a friend to help you check this—the center of the forward pedal spindle should be in a vertical line with the back of your knee, or possibly a line passing through the center of your knee. There is that much variation, mostly due to differences in foot sizes, but the line should not be farther forward or to the rear.

This rule is followed religiously by the best professional road-racing coaches in Europe, but it will work for anybody with normal anatomy for any cycling purpose. It creates by far the most efficient, powerful pedal stroke and reduces knee problems; it is

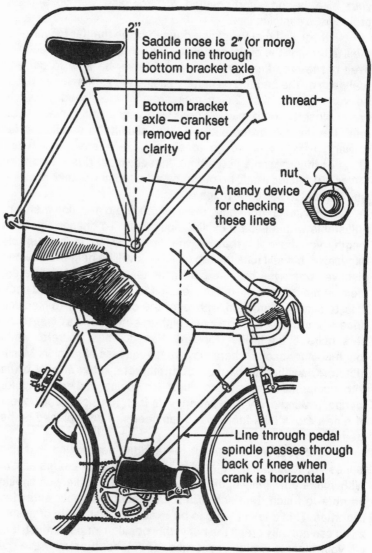

2"

Saddle nose is **2"** (or more) behind line through bottom bracket axle

Bottom bracket axle — crankset removed for clarity

thread→

nut

A handy device for checking these lines

Line through pedal spindle passes through back of knee when crank is horizontal

Proper rider position and saddle height.

particularly valuable in climbing mountains. It would be possible to write a whole lengthy treatise on why this is so—and it has been done—but take it from me, *it works*.

If you find that your knee sticks out considerably forward of this line, slide the saddle back. If you can't get the saddle back far enough without a really gross maladjustment of your position, your bike is too short-coupled for you and will pose many problems in camping use.

If you find that your knee doesn't come that far forward—if the line through the pedal spindle passes through your kneecap or even misses the knee entirely—you'll never be able to get any real push on the pedal. You can try sliding the saddle forward, but be very careful; that 2-inch measurement mentioned above is pretty close to a minimum, except with very small frames. If you can't get the proper leg angle without sliding the saddle too far forward, it may help to go to shorter crank arms, which are cheaper than a whole new frame. Indeed, most riders who take 19″ or 20″ frames would be better off with 165mm. cranks anyway, which are also better on rough roads.

Moving up front now, *stem length* is a dimension that isn't adjustable with standard cycling equipment. To change the stem length, you have to replace the stem, which is not terribly expensive, but still runs the tab up a bit. It will be helpful if you can discover when you buy the bike whether you'll need a different stem; some dealers will make the change for you at reduced cost. It is a common problem with over-the-counter, low-to-medium-priced "club" bikes. Racers and high-speed "tourists" want their bars quite a bit farther forward than do most tourers, while rough-country backpackers may want even less extension. Manufacturers, wanting to capture both markets, often fit new bikes with compromise stems too short for racing and too long for touring, making everybody unhappy. In fact, the single component of a new stock bike that most often needs to be replaced is the stem.

Put your elbow against the saddle; never mind that this makes you look like the guy who doesn't know it from his elbow. With your elbow firmly against the nose of the saddle, you should be able to touch the back of the handlebar with your extended fingertips. This doesn't have to be exact; it's just a rule of thumb. If you can actually grasp the bar in this position, or can't touch it at all, your stem is wrong—assuming, of course, that you have got the saddle in the right place first.

Experience will help you work this out; a few long rides and you'll soon know whether or not you can ride comfortably in the full range of positions, which is the point of all of this.

Note: If you're having trouble reaching the bars, the way to correct the problem is with a shorter stem. The saddle must *not* be slid forward or backward to compensate for incorrect stem throw; you set the saddle where it goes according to the principles outlined previously, and then adjust forward reach by changing the stem length.

People with small bikes—especially women, who seem to have less forward reach than men of the same size—sometimes cannot reach the bars without strain, even with minimum-throw stems. They may try to correct this by sliding the saddle very far forward, until the nose is over the bottom bracket. This is an extremely poor practice and results in a harsh ride and poor bike control. If this is your problem, your frame is improperly proportioned—not uncommon with stock frames below 21". If you cannot afford a custom frame, you might be better off fitting your bike with regular flat handlebars. These bars are adequate for touring, and rather nice for looking around at the scenery; some people even find that they give a bit more control on extremely rough roads.

Stem height is usually set so that the bars are about level with the saddle or even a trifle higher; this is another point that differs from racing or fast-touring practice. With randonneur bars, you may find that you want to set the stem a trifle lower. Remember that you must leave a couple of inches inside the headset for safety's sake. Make that 2½ inches; you've got that handlebar bag up there. So your setting may be determined by this, rather than by exact preference.

Handlebars should be set so that the upper part of the hooks will be horizontal; this gives you more riding positions. The straight ends of the bars will point in the direction of your back hub. Put the brake levers up where you can rest your hands on the rubber hoods for "honking" up hills. At this point, you may decide to rewrap the bars with one of the cushion tapes; it's the perfect time to do it.

Remember, make all adjustments gradually until you get them right; tighten everything securely, use the right tools, and make sure you know what you're doing or you can ruin your bike. See the reading list if you need help.

Riding Techniques _____

Pedal spin is, of course, basic to all cycling. Presumably you already know that the correct technique is to spin the pedals in a smooth circle, rather than in the clumsy up-and-down reciprocating motion used by novices. Even at low speeds, the smooth spinning motion used by racers is far more efficient, less fatiguing, and less likely to cause strains and injuries.

A great deal has been written and stated to the effect that the foot should be kept absolutely horizontal and flat throughout the stroke and never extended downward at the bottom of the cycle. One prominent authority even wrote, "If I've screamed it once I've screamed it a thousand times—*Drop your heels!*" Almost as many other authorities have produced arguments in favor of a pronounced ankle motion. Actually, I doubt if it really matters, as long as the style is matched to the individual and the bike set up to fit the style. I think it comes down to personal body build, ankle flexibility, and other variable factors. To give but two counter-examples: Rik van Looy, one of the greatest racing cyclists ever, pedaled in the flat-footed style, while Jacques Anquetil, another racing great, particularly noted for his fine bike-handling technique, pedaled in the toes-down style that the aforementioned authority describes as, "*Wrong, wrong, wrong!*"

So, if you've encountered some of this conflicting and possibly confusing advice and counteradvice, my own suggestion is to pedal whichever way seems more natural to you, and set your saddle height to suit. Those who "ankle" pronouncedly usually take a slightly higher saddle setting.

Gear selection has a lot to do with pedal style. Most novices especially young men, tend to pick too big a gear, which forces them to use a slow, clumsy pedal technique. This is especially foolish for people who are not in a competition. In fact, most faults in pedal style can be traced either to an improper riding position or to pushing an excessively high gear—or both—and I suspect that these two errors also lie at the root of most of the discomforts and strains of inexperienced cyclists (as well as a good many others who do not have the excuse of inexperience).

Actually, a gear between 62" and 72" is plenty high enough for normal cycling on a flat surface. Some people may not even need to go that high at first. In the old days, before multi-gear bikes were invented, people rode all over—often at speeds that would be considered respectable even today, and on very bad roads—on bikes with a single 67″ fixed gear. When I raced, I spent February and March riding around mostly on a single fixed gear, 63″ or 67″, to loosen up my legs and develop my spin, and I found that I covered quite a bit of real estate in these low gears and had fun doing it.

Oh, sure, nobody's questioning that you *could* push a much bigger gear; that's not the point. It's just that you'll wear yourself out less, have fewer knee problems, save your energy better for the hills and headwinds, and probably cover more ground in the long run if you gear conservatively and deliberately choose a gear lower than the biggest one you can push. As I remarked elsewhere in this book, most people find that with a loaded bike, they need to gear down one step from what they would choose for bare-bike riding.

Keep those gears down and strive for a smooth spin. It may feel funny at first if you're used to honking along in a gorilla gear, but in time it becomes the natural way to pedal. Of course, individuals differ; big, powerful, long-legged men sometimes find it more natural to gear a bit higher and pedal a bit more slowly than the short, "nervous" type. While we're talking gears, make sure you can shift smoothly and precisely without having to look down at the levers or the mechanism. Elementary, yes, but quite a few people have trouble doing it.

Cornering under a full load takes some getting used to, even if you're a good bike handler. The only good answer is practice; it also helps if you can strengthen your arms and shoulders a bit with some exercises. Remember the racer's rule: Use your brakes *before* you go into a turn, not halfway through it. Trying to brake or tighten the radius of your turn, once you've committed yourself to a given line through the corner, is a sure ticket to a painful crash. The obvious lesson here is to look ahead and never let your bike get going faster than your eyes and reflexes.

Concentrate on keeping that back wheel on the road and tracking right. There is a tendency, probably somewhat psychological, to try to "steer" the front wheel with the handlebars as you would operate the steering wheel of a car, and more or less expect the back wheel to follow. That works okay at low speeds and with no load to speak of, but when you're moving fast and loaded up, the bike may tend to try to swing around the front end of the frame, with the back wheel sliding loose and possibly going right out from under you. Slamming on the brakes merely intensifies the skid. At any kind of speed, a bicycle is primarily steered by the weight of your body; those handlebars are mainly there to hang onto. You *lean* the bike around turns, in a manner of speaking. Try to "muscle" it around at any real speed, and down you go.

If you aren't used to handling a loaded bike, put all of your stuff on the bike or substitute something of equal weight but no value, if you don't want to risk messing up such items as your stove. Then get in some practice in a parking lot or even going around the block where you live, and feel how the behavior of the loaded bike differs from that of an unloaded machine. If you just take it out on the road and try to ride in your usual style, you might get a nasty surprise.

Brakes probably cause as many crashes as they prevent. We just noted a common problem in the corners; even on the straight bits, looking and thinking ahead will eliminate many of those screeching-halt situations.

Contrary to what you may have been told and may even have read in some of the more unfortunate literature for beginners, *the front brake is your main brake!* Trying to stop primarily with the back wheel is, in the first place, ineffective—the back brake cable has to travel farther and thus develops less power—and it's dangerous besides. If you slam on the back brake at speed, the back wheel is very likely to slide right out from under you. It might seem that if you put your main braking force on the front wheel, you would go over the handlebars, but it doesn't work that way—certainly not with 20 to 30 pounds behind you! Of course, you counteract this over-the-bars tendency by pushing back hard with your arms to keep your weight on the saddle.

Remember that every pound on the bike makes it harder to stop. Keep those brakes adjusted, with good cables and shoes, and hold your speed down if the road is slippery or loose. Your primary bit of safety equipment is not on your front wheel or your back wheel, but between your ears.

I shouldn't have to say it, but in view of experience, I'd better: Don't hit your brakes without warning when riding in a group! If the mass pileup doesn't put you in the hospital, your buddies probably will.

Climbing is the tough part for most bikies. A modern bike on a level surface may be a supremely efficient machine, but load it up with camping gear and aim it up a steep slope, and its efficiency falls off spectacularly. Low gears may ease this problem but will never fully relieve it. In fact, some quitters (such as the author) have been known to say the hell with it and get off and push the bike to the top—but do not spread this fact around; I don't believe it is generally known. . . .

Barring that desperate and ignominious alternative, climbing hills is mostly a matter of pacing yourself. "To climb steep hills requires slow pace," wrote William Shakespeare. The inept cyclist rushes violently at the hill, usually already overgeared and waiting too long to shift down, and then runs out of steam halfway up. The old pro shifts down well before he feels any strain, sets an easy but steady pace, and twiddles smoothly to the top. Of course, when crossing rolling country, you can use the speed and momentum of a downhill run to get a rush up the next hill. But on a long, steep climb, the rider who gears down early and takes it slow is usually the first to the crest.

Try not to get off halfway up a hill unless you're sure you'll have to walk the bike the rest of the way; it is terribly hard to get a loaded bike started again on an uphill grade. If you're in one of those superlow gears, it is nearly impossible to get started at all, once stopped. If you must stop for a breather, try to find a relatively level bit where you can remount and restart.

Climbing is really largely psychological, given that the rider is fit and the machine properly geared. Usually your mind tells you that you can't possibly make it any farther, when actually your legs and lungs are far from exhausted. If you climb while thinking what agony this is, you'll never be much good in the hills. Think about other things—the fresh air, the scenery, the birds. Look at things along the shoulder, the road itself, the view, but never look at the top; it will seem to recede cruelly as you approach, due to a trick of your sadistic eyesight. (Of course, sometimes you see things by the roadside that depress you—empty beer cans that evoke visions of their cold, foaming erstwhile contents, say—or like the time on a mountain road when I saw a big spider on the shoulder and realized he was passing me!)

Promise yourself a break at the top. Think about what a lovely fine downhill run there's going to be on the other side. Count pedal strokes. Anything to take your mind off of the remaining distance to the top. If you get to thinking about that great mass of rock and earth beneath you and what you're trying to do, you'll probably collapse. (People are too different to make this more than a tentative suggestion, all the same. I'm sure there are people who climb by concentrating on what they're doing and, as runners put it, pushing their way through the mental barrier. All I can say is, you'll have to find out what works for you.)

Standing up and "honking" the pedals may be okay to get over short rises or the last few feet of a climb, but basically it's a poor practice with a loaded bike. Unless you have very powerful shoulders and arms, it is difficult to maintain control and balance in this position, and it presents the distinct possibility of injuring a knee.

Speaking of knee pains, if you do get a sudden sharp twinge in a knee while climbing, don't try to push it—get off immediately and rest a moment. Then walk up the hill slowly, and keep your gears low for the rest of the day. The human knee is very easily injured and doesn't heal well, and once you strain a knee, it will give you hell for the rest of the trip.

Downhilling is, in W. C. Fields's phrase, "fraught with imminent peril." An adult cyclist on a bike loaded with 30 pounds of gear can quite easily hit speeds in the 50-mile-per-hour range without even turning a pedal if the grade is steep and long enough. A slick spot on the road, a burst tire, a misjudged turn, and you could be very badly hurt or even killed.

It's too bad, because the sensation is fantastic while it lasts—the wind in your face, the high-pitched whine that fine hubs give off at high speeds, the feel of the bike under you as it lunges down the grade . . . and with an unloaded bike, you can engage in quite a bit of this kind of whoopee, using the brakes to slow for the sharper turns. But with camping gear aboard, you'd better put a tight lid on the whoopee impulse if you want to live to even a moderately ripe middle age. We're dealing with some irrevocable laws of physics here. As Isaac Newton figured out a long time ago, the heavier a moving body is, the more energy it will develop, especially when the motion is partly downward, and the harder it will be to stop. Also, the stronger will be its tendency to travel in a straight line and resist attempts to turn it into another line.

In simple terms, it's much better to keep your bike from building up too much speed in the first place. Once it gets going past a certain speed, it's pretty useless to start hitting the brakes. All that will get you is a skid to complete the disaster. If you try to turn at such a speed, chances are the bike will just keep on going in the same direction—sideways. You aren't driving a car or truck; you don't have four fat tires on the road, just a couple of spots of rubber about the size of quarters. You're not going to stop or redirect very many foot-pounds of energy with *that*.

However, you don't just ride your brakes all the way down a tricky fast descent. That will cause heat to build up, and then, suddenly, you won't have any brakes at all—a terrifying sensation, I imagine. Instead, you pump the brakes in alternation—front, back, front, back, just a gentle rhythmic squeezing, and a light touch does it. Now you are being repaid for getting a good set of brakes and spending some time adjusting them—or, if you couldn't be bothered, now may be the time you get another kind of payoff.

There is a tendency, going downhill, for the body's weight to come forward onto the handlebars. Using the brakes seems to increase this tendency. Resist it; it is very dangerous. With dropped bars, you'll have to make a conscious effort to keep your weight back on the saddle. If you don't the back wheel can easily come loose from the road and dump you, especially during a turn. Here is another payoff for all that fussing around with weight distribution.

Using this set of techniques, I have taken a fully loaded bike down a steep mountain road, with 180° switchbacks every few hundred yards and nowhere to go but a lot of treetops and air if I missed it, *in a rainstorm,* without incident. I tell this, not to impress anyone with what a hairy-chested hero I am (well, maybe a little), but to demonstrate the value of learning correct downhill techniques.

Sometimes there are long, fast, straight downhills with no real curves and a hard clean road surface and no side roads from which a car or dog may appear. Then, if you're sure of your tires and your brakes, you may open up and revel in that glorious sensation of silent, effortless speed. We all need a little adventure now and then. But on a sharply winding road lined with houses and intersections, especially if it's wet, going all-out downhill is a very foolhardy thing. Most of us get silly and do it now and then, and usually we get away with it, but every now and then we don't. Every time the weather turns cold, the little cracked place in my wristbone gives me a twinge to remind me of the time I didn't quite make it. It could have been worse. Don't you do it.

Practice

You can't learn to ride a bicycle from a book—even a book as wonderful as this one. You've got to get out there and do these things. A little experience is worth any amount of theory. Dave Gardner used to say, "How in the world you going to explain anything to anybody that ain't never?"

Do some riding with your camping outfit aboard. Start with

little rides around the block to make sure nothing is going to fall off or break; work your way up to some real distance runs, even 100-milers. (Sure you can; I've seen an eight-year-old kid do it on a 40-pound high-rise clunker—in 90°F. heat.) If you can, have somebody in a car come check up on you on your first long efforts, in case you give out; you may be fairly experienced on a bike, but if you're not used to a load of gear, you may badly miscalculate your own range.

No doubt you'll feel silly going out for a two-hour ride over to the next small town and back with a full camping outfit aboard. No doubt you'll look pretty silly, too. But what of that? If you worry about what people think, you'll never amount to anything. George Bernard Shaw, an avid cyclist, wrote, "A man progresses in all things by resolutely making a fool of himself." By doing these little local rides with full kit, you'll get the hang of handling your bike under full load, and learn its limitations and capabilities. You'll find out what gears you need to climb a given type of hill, and when to start pumping the brakes, and what line to take through a tight corner. As you progress, you can start riding on some dirt and gravel roads—surely you can find something within range—and develop your skills there. You can even improve such ancillary matters as your dog-hitting technique.

If there is a touring bike club in your area, go on some of their rides with all of your stuff aboard. They won't ridicule you—just explain that you're getting used to a lot of new equipment and testing your setup, and if they know anything at all about cycling, they'll respect what you're doing. In fact, they will almost certainly offer helpful advice, of which one or two bits may even be of some value. (You can go crazy, though, if you try to take all of the advice you get from cyclists. There is an old gag: If you ever lose your way in the backcountry, just get off and start adjusting your saddle, and immediately ten people will show up and tell you how to do it, and you can ask them for directions.) Try going on one of those League of American Wheelmen century runs with a full load; even if you only make half the distance, you'll learn a lot about your capabilities.

Besides the practice, you'll get a chance to test your equipment and your bike's layout under field conditions and still be close enough to home or assistance to survive any failures. After all, if your derailleur won't go into the lowest gear or your rack wobbles or your stem is too long, you're better off finding out 20 miles from home than 200!

CHAPTER **9**

_____ Special Conditions

If it were just a matter of riding a bike down a smooth, paved road in mild weather, with the sun out and nobody else on the road, there would be little need to discuss riding techniques at all in this book, except perhaps for climbing and downhilling. Anyone who can ride a bicycle at all should, with a little practice, find the whole business simple enough.

Life, however, is not always so ideal. Complicating factors arise, which is a nice way of saying that things go to hell. Within reason, that's okay; it's part of the challenge. Difficulties, after all, help us to enjoy the good stuff, as we have so often been told. Anyway, nature operates in such a way that it takes one possibly troublesome force to cancel another—in the summer, a rainstorm may create problems for you, but if it doesn't rain, the heat and dryness are even more unpleasant.

Sorry if I seem to be belaboring an obvious point. It's just that we see all these nice pictures of people riding their bikes along the road in the sunshine, and perhaps we get to thinking that this is the natural order of things. Then, when the wet or the cold or the dark comes down, we feel somehow that something unnatural and perverse is being done to us, and we get depressed. One of the secrets of enjoying the outdoors is learning to accept such things as part of the natural world. Still, some situations do call for special equipment and/or techniques, especially aboard a bike. The following are some of the most common special conditions that affect bikepackers on the road.

Wetness

Sometimes riding in the rain can be rather pleasant. If it's been a long, hot day and the road is good, level, and empty of traffic, and you'll be in camp changing clothes in a short while, then a light shower can be a real pleasure. Even riding through a full downpour occasionally generates a kind of hey-isn't-this-crazy gonzo euphoria, and there are a few amphibious types who apparently enjoy riding in the rain. There are also those who come from regions where it rains all the time, such as England or the Pacific Northwest; they don't seem to think much about the rain at all. I sometimes have an impression that the average British cyclist has to stop and think about it before he notices whether it's raining or not. Such people don't necessarily like it, but they accept rain as a normal, almost daily, condition of life.

For most of us, however, rain is basically a nuisance or worse. It makes the pavement slippery; if the surface isn't paved, it makes mud, which plasters you and your bike and slides treacherously under your tires. It washes the lubrication out of the bike's moving parts, while the wheels throw dirty water from the road onto those parts, embedding bits of dirt and grit, and shortening the life of these expensive mechanisms. (The cycling cartoonist Art Read, in an inspired moment, wrote, "The rain, insane, falls plainly on your chain!") It ruins your vision, reducing your world to a tiny blind circle, too small to see what you're getting into before it's too late, particularly since the braking powers of your bicycle deteriorate as fast as your visibility.

Worst of all by far, it has a similar effect on automobile drivers. Behind their rain-blurred glass, they can't see you in time—if they ever see you at all—and they can't stop quickly either. The wet road also has a deleterious effect on their driving, which, in the case of most American drivers, was never exactly at the Jackie Stewart level to begin with. Moreover, as Tom Cuthbertson has accurately pointed out, it makes a lot of people act crazy—they get in a hurry to get home and bring in the wash or pick up the kids at school or something, and they go into a kind of panic and lose any fine edge of judgment that they might ever have possessed. I don't want to get into a thing about auto drivers here, because we're going to talk about them in the next chapter, but it is important to understand this point. It has been treated rather casually by some cycling writers, who prefer to dwell on things like fenders and rain capes. The main reason any experienced cyclist dreads the rain, if there is any traffic whatever about, is not that he or she may get wet, but the enormously increased danger of getting into a terminal encounter with an automobile.

For this reason, the very best advice is: On roads with any appreciable amount of auto traffic, don't ride in the rain if there is any way you can possibly get out of it. If you're riding through an area where it's clearly impossible to make camp, and the rain seems likely to go on all day and into the night, then you haven't much choice in the matter. If you can take shelter until the storm passes, or stop and make camp and call it a day, it's far better to do so. You might lose a few miles and have to go hard next day to keep on schedule, but that's better than having a bad crash or getting run over—not to mention the wear and tear on your bike. Anyway, you should have planned your trip schedule to leave room for weather-induced delays.

If you're just looking for a temporary shelter in which to sit out a short summer cloudburst, something will usually turn up, if you aren't too hard to please. Look for abandoned houses and farm buildings. Try roadside rest areas, gas stations and stores, and country churches. Or try a rural school closed for the summer, with a porch where you can huddle. People seldom make much fuss about "trespassing" when you're obviously just taking shelter from the rain. For that matter, country people generally have a tradition of generosity toward travelers in distress. If you knock on a door and ask politely if you may sit on the porch or in the barn until the rain passes, often as not you'll be invited in and plied with hot coffee and photos of the grandchildren. (This varies widely according to a lot of factors. A woman or group of women will seldom have any trouble finding shelter, though they may want to be cautious on their own account. A couple of big, rough-looking young men might do better to avoid going up to houses in isolated areas, especially on weekdays, however innocent their intentions.

Nowadays a lone woman in such a house is likely to be very nervous about strange visitors, and who can blame her? Also watch out for farmhouse dogs, which will eat you up, bike and all.)

If you're out away from man-made structures—which is, after all, the point of this entire exercise—you can usually improvise something. Keep your tarp or tent fly stowed where you can get at it easily, and you can extemporize adequate shelter for a short summer storm. Drape it over some bushes or a fence (beware of barbed wire) or use your bike as a supporting member. Or even get out the poles and stakes and rig the fly by itself without the tent—with most models this is possible. If you have also squirreled some snacks away in a handy jersey or bag pocket, you can settle down for a rather pleasant little break. I can recall a couple of times when I've managed to make myself so comfortable on one of these hasty roadside bivouacs that I was sorry to have to move on.

You may find natural cover that you can use. If there's no lightning or high winds, just rain, then a grove of trees is okay, but beware of falling dead limbs. A fallen tree that rests partly off the ground on its massed branches can form a very good little shelter. Evergreens are particularly good this way, as their thick, waxy needles shed water. Lots of Indians and mountain men made their bivouacs by crawling under a fallen pine—it's almost like a little cave under there.

Caves, rock overhangs, and mine-shaft entrances offer excellent protection in mountain country. If there's lightning, don't stand or sit near the entrance of a cave or mine entrance—lightning sometimes does screwy things, such as tracking down the face of a mountain and blasting people right out of cave mouths. Several rock climbers have died this way; in fact, most climbers fear lightning more than any other natural force except, perhaps, avalanches.

Speaking of lightning: If there's lightning about, *get off the road.* Perched up there on that steel bike, you make the ultimate target. This is true whether you're in the mountains or crossing open, flat country. People go into the outdoors scared silly of snakes but regard lightning as a rather farfetched danger. Your chances of being hit by lightning are a good deal higher, statistically, than those of being bitten by a snake, and the consequences are much more severe. (While we've got the snakes on camera here, remember to watch where you sit or put you hands when taking cover under rock overhangs or fallen trees.)

Depressions and gullies might appear to offer protection from the wind, and certainly they reduce the chance of being hit by lightning, but such places can flood very, very rapidly. Even if it is not raining hard where you are, a harder rainstorm a mile away can send a wall of water raging down a gully in desert or plains country. Flash floods are nothing to fool with. NEVER take cover under a culvert, except just possibly from a tornado—heavy rain can flood a culvert faster than you can get out. Up under the ends of a high bridge or overpass there is excellent shelter. In fact, I once spent a night under the end of an overpass near Memphis, though it got awfully noisy when trucks passed overhead.

If you absolutely must ride in the rain—and sometimes there's no help for it—go quite slowly, turn on every light you've got, and don't be too proud to take to the shoulder if something motorized seems to be coming up fast from astern. Avoid slamming on your brakes; instead, pump them on and off very lightly, as you approach a descent or a curve, so that the brake shoes can wipe the worst of the water off of the rims. (If you're using steel rims, this is when you're going to wish you weren't. Steel is slick when wet, and brake shoes simply cannot get a decent grip.)

Much technology has been expended on this problem of wet bicycle brakes, without really spectacular results. The composition brake pads, such as Mathauser, seem to be of some help. But here we're up against the basic nature of the beast. Even if you fitted some sort of brake that could exert a full and absolute stopping power, no matter how wet it got, you'd still have trouble stopping the bike because, in the final analysis, there just isn't that much rubber in contact with the road. Lock up the wheels, and the bike will slide and skid on these two peso-sized spots. (Ask the owner of a moped; their drum brakes are enormously powerful compared to anything you've got on your bike, and wholly unaffected by rain, but any expert moped jock knows to take it very easy on a wet street.) The basic function of those brakes in rainy conditions is to slow you down so you don't have that necessity for a sudden brick-wall stop in the first place.

We'll be talking about lights in a minute, but note here that heavy rain or fog may create a need for lights to make you more visible—and reflectors work very poorly under such circumstances. So one criterion for choosing your lighting equipment should be reliability under wet conditions.

Riding a dirt road in the rain is nothing short of grisly. Mud accumulates all over the bike and rider until you look like a contestant in one of those mud-wrestling shows. You may, depending on the composition of the mud, have to use your water bottle from time to time to help get the mud out of the brakes and off your chain and freewheel. Get in a nice low gear, because you probably won't be able to shift worth a damn until you get it cleaned off. Do everything possible to avoid this situation; if you're going on a dirt-road trip, allow for extra time to sit out the rain and let the road surface dry. Luckily, the places where you might be riding dirt or gravel are also usually places where you can easily find a place to put up camp for a day or so. You may also find rain-swollen creeks blocking your way, potentially a very dangerous situation if you try to cross, but more of this in another chapter.

Getting back to the pavement: If you can't sit out the rain, at least try to sit out the first 15 minutes or so. Paved roads are always dirty with oil and grease from cars, and the first rainfall causes this stuff to float up from the pavement, and it creates an extremely treacherous film—it is like riding on a bar of old soap. After a few minutes of steady rain, the oil washes away, and you'll have a safer surface to ride on.

After the rain, or in the later stages of a long rainstorm, remember to keep an eye on the road for various hazards. Dead limbs, piles of mud and gravel washed down from overhanging cutbanks (these can actually block the road, and seem to be especially common on the outside of sharp, blind turns), and piles of wet leaves all pose threats to the unwary. Wet leaves will slide out from under you in a particularly treacherous way. Remember that after a rain, motorists sometimes drive faster to make up lost time and may not be alert or considerate, so keep your ears open.

One good thing about rain, though—it really keeps the dogs quiet. I've never yet met a dog mean enough to go after a cyclist in a rainstorm. It's enough to make you do a rain dance.

Darkness

Woo. Scary. Riding in the dark gives a few cyclists a kind of weird Dracula-rides-again charge. But it scares most bikies silly, and with excellent reason, at least in urban areas or on highways with heavy late-night traffic. Contrary to the more extreme statements made by a few, it is certainly possible—and not even difficult—to get a lighting set that will let you see where you're going at any reasonable nighttime cycling speed. Rather, the chief problem is that it is very hard to compete with the powerful lights of the motorists; the difficulty in many cases is not in seeing but in being seen.

Many systems of lights and reflectors are offered to deal with this problem, the most effective of which seems to be a powerful flashing beacon that goes on a belt at the cyclist's back. I question the validity of the basic concept, however; my own experience has convinced me that while a cyclist may be hit if drivers don't see him well, there is at least an equal degree of danger in being too visible after dark in urban areas. Deliberate vehicular assault by young male drivers, especially with a few illegal drinks or dope hits churning their already unstable brains, is a very real problem, and at night they know they'll never be caught. I suspect that these super-lighting systems just make you a better target.

This is all rather irrelevant here, fortunately for us. These problems mostly affect cycle commuters, who have to ride in urban or suburban areas during peak-traffic hours of early evening (poor devils). Bike campers have different needs. When a bike-packer has to ride in the dark, it usually is because he or she got caught out unexpectedly late due to a flat or accident, rain, or a miscalculation. Or, on occasion, a bikepacker may be setting out early to beat the afternoon heat or to get an early start on a long day's ride; some desert crossings may be safer by night.

In such situations, riding by night is a far less risky affair. Traffic is much lighter out in the country at night, if you sit out the peak-traffic hours when people are coming home from jobs in town, or the early-morning period when farmers and loggers are on the road with their trucks and not expecting to encounter cyclists. True, you do occasionally get a car or pickup full of aggressive, boozed-up, small-town punks out tearing up the roads, and they can be bad news, indeed—worse than the urban variety, since they know that there are no cops around. On an empty country road, you can see headlights and hear a car coming for a long way and can judge by the tone of the engine and driving style and probable state of sobriety of the operator, so it is usually simple enough merely to stop, get off the road and the shoulder with your bike, and stand quite still until they pass— blinded by their own headlights, they will not see you if your lights are switched off and you have no reflectors pointing toward them.

This may happen once or twice in a long night; it's just not common enough to worry about. There are roads too, on which you can ride all night and never encounter a moving vehicle.

All the same, riding in the dark is essentially a poor idea. You can't see small, tire-damaging objects, such as glass and rocks, and fixing a flat by flashlight is nearly impossible. And you can't see the scenery at all, which is usually the reason for being there in the first place. So, for most bikepackers, any night-riding equipment such as lights will be classified as emergency gear, like the spare tube or the first-aid kit.

I must admit that I probably ride at night on these trips more than most, because I live in a city which is pretty well surrounded by industrial and other heavy-traffic zones. I prefer to start a trip at about three in the morning and ride through these nasty areas—which are deserted and safe at this hour—and by the time the sun comes up, I'm out in the country. I only do this for the first day, unless I've got some other compelling reason to make early starts. The point is, there are places where it is safer to ride after dark than during daylight hours.

In any case, the cycle camper, who faces lighter traffic but possibly more demanding road conditions, is less concerned with being seen than is the commuter or other urban bikie, and more concerned with being able to see. For this purpose, we may do well to go back and take another look at the more traditional lighting systems, which had this purpose.

The old standard is the small generator that runs off the tire or the hub (rarely). Despite a lot of harsh words about it to the contrary, this is an excellent system. It provides adequate light at sane speeds; it does cut out when you stop, but while this is a serious hazard at a city intersection, it is irrelevant to rural riding conditions. A bulb can burn out at high downhill speeds, but if you're silly enough to go downstairs at speed in the dark, you deserve anything you get anyway. The drag of a good dynamo is not much, and the best units are very light and compact. Cheap dynamo rigs, however, are unreliable and worse than worthless, since they may work just long enough to get you out into the middle of nowhere in the dark and then quit working forever.

The best dynamo set I've ever used is the French Soubi-tez; it works beautifully and weighs little, and if you want a generator light, this is the one I wholeheartedly recommend. Some of my friends have used Union dynamos successfully, but the only one I ever had didn't work worth a damn. (That was five or six years ago, and they may have improved them.)

Generators come in block models, with the light and dynamo housed in a single, solid casing that clamps to the front fork, or in sets with a separate frame-mounted dynamo that's connected with wires to the headlight. The block type is far better for camping; wires always present some added possibility of failure, especially under backcountry conditions.

A taillight may be powered by the same generator, but this creates more problems of reliability and provides more wires to get messed up. I've never found one that worked reliably except one on a French touring bike that had all the wiring built inside the frame tubes. A taillight isn't really essential for rural-road night cycling, though in fog or rain it is well worth having. One of those little plastic leg lights works as well or better.

The alternative to generator lights is, of course, the battery light. There are certain problems with these rigs, primarily having to do with weight and duration of service. Batteries are quite heavy; the weight of such a light may be no worse than the drag of a generator, but you only have to fight generator drag while you're using the lights, whereas you have to lug the battery around all day. It's hard to make yourself pack something that heavy up and down mountains for a week on the off chance that you might need it for a couple of hours some evening. Batteries also run down, whereas a generator keeps creating its own energy. If batteries die on you unexpectedly, you're out there on the road in the dark with no chance of relief—a terrible sensation; I've had it happen to me. But if you carry a lot of spares, your weight total gets to be astronomical, to say nothing of the expense and the environmental implications of using up batteries and throwing them away.

But there is one special consideration that comes into play for the bikepacker. If you're going off the pavement, generator lights, or any other lights mounted down there on the bike frame, are very vulnerable to damage from water, mud, and flying gravel, while wires can be ripped off by brush. For rough-stuff cycling, the only practical answer is a battery rig that can be taken clear off the bike and stowed in your bags. (You won't actually ride on such tracks in the dark, unless you are entirely demented; you just need something for emergencies when you hit the highway.) For such trips, a good possibility is the well-known, French-made Wonder Light. This is a very light and compact unit that is easily mounted virtually anywhere about the bike and just as easily unscrewed and stuffed into a bag, where it takes up little room. The batteries are excruciatingly expensive and hard to obtain, and the duration is not great, so this light should be used only if you do not intend to ride by night and merely want something in case you have no choice.

Most battery lamps using flashlight cells are heavy, unreliable, and underpowered. I have heard that the English Berec, which uses D cells, is reliable and gives a good light, though I have never used one.*

If you envision a lot of long night rides—desert crossings, say—get a good generator light; batteries just aren't up to it. In the weird eventuality of a trip that includes a long night ride or two and some rough stuff as well—a desert crossing followed by a few days exploring old mining roads in the hills, for one far-out example—a block-type generator lamp can be unclamped from the front fork and stowed in your handlebar bag when things get hairy.

Many cyclists like a headlamp. I like them myself in many ways. The light shines where you want it to, whether or not the bike is pointing that way, which is great for reading signs and checking out ominous canine sounds at night. They're also absolutely invaluable in case of flats or mechanical problems. Drivers can see you at a great distance, in situations when this may be important. (There is an old Justin Wilson routine that ends with the punch line, "Man, if you're as wide as you are high, I'm gettin' off the road!") The headband used with most models will fit neatly on an MSR or Bell helmet, and the battery pack will fit in a jersey pocket. The light from some models is enormously powerful.

The problem is, of course, those batteries again. The most common headlamp, the type used by nocturnal hunters, uses a huge, boxy dry cell that has a good long life and is unaffected by damp or vibration but weighs a short ton. Some of the light models for cave exploration use batteries not easily obtained in the U.S., especially at rural stores (which do have the big Eveready cells). If you know anyone who is into caving—an activity that I find terrifying even to think about—ask about headlamps, because

---

*Since writing the above, I have acquired a Berec. It is an entirely admirable light and is now my number one choice for most trips. However, the mounting bracket is poorly designed, and the recommendation to mount it on the handlebars doesn't work well with a handlebar bag. With a little careful bending, you can, as I did, modify the bracket so that it mounts on the left front fork blade—a much better setup.

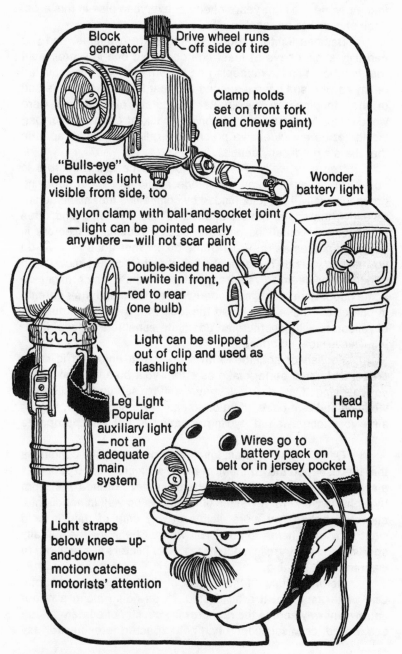

Block generator

Drive wheel runs off side of tire

Clamp holds set on front fork (and chews paint)

"Bulls-eye" lens makes light visible from side, too

Wonder battery light

Nylon clamp with ball-and-socket joint —light can be pointed nearly anywhere—will not scar paint

Double-sided head —white in front, red to rear (one bulb)

Light can be slipped out of clip and used as flashlight

Leg Light Popular auxiliary light —not an adequate main system

Head Lamp

Wires go to battery pack on belt or in jersey pocket

Light straps below knee—up-and-down motion catches motorists' attention

A variety of useful bicycle lights and features.

these people are light-years ahead of everyone else in this area. Their stuff *has* to be reliable.

Besides lights, various reflectors are available, and you certainly should have at least one good, big one in a prominent rear location. I find my sleeping bag overhangs the one mounted on my carrier, so I have a second one that is fastened to the end of the sleeping-bag bundle itself. (Safety pins, if you were wondering.) A reflector or two on the back of each pannier bag would not be an excessive precaution; reflectors weigh so little that there's hardly any penalty.

You may well be required to have certain reflectors in some states, even if you never ride at night. Various lobbying groups (usually, I am told, funded by companies that manufacture reflective materials) have managed to get confusing and often ill-conceived regulations onto the books, requiring reflectors in such odd places as the front of the bike. What good this will do you, unless you ride head-on at a car at night, I do not know. Such codes never seem to require the use of lights, which might do some good. As a result, many people—children and their parents in particular—have developed the idea that a sufficient quantity of reflectors will constitute an adequate substitute for real lighting. This is most unfortunate.

Foolish or not, these laws are being enforced in many areas, and you'd better make sure that your bike is legal where you're going. One day you may want to set up a deliberate violation-and-test-case situation to challenge such a law, but I'm sure your long-awaited cycling vacation is not an appropriate time.

One good safety item for night or poor-visibility conditions that has escaped the attention of these well-intentioned people is a simple plastic safety vest—the familiar blaze-orange vest worn by highway workers. It weighs little, shows up well in headlights, and also makes you more visible at any time of day; in cold weather it even helps to keep you warm. Check for them in any sporting-goods store; in most states, deer hunters are required to wear this sort of thing.

Before getting off the subject of night riding, an anecdote. One winter morning at around 3:00, I was riding along a rather narrow highway across the rice-growing country of eastern Arkansas, bound for Mississippi. I had not expected to encounter any traffic at all during the night, the area being very thinly populated, so I had only a small battery lamp, with a couple of reflectors on the bike and some reflector tape stuck on my helmet and on the back of my windbreaker. I had minimal stuff, in other words, the kind of thing you use when you've convinced yourself that you don't really need it anyway.

Unfortunately, what I didn't know—having quit hunting a decade earlier—was that it was opening day of duck season. At about 3:00 A.M., that road became a solid parade of trucks and jeeps bound for the duck blinds. It was freezing cold, so I couldn't get off and wait till morning, and there was no shoulder. All I could do was ride straight and hope that they could see me.

A lot has been written about the American hunter, some of it bad, and I've thrown my share of rocks, but those guys were superb. At least a hundred vehicles must have passed me before dawn on that narrow road; not one came close enough to be even unpleasant. When there was traffic coming the other way, the vehicles behind me slowed and matched my speed until they could pass safely, a courtesy you rarely get even in broad daylight. Several people honked and called out cheerful greetings.

Why all the skill and courtesy? I've thought about it. They were all awake and alert, keyed up by anticipation of the morning's sport. They were expecting to engage in something that would involve good eyesight and reflexes, and had subconsciously adjusted their perceptions to suit. (After all, anybody who can't miss a man on a bicycle is hardly likely to hit a duck.) And they were largely in a good mood, since they were going to be doing something they liked, as contrasted with the sour attitude of an office worker who might take out on a hapless cyclist the resentment he feels for his employer.

What I am getting at here—besides showing another side of the much-maligned hunter; some of them are no doubt sadistic swine, but a lot of them are basically excellent fellows—is that any trouble cyclists have with nighttime highway traffic is probably based on the mental state of the drivers, and you can't affect that very much by fiddling with lights and reflectors. Whatever the problems of the late-hours cycle commuter in the city, I don't think the cycle camper needs to be encumbered by a lot of elaborate strobes, flashers, and reflectorized tires.

Heat and Dryness

The desert is a fascinating place, but a dangerous one. Many people have gotten into trouble crossing it in cars, let alone by bike. If you try it, carry lots of water, refill your containers at every possible opportunity, keep your head covered, and let somebody (such as the cops) know you're going. What am I *saying* here? If you don't have sense enough to carry water on a desert crossing without my telling you to do it, you shouldn't be going in the first place.

Even in nondesert regions, the heat is nothing to trifle with. If your schedule will accommodate it, try to do your riding early in the morning, take a break during the hottest part of the afternoon, and perhaps ride on a bit more as it gets later. "In Rangoon the sun at noon is just what the natives shun," goes Noel Coward's catchy verse, and if you're smart, you'll shun it too, even in our allegedly temperate summers. Keep your head covered, seek out shady spots for regular breaks, and drink lots of water, sipping frequently rather than waiting long intervals and then gulping. Remember, also, what I said about meats and fats for lunch.

For many years, it was taken as axiomatic that you should take salt tablets or otherwise replace salt lost through sweating in hot weather. This idea, however, has come under some fairly authoritative fire in recent years. There is also a theory that you should replace other minerals—potassium and magnesium, mostly—lost by the sweating process, with its adherents and opponents.

My own highly inexpert view is that it is a matter of personal body chemistry rather than anything on which general rules can be laid down. I worked for over a year in an old-fashioned iron foundry; the temperature never got below 120°F. during working hours and often went well above that. There were salt tablets in wall-mounted dispensers—the *only* effort made by the management toward worker welfare—and we used to talk among ourselves about whether or not they worked. Some of the men got violently ill if they didn't take salt tablets, often as many as two or three an hour. Others got just as sick if they took them at all. I myself could take them or not with no discernible effect, but I usually took them just in case. I saw the same thing—different reactions among different men—in the Army, and I note that Colin Fletcher, surely an expert on hot-climate travel, seems to agree that individuals vary in their need for salt replenishment.

So I suppose each person must experiment—very cautiously—to find out his or her own needs.

Various commercial preparations are said to replace body minerals lost in sweat. Dr. Rich Hammen, biochemist and former international bike racer, raises an interesting point: Are we to assume that evolution has produced a defective cooling-and-excretion system whose "mistakes" we must "correct," or isn't it at least equally likely that the body knows what it's doing when it flushes these substances out through the skin? A provocative point, at least. It is rather amusing to hear people talk about "natural" diet and then turn around and gulp quarts of synthetic mineral-replacement drinks.

You can't get around experience. I drink Gatorade in considerable quantities in very hot weather; when I stop at a store on a summer run, it is the first thing I look for. I also carry envelopes of Gatorade powder on my summer runs, and I definitely think it makes me less prone to nausea and heat cramps, whether or not it is actually valuable for other reasons. However, as noted earlier in this book, sugar content in any drink will slow the absorption process in the stomach, so I mix Gatorade powder at half the strength recommended on the package. At the foundry, I drank Gatorade a lot, and it seemed to help. Again, individuals must be presumed to differ.

Heat stroke is no joke. If you start to fell faint, dizzy, and weak, get off of that bike fast. This isn't one of those things that you can tough out; it's tougher than you are. Drink water or some other liquid at least every hour, and drink *before* you feel thirsty; in hot weather, by the time you start to really feel the thirst and the sickness, you've already gone too long—better start looking for a shady spot to take a good long break.

Cold

Bicycle camping isn't really a cold-weather activity—not if you're talking about serious, freezing cold. Icy roads and head-high snowdrifts simply aren't an appropriate environment for the bicycle, and very few cyclists will want to carry the heavy loads required for winter camping. Thick sleeping bags, snow tents, and lots of high-calorie foods add up to more than our lightweight bikes ought to carry, and cycling in very heavy clothing isn't much fun either.

If you're speaking of riding when it's somewhat colder than the usual spring or fall day, however, that's another matter. I've had some pretty good times in January without carrying too much junk. Several layers of relatively thin clothing, rather than single heavy garments, will keep you warmer and permit flexiblity in adjusting to temperature. Wear a windproof shell layer over everything; wind chill is an especially severe problem when you're moving rapidly through the air. Be sure to keep your head warm, since this is a big heat-sink area. You can wear a knitted cap under your helmet or try one of those ski mask–caps that makes you look like Darth Vader. Mittens are warmer than gloves, and with bar-end shifters, you can still change gears. Ski clothing is well adapted to cold-weather cycling.

Feet are particularly hard to keep warm, and heavy insulated boots won't work with pedal clips and straps. Thick, wool boot socks will help. There are available little windshield gadgets, sometimes pile lined, that are meant to go over your toe clips to keep your feet warm; I've never tried them, but they look useful. A few people report good luck with the battery-operated electric socks meant for hunters.

As for camping gear for such conditions, be a bit cautious about accepting the listed temperature rating of any sleeping bag. Nowadays this rating is usually meant to refer to use inside a tent and atop a thick foam pad, and even then it only means that you won't freeze to death—it doesn't necessarily mean that you'll feel warm and comfortable. I'd tend to knock about 10 degrees off of the bag's temperature rating just in the interests of safety and comfort. If a bag is rated at 10 degrees above 0, I think I'd try to avoid getting into a situation where it might get much below 20. Of course, in a pinch, you can sleep in your clothing, and things like sweaters and long thermal underwear will cause a spectacular improvement in performance, even with a mediocre bag. (Cheap thermal underwear that isn't really adequate for serious outdoor wear still makes warm sleep gear.) Still, it's rather confining inside a mummy bag at best, and with all that stuff on, you can become very claustrophobic.

In very chilly weather, there is a temptation to cook inside the tent, and also to close all of the tent openings. Don't ever yield to both of these temptations at once, especially with a fully coated, single-wall tent, or in short order you may become somebody's late lamented. This is a surprisingly common cause of death among outdoor people in winter. The same is true with lanterns. Last winter in a town near where I live, two men went out on an overnight hunting trip; they had a large tent and a Coleman lantern, and they shut all of the flaps against the cold and left the lantern burning. They either fell asleep or passed out; they never awoke. So useless. If you must burn a stove or lantern inside a tent—and the fire hazard alone makes it a moderately foolish thing to do except in heavy rain—make sure you have full ventilation.

In cold weather, your food should have a considerably higher fat content, even to a point that many people may find unpleasant. On a cold day, I've seen a man lick a stick of margarine like candy—and I've also done it myself.

If you get caught out in a cold snap for which your outfit is simply not adequate, *abandon the trip,* unless, perhaps, you can buy some warmer clothing and more suitable food at a nearby town. If you have to keep warm until you can get to shelter or reach home, try newspaper; as generations of old winos have known, newspaper is the cheapest insulation around and one of the most effective. Stuff it down your clothing, wrap it around your feet. Never be too proud or stubborn to call off the trip if you really aren't equipped for it. Hypothermia and pneumonia are not romantic ways to go.

Even in relatively mild weather, hypothermia is a danger you must never overlook. Wet clothing and wind can lower the body's temperature at great speed, even if the day isn't particularly cold. This is one reason why I am such a believer in a complete rain suit—a poncho does not protect you against windchill and the cooling caused by evaporating water. Even if you get off the road and make a bivouac to sit out the rain, make sure you keep warm. Get a sweater or wool shirt out of your bags and put it on, even though you don't really feel all that chilly, because it can sneak up on you. This is one time when a wool jersey is a welcome thing to have.

The first obvious effects of hypothermia are poor coordination, mumbling speech, irrationality, and at times an illogical euphoria—"No, really, guys, I feel fine!" In fact, the behavior pattern is very similar to that of drunkenness. If you're riding along on a chilly day, or you got wet in a shower and now the wind's up, and your buddy starts to act as if he's had a few too many, don't assume he's been hitting a private supply of Old Crankset—get him off that bike! At any minute, he may lose control, crash, and go into a very dangerous unconscious state; time is extremely precious in treating hypothermia. If you can get the victim off the bike and into warm, dry clothing (modesty should take a back seat to survival here), get out the stove and fix a hot drink, and perhaps give a bit of fast-heat food, such as a cup of instant soup, a mild case of windchill hypothermia can be arrested and cured. If you wait until the victim goes into severe hypothermic shock— and this can happen, due to wet clothing and wind, at surprisingly mild-seeming temperatures—it may become a case for the hospital . . . or the coroner. Don't let considerations of politeness or diffidence stop you from *making* an obvious hypothermia victim accept treatment—he'll thank you later.

In the final analysis, the only people who should go on cycling-camping trips in extreme conditions—long rides across deserts or deep-winter runs—are those who are already experienced and expert cyclists *and* campers, whose knowledge and confidence are such that they can work out their own equipment and techniques. If you're still having to learn from books such as this estimable volume, I suggest you stay with less brutal conditions for now.

The fox knows many things, but
the hedgehog knows one big thing.

—Archilocus

CHAPTER **10**

_____ Scary Stuff

Besides the normal and natural situations described in the preceding chapter, other special problems can arise that are harder to cope with, mainly because they depend somewhat on the behavior and attitudes of other entities, rather than on your own technique or predictable natural forces. Sometimes the consequences are comic; occasionally they can be tragic. Nearly always the situation is at least a little frightening at the time, even if it seems less so in retrospect.

I hate to write about these things, and I do hope that nothing in this chapter scares anybody away from cycle camping, which is really a very safe and rational pastime. But it would be dishonest to pretend that these problems do not exist, or to ignore them in the hope that they will go away. I think that talking about them and considering them in a dispassionate way may help make them less demoralizing—if only by reducing the element of surprise and letting the inexperienced bikie know that others go through this sort of thing all the time and survive.

However, experienced cyclists take note: This chapter is mostly about highway hazards. If you've been riding a bike around the country a lot and are reading this book mostly for the camping

199

part of it, you already know about most of the stuff in this chapter—traffic, dogs, hostile people—and have already developed opinions of your own on the subjects. You people can skim or skip this chapter if you like. See you next chapter.

Traffic

If there's a single common factor that unites American cyclists—tourists, racers, commuters, everybody down to your grandma riding her Huffy to the disco—it is a deeply rooted and fully justified fear of the automobile, as operated by the American driver. Some feel it more than others; some have allowed it to become a paralyzing terror that ruins the whole thing for them, while others practice an aggressive go-for-it style, as if daring motorists to deny them their full rights on the road. Whatever, at some level we all feel it.

There is good reason. The overall level of driving skill in most of this country is outrageously low. Many cyclists feel persecuted, as if motorists single them out for inconsiderate or even hostile treatment. In most cases, these drivers are behaving no worse than usual; it's just that cyclists are more vulnerable. An incompetent or inconsiderate driver who sideswipes another car seldom causes anything worse than a dented fender, but if he or she does the same thing to a cyclist, somebody can be killed. I've noticed that every time I've ever been involved in a brush with a car, the car itself bore marks—bent fenders, broken taillights, bashed-in doors—of previous encounters with something less yielding than a bicycle.

Some drivers do seem to respond differently according to the nature of the other vehicle or its operator. They will cut across in front of a bike more readily than they will a car and they'll do it to the car before they'll do it to a big truck. Motorcyclists tell me that the same type of jerk will harass a well-dressed person on a light motorcycle or moped but becomes remarkably courteous in the presence of a mean-looking, outlaw motorcycle gang. (I have had experiences like this myself. Some years ago I used to cycle out to an old gravel pit for rifle practice, and, as was legal in that state, I carried my rifle slung across my back. Though I had to ride along a very busy road that I usually tried to avoid, I discovered that people became amazingly considerate; nobody passed at close range, honked, or anything. If you're one of those cyclists who worries about being seen by drivers, take it from me—throw away the reflectors and flags, and sling a .30/06 Springfield across your shoulder blades. I guarantee you, *they'll see you*— and exhibit a remarkable tolerance toward your life-style.)

Still, truck drivers will tell you quickly that plenty of these dummies drive recklessly even in situations in which they are obviously bound to be the losers. So my own opinion is that cyclists are mostly the victims of a broader national problem—the wretchedly inadequate testing, licensing, and legal regulation of the American driver.

If you're wondering by now why I've gone off into psychology, sociology, and legislative issues, it's because some of the safety measures or "solutions" pushed by some cycling factions strike me as having missed the point, and some of these matters impinge on the bikepacker in his or her relationship with the motor vehicle. We don't ride in urban areas on our trips, so we aren't concerned with the main bikes-in-traffic nightmares. We do have our problems, chief of which is that of high-speed, overtaking traffic that endangers the cyclist by passing improperly. An actual tail-end direct hit is rare (I've had two, but only in town). More commonly, cyclists are forced off of the road into a ditch, or they receive glancing, sideswiping blows.

The popular theory is that drivers are basically competent and want to avoid the cyclist, and that the main defense is to get their attention by using various devices, mostly visual—and also to stay out of their way. *I* believe that the line, "I didn't even see him!" is usually just an attempt to avoid a charge of reckless driving. (Cops I've talked with agreed; they say they get the same excuse when a driver hits anything, from a pedestrian to a truck to a tree.) Usually, when a motorist hits or narrowly misses a cyclist on an open, level, straight highway, it's because the motorist either misjudged distances and speeds, a common weakness among U.S. motorists, or simply didn't figure a person on a bicycle had any right to be on the road.

Think I'm being unfair? All right—when they miss you, do they yell, "Hey, I'm sorry, I didn't see you!"? Or don't they more often give you an angry honk and maybe, "Get that thing off the road!" It's only when they find themselves facing the chance of a ticket and an insurance claim that they whip out that tired old, "Gee, officer, I didn't see him. . . ."

By all means, deck yourself and your bike out with reflective devices, fanny bumpers, and the like. In a few marginal cases it helps—in rain or fog, or with a tired driver who actually needs that flash of color to notice you. Don't expect miracles, and don't ride passively, depending on your flag and your fanny bumper to save you.

On a wide, straight, flat road with light traffic, you aren't obliged to inch your way nervously along the edge of the road, and if you do it, you are asking to get run off the road, or even clipped. If you hug the edge, drivers assume that you have surrendered your place and are getting over, out of their way, and they will blast by you without trying to give you space, even if there is nothing coming in the other lane. If they miscalculate, or, worse, have those big protruding rearview mirrors, you could be clobbered.

So, though this may sound foolhardy, *move out into the road.* When the road is clear and straight, and traffic is light, take yourself some space—and refuse to yield it unless the alternative is clearly suicidal. If the traffic grows so intense that you are clearly endangering yourself and others, okay, move over. Though as long as it's just a matter of the odd car or truck overtaking you and there's plenty of safe passing space in the other lane, stay out there a couple of feet and make them go around you.

It's odd; if you're over at the edge, they'll pass you with no room at all, but if you're a couple of feet into the lane, they'll almost always swing way over into the other lane and pass you with yards to spare. I don't know why this is so; maybe more subtle maneuvers are beyond their skill.

This procedure does take a certain amount of guts; you feel very naked and vulnerable out there. You have to be prepared to accept and deal with a certain amount of hostility, because some people will never accept that you have any right to do it. If you can steel yourself to try it, however, you'll find that the occasional angry driver is less frightening than all of those perfectly nice people who streak by an inch from your earhole.

Of course, some judgment is called for here; you don't want to be crazy about this. On very rare occasions, you may hear a motor coming with increasing volume and undeviating course, and realize, "This guy is going to run right over me if I don't get out of the way." There are a few authentic loonies out there. Such incidents are very, very rare. Much more often, what you get is an angry honk of the horn and a hoarse shout demanding that you get that thing off the road, while the driver roars past doing horrible things to his transmission. Don't be bullied—by the time these louts honk they're already pulling around to pass anyway. You may, if you like, respond with an appropriate gesture and one of the terser Anglo-Saxon equivalents of, "Bad show, sir!" (If, however, the driver immediately begins slowing to a stop, you'd better be capable of dealing with whatever follows. Don't let your digits make dates your fist can't meet.)

Even the horn honkers and shouters are quite uncommon in most parts of the country, though of course it only takes one to upset your nerves for quite a while. Most of the horn honking is of the friendly variety, or done by nervous, well-intentioned people who simply want to make sure you know they're there before they pass you. A lot of drivers, especially older ones, basically regard bicycles as children's toys, and even though they see you, an adult, on the bike, subconsciously they still regard you as a little kid on a bike who may unexpectedly dart across their path.

On a narrow, two-lane road with heavy traffic going both ways, it's a whole different scene. With the best intentions in the world, a motorist may not be able to pass you except very closely, and it's not too good for public relations to get a whole string of cars and trucks backed up behind you. Usually you'll just have to get over as far as you can, ride very straight, and try to get off onto another road as soon as you can. In extreme situations, you may even find it necessary to take to a gravel shoulder. Normally I'm one of the loudest defenders of the bicycle's right to equal status on the highiway, and I live in a state in which the law declares that a cyclist has a right to a full lane if he wants to occupy it (and you thought Arkansas was backward!), but you have to be practical. It just isn't worth taking up permanent meditation in a ditch to defend a point of pride. In a lot of states, the law says that you have to ride as far to the right "as practicable," whatever that may mean; block a lane and hold up traffic, and you might get a ticket.

Now trucks make this sort of situation much, much worse. It's not that trucks are likely to *hit* cyclists; this is so rare that I've never even heard of a case (except for a race run over an improperly marshaled course, and that wasn't the truck driver's fault). But a truck passing at close interval stirs up tremendous air turbulence and a cyclist can easily lose control. Depending on speeds, intervals, and crosswinds, you may be blown off the road onto the shoulder or sucked out into the road behind the truck, where a following car may hit you. (It has even been claimed that a big, fast-moving truck can suck a cyclist under its own wheels, but I must say I've never actually heard of this happening. The story seems to have originated with California highway patrolmen seeking to justify ordering cyclists off certain highways, so I have my suspicions—but I've got to admit that the idea has bubbled to the surface of my subconscious more than once when being passed by trucks. It's a hideous thought, anyway.)

Truckers, on the whole, are sympathetic and will try to slow down and pass wide around you; they are well aware of the wind-blast effect of their giant vehicles. It is very rare that you'll encounter a sadistic joker who deliberately blows you off. For all their manic behavior at truckstops and the gonzo image generated by certain stupid movies, most truck drivers are actually rather introverted, gentle people, like most men in solitary occupations. As with so many groups, an obnoxious minority has given them all a bad name.

Yet, in a lot of situations, they *can't* slow down—a big truck just doesn't respond that quickly—and they often have no room to pass. It is also probably true that some of the younger drivers have an exaggerated confidence in their own skills, which may lead them to pass closer than they should, even though meaning no harm.

On the whole, then, it's best to avoid truck routes. If at all possible, try to get some information about this while planning your trip. You can consult the Highway Department, the state troopers, or some other authority of the sort. Most truckers follow well-established routes that are known to everyone connected with the business. You will occasionally encounter a solo truck off of these routes, but it's only in heavy numbers that they're really dangerous. While you're at it, try to figure out ways to avoid narrow roads with lots of traffic of any kind. This is a problem in planning rather than in bike handling.

If you find yourself with a problem of this sort while out on the road, you might try doing what I do—stop at a truckstop and talk with the drivers over a cup of coffee. Explain what you're doing and how you need to find a route without much traffic. Most of them will help you work it out. They'd rather not have you on the road to worry about anyway, and besides, truckers love to talk about ways to get from one town to another. Around any truckstop there will be a driver or two who has had occasion to seek out an obscure back road—trying to sneak an excessive load past the authorities, for example, I've even had them get on their CB radios and ask colleagues for their opinions and information on the traffic situation on this or that road. They usually seem delighted that some member of the nontrucking public respects their opinion on something.

Another source of advice is the highway patrolman, but I must add that there have been reports of a few individuals who were hostile to cyclists and even tried to order them off the road. I don't know why; there's probably some kind of mental association there that I don't understand. Most of the troopers are decent, polite, helpful men, much better than some of their urban equivalents.

If you absolutely cannot avoid a high-traffic road, then consider whether there may be some time of day when traffic would be at its lightest. It may even be best to make the run after dark, if your schedule and equipment will permit it; some extremely busy roads become almost deserted at night. Trucks run at night, of course, but you can hear them coming so far away that you can take to the shoulder.

Usually, traffic is something a bikepacker has to worry about only on the main highways or when passing through built-up areas. Once you reach the backcountry, there is seldom any "traffic" in the usual sense of the word—just the occasional individual vehicle coming along the road at long intervals, with plenty of time and space to avoid problems.

There is one exception, a weird product of our mad times. In some areas, there exists a little-known but troublesome form of vehicular hazard peculiar to the bikepacker's world. This consists of a growing invasion of scenic backcountry areas by city people driving pickup trucks, vans, motor homes, or family cars towing trailers, in search of the Great Outdoors. Most of them are heading for some public campground or park where they will park their vehicles, set up elaborate living arrangements, deposit their adipose buttocks in folding chairs, converse with others of the same persuasion who have packed the area like a Hong Kong rooftop slum, and fondly believe themselves to be camping out.

This is all harmless enough in itself—their impulses are in the right place, they just don't know what to do about them, or can't imagine doing it without motorized transportation and all of the utilities of home. (One of these people complained bitterly to me about the lack of electric hookups at an Ozark campground; I pointed out that when I was a boy growing up in the same area, we didn't have electricity in our *houses*.) The problem for us is the hair-raising business of sharing the roads with them. The places where they go are often accessible only by narrow roads, sometimes with only one real lane, and in some popular areas the numbers of these motorized "campers" have created serious traffic problems. This is especially severe in some National Parks—Yosemite on a peak weekend is worse than downtown L.A.—and bikepackers are advised to keep clear.

Even in less daunting numbers, they can scare you silly, because so many of them are such wretchedly bad drivers. Or, rather, they're so bad at driving what they've got. In many cases, a person whose entire training and experience has been in family cars is trying to operate the equivalent of a good-sized truck, often on a road that would make a professional truck driver turn pale with horror. Their whole attention is absorbed by the mere business of controlling their unfamiliar and oversized vehicles; they have none left over for bicycles. Their vehicles invariably sport enormous "Texas" mirrors on either side, and they rarely have any idea of how much room to allow for clearance (not just for passing bikes, either; as any ranger can tell you, they're always wiping those things off on trees).

If you ride along the edge of the road and let one of these Bloatmobiles pass you, be prepared for a memorable, if not terminal, experience. They'll often squeeze by you with no room to spare, even when there is another lane and nobody coming. They don't actually mean to crowd you; it's just that the driver usually has all that he can do to keep the thing on the road at all (though he belives he's doing a masterly job), and moving over to pass you is far too complicated a maneuver.

So it is vital that you take a good piece of the road and refuse to give it up. You'll be subjected to a good deal of honking—and these beasts have monster horns—but they won't do anything worse; these are very respectable, law-abiding people, very upper-middle-class and conservative, certainly not given to overt antisocial behavior. They'll crowd you if you let them, or honk if you won't let them waddle past without changing lanes, but you won't have to deal with the submerged potential for violence that you sometimes get with, say, a pickup truck with a rifle rack in the cab and a KKK bumper sticker, or a Corvette full of drunken college boys.

You may find yourself (horrible fate) sharing a campground with these people, and if you are a diplomatic and persuasive person, you may be able to engage them in conversation and explain your point of view. My own efforts at reeducation have not been crowned with success, but others are no doubt better at that sort of thing. The first time I saw a family park a Winnebago at a public campground, unload a power mower, and *mow the grass* around their site, I knew there was no way I would ever establish any sort of "meaningful dialogue" with these people.

People towing trailers are a different problem. They often fail to allow for the length of the trailer when pulling back over after passing you; they do this when passing cars, let alone bikes. Any time a car or a truck with a trailer in tow passes you, watch out for this and take to the ditch if necessary. (Rental trailers are worse, because the driver is less likely to be used to it.) Boats on trailers are a particular menace—and people who operate big, ugly, overpowered boats on lakes tend to be crazy drivers, for some reason—so any time you're riding near a lake or a big river, be alert for this hazard.

Urban traffic is much nastier. You shouldn't have to worry about this on most bikepacking trips, but on occasion you may have to go through a city to get where you're going. Try hard to find a way to bypass the place, even if it adds a day to your trip.

Cities—crazy drivers wall to wall, predatory gangs of punks, unbreathable air—stay away, stay away.

If you do get caught in a city, even briefly, watch it. The business of cycling in an urban environment is a whole complex matter that can't be dealt with in a book of this kind—check the reading list for more specialized works. There is one point I want to make, in case you're a fairly experienced traffic-buster: *Remember, you're on a loaded touring bike!* You can't cowboy it up in traffic the way you could on a stripped-down racer; your bike lacks the necessary agility. You can't turn tightly or accelerate fast, and you can't stop as quickly, either. Just maintain a low profile and get the hell out of there as fast as you can.

Let me say it just one more time: The best solution to the problem of riding with traffic is to ride where the traffic isn't. Fortunately, this country contains many hundreds of miles of roads with very little vehicular traffic, and these roads often pass through the very kind of country where bikepackers like to go. The Invasion of the Winnebago Monsters does create some problems, but only in a few areas, and they'll probably thin out as the cost of gas goes up. With a little careful planning, traffic needn't be a big worry on your bikepacking trip.

Beasties

Dogs are an ancient enemy of cyclists; they were after us before cars even were invented. When the last car sputters to a stop with its gas tank forever empty and people go back to rational vehicles like bikes, horses, and their own feet, dogs will no doubt continue to chase us. In fact, they're probably looking forward to it.

Even a small dog, no danger as far as actual biting, can get under your wheels and cause a crash, and a big dog is an authentically dangerous animal. Cyclists tend to treat the dog problem as a joke, and it has its comic aspects, but at times it quits being funny.

Out in the country, the dog problem is less severe than in urban or suburban areas. Farm dogs are mostly good-natured louts, lazy and not terribly bright, with plenty of opportunities to work off their hunting instincts chasing rabbits and the like. A passing cyclist is worth a bark but rarely a determined chase. They're usually fairly docile and well trained, since country people are pretty responsible about animals. Even if they come at you, a good shouted "NO!" will usually bring them to a halt. Very rarely will they press home an attack.

However, there is in this country today a strange vogue for large, dangerously aggressive dogs of the sort that used to be associated with prisons, military installations, and the secret police of totalitarian countries. Unfortunately, not all of the people who buy them are responsible enough to have them correctly trained and to keep them under proper restraint. This problem is mostly a suburban one, but in some areas, people from the cities are buying property out in the country and bringing their big, vicious dogs with them, so you have to keep your eyes open. One particular danger spot: mobile homes. People who live in mobile homes in the country tend to have the biggest, meanest dogs around. I don't know why—there's probably a Master's thesis in it somewhere.

Usually a cyclist can outrun a dog, especially in the country, where houses tend to be set well back from the road. But if you've got a full load on the bike and perhaps are a bit tired, or

there's an uphill grade, you may not be able to make it. Try yelling, loud and rather arrogantly. Bellow from deep in your stomach, like a karate fighter. Yell, "NO!", which most dogs recognize. Reinforce this with a threatening gesture, as if throwing rocks, or brandish your pump like a club. Or make a pointing motion at the dog.

If you think the dog may be coming on anyway and you can't outrun him, you'd better get off the bike and face him on the ground. This movement alone sometimes stops the attack— perhaps he realizes that you can defend yourself better now. Continue to shout and threaten. One thing that often works is to take your pump or a wrench and strike the saddle sharply—not enough to damage anything, just enough to make a sharp, whacking sound. Dogs are usually trained as puppies with a rolled-up newspaper, and a whacking noise seems to trigger memories. I've stopped very big, aggressive dogs this way.

If he does come at you, use your bike to block the charge and clout him a good one between the eyes with your pump. Or do what I do—carry a can of Mace, good for man and beast. (More about this shortly.) You will find that things very, very rarely get beyond the yell-and-threaten stage, though, if you really put yourself into it.

Some people who are good with dogs just stop and make friends with the animal. Every now and then I do it myself, if I'm not in a hurry and it seems to be a basically likable dog. A few dogs will come out and seem to be going for you when all they want is some conversation and attention. You do have to have a good feel for canine dispositions to bring this off.

I do not buy the common argument that dogs fail to recognize a cyclist as a person; the same dog often ignores local kids on their bikes. He's just defending what he views as his territory and responding, too, to an ancient instinct that tells him to chase whatever runs away. That same instinct also tells him to stop and refuse to close with whatever turns and shows fight. This is part of the hunting pattern of dogs and wolves, going back to Pleistocene times.

If you are bitten, report this to the legal authorities (usually the Sheriff's Department) at once, and make sure that the dog has been vaccinated for rabies. Demand to see the certificate of vaccination. If this cannot be verified and the dog cannot be located, painful rabies shots must be started immediately. Don't take a chance on *any* dog bite, no matter how slight. Rabies is a killer—much more certainly lethal than the bite of any snake in North America.

Dogs are the only animals likely to attack a cyclist. Wild animals stay off the roads in the daytime and, in any case, are very shy of man. Domestic cattle can block the road, and an occasional bull may even charge a cyclist, but they don't run even as fast as dogs, and you can easily sprint away. In grazing areas, if cattle are crossing the road up ahead, wait until they're across—if you come close, the stupid beasts may stampede right over you.

Horses aren't dangerous, but if you meet horseback riders, stop and stand quietly by your bike until they pass. Horses are nervous, brainless creatures, and the sight of a cyclist can send them into fits. There's no point in endangering the horseman's life. Watch out for little souvenirs on the road, too.

The only wild animal in the U.S. that may endanger a camper—and then very, very rarely—is the bear. They are no threat to a rider, but might be a problem in camp in some areas. Nobody really knows what makes a bear decide to attack. The black bear is generally a peaceful, rather timid animal and will run from man. When a black bear becomes dangerous, it is nearly always because it has been fed, teased, or injured by humans. People who feed bears ought to be recycled; the bear begins to assume that people are all good for handouts, and when somebody doesn't feed him, he turns nasty. This is a problem mostly around certain national parks, and, given their congested traffic and Byzantine regulations, these places have become unattractive to most bikepackers anyway.

Bears have been known to rip into tents looking for food, so don't keep food in your tent in bear country—hang it from a high tree limb by a nylon line. Thinking back, I've never bothered to do this, and I spend ridiculous amounts of time in bear country, yet I've never been bothered—though raccoons have scratched around the tent a few times. The bears where I hang out haven't been fed or otherwise led to believe that people exist to feed them. Still, this is one of those cases of "do as I say, not as I do"—I ought to quit sleeping with food in the tent, period.

The grizzly is a wholly different matter. This great, powerful, magnificent creature considers himself *numero uno* on his home turf and may swat the occasional human just to make a point. Obviously, this is one endangered species that declines to go quietly. Good for him. But if you should cycle in grizzly country—and only a very small bit of their very limited U.S. range is negotiable by bicycle—give him a wide berth. A few cyclists in Idaho and Montana have reported seeing grizzlies crossing the road. No doubt, it's an inspiring sight, and one the rest of us can only envy.

One wild animal you'd better not mess with is the skunk. He just doesn't give a damn; he *knows* he's got the drop on you. If you encounter one, give him a respectfully wide berth, and make no sudden movements. If he begins to stamp his feet and glare at you while switching that beautiful tail, start backing away and try to get trees and bushes between you and the skunk. One night, back when I was a kid, I had a skunk come right into camp and go through my stuff looking for food while I sat shivering in a tree, which I had climbed with astonishing agility even though it was dark. I'd do it again if the situation came up. Get a whiff, just once, of a dog that's been sprayed; you'll see.

Any wild animal that behaves strangely—especially one that shows no fear and comes straight at you—*must* be presumed to have rabies. Get away from it at all costs.

Poisonous snakes constitute an overrated hazard, except perhaps in a few limited areas, chiefly desert and swamp regions. If you watch where you put your hands and feet, and where you sit, you'll be fine. Be especially cautious when dipping water from a stream or lake—the shoreline is a good place for snakes, and you'll have your bare hands right down there in biting range. Snakes are basically very nervous, timid creatures and will run if they can. They are also useful animals, destroyers of rats, and very beautiful if looked at with open eyes. So do not harm them, ever.

Even if you should be bitten, the chance of fatal results is very low. Statistics show that nearly everyone recovers, except children, very old people, drunks, and those with heart trouble or allergic reactions. Still, a little snakebite kit is worth carrying along.

The hairy tarantula is a coward, and his bite is no worse than a wasp sting. A black widow is something else, but they are a problem chiefly around old houses—watch where you put your hands if you go poking around old home sites or abandoned barns.

With the exception of dogs, animals generally pose no danger to the cycle camper. Indeed, for most people, the chance to see wildlife is one of the greatest attractions of outdoor travel.

Of course, anything can be dangerous under sufficiently freakish circumstances; I once had a bad fall when a flock of birds suddenly flew up off the road in my face and momentarily blinded me.

Hostiles

If birds sometimes fly too low, humans sometimes fly too high.

This is one of those things I hate to bring up at all, because in most cases the danger has been greatly exaggerated, and some people have become almost paranoid. Yet honesty compels the admission: If you ride a bicycle around this country, there is a fair chance—not a high probability, but a fair chance—that sooner or later you will encounter hostility and perhaps worse. Not just the honk-and-curse business on the highway; most aggressive drivers are perfectly ordinary people when not behind the wheel. I'm talking about people who resent you for no apparent reason, except that you look different, you're doing something they don't understand, you're clearly from another area or a different racial or ethnic group, or some such cause.

Generally this takes the form of open but nearly silent hostility—dirty looks, or deliberately rude service at a cafe or store, and perhaps an occasional shouted insult or loud remark. Groups of young louts with nothing better to do than hang around a roadside rest area, campground, or small-town square may amuse themselves by surrounding you while you make camp or eat lunch, and ask you a lot of smartass questions amid general guffawing. They might drive past you on the road and shout various pleasantries. These things are infuriating, of course, but they're no worse than much more common incidents of the same kind in urban areas. The obstreperous idle young are with us wherever and however we go (and have always been, it would seem; see the Old Testament account of Elijah, a great shaman who spoke with birds and bears and knew how to deal with small-town punks. If you can figure out a way to travel with a couple of bears . . . but I digress).

In a rarer but more unsettling type of incident, cyclists, like other minority travelers (hitchhikers, motorcyclists, and walkers), sometimes come upon small, usually isolated towns where *everybody* seems hostile and bitter, and even the cops try to make trouble. I've had this experience a few times, as have others of my acquaintance—Louisiana, Texas, and Kansas seem to have an unusual number of little towns like this, and some parts of northern Colorado—and I don't know the reason for it. If you find yourself in such a place, stay very cool and get out fast.

On very, very rare occasions, a cyclist may face actual violence. This is nearly always an urban phenomenon, with theft the motive, but there have reportedly been instances of attacks against cyclists on country roads. While there are a few stories of unprovoked, totally unexpected violence against cyclists—by, no doubt, psychotics—this sort of event has to be considered as one of those X factors of the human condition. I mean, you could just as easily be walking down a street in your hometown and be blown away by a crazed sniper, go to the beach and get eaten by a shark, be struck by lightning, catch a rare, incurable disease—or the crazy people who run our world could start a war and blow us *all* to confetti, as far as that goes. Some things you just can't allow for or predict, so there's no point in worrying about them. While riding a bike along a quiet country road, you're certainly less likely to encounter homidical nuts than in most cities.

Much more often, when a cyclist gets involved in a violent brush with hostiles, it is as the climax of an escalating pattern. A common example: A carload of beer-swilling young rednecks pass a cyclist on a country road. They honk, hoot various derisive epithets, and perhaps go so far as to toss an empty beer can, which may or may not miss. Cyclist, justifiably enraged, responds with a finger gesture and perhaps some nouns, adverbs, and adjectives of his/her own. Car screeches to halt and occupants emerge. Loud confrontation ensues, leading to fist fight or worse. Alternatively, car makes U-turn, comes back, and attempts to force cyclist into ditch, or some other sociopathic manifestation.

Well, what *do* you do? It's very hard to tell the cyclist that he ought to just ride on and ignore them, because all he's going to do is get it kicked off, and yet, on the other hand, not many people have any business trying to fight two or three guys at once. (Cowboy-movie notions of "one on one" or "fair fight" have absolutely no relationship to reality anywhere I've ever been; the Hell's Angels, with their "all on one" rule, merely articulate a universal rule of their peer group.) Even in a fairly well-matched situation, you're going to get banged up at least a little, which you don't need—to say nothing of possible trouble with the law.

I've tried to think of what I should write here, and I've drawn a blank. Look: I'm 6'3", I weigh 200 pounds, I've spent most of my life among fairly rough people, and I used to be the regional correspondent for *Black Belt*. For all I know, you weigh 125 pounds with boots on, had mono last year, and have never even seen a serious fight in your life. So who the hell am I, and where the hell do I get off, to tell you how you ought to deal with a potentially violent situation? No way; you're going to have to work this one out for yourself.

The one bit of advice I offer is to keep your mouth shut, unless you seriously intend to fight. Never bluster, bluff, or threaten. Most of these characters are merely arrogant bullies with infantile ideas of humor, rather than outright sadists or psychos. They do not see themselves as truly bad people, just as a lot of good fellows out having fun. On another level, they are engaged in a very ancient custom whereby young males establish group status by getting tough with vulnerable outsiders. The one thing that turns them really ugly is any sort of empty bluff. The man who, in their terms, "talks big but won't fight," is at the bottom of their social hierarchy, and they consider themselves justified in anything they do to such a person.

This is particularly true of bluffing with a weapon. Most campers carry some kind of knife and might be tempted to brandish it to frighten off attackers. Unless the situation warrants the use of deadly force—an attack by an armed person being the only example the law would recognize—and you are prepared to go through with it, *and know how,* don't even think about it.

Most people, most of the time, are better advised to remain calm and ride on. An exceptional person may challenge such people and pull it off—the legendary Steve Woznick, a monumentally tough track racer who used to dominate the kilo event in the U.S., once took on three guys in a pickup truck and put all three in the hospital—and for all I know, you may be in that class. (If you are, you'll find that these people tend to give you a very wide berth; they have an unerring radar for detecting the unbullyable. The three rednecks just mentioned had just attacked a bunch of young riders and didn't see Woz coming until it was too late. . . .) Be realistic and don't get any ideas about whipping a carload of guys because you once took a few karate lessons.

Of course, if you are actually attacked despite all you can do, then fight like hell and at least make them pay for their fun.

With your helmet protecting your head and your muscles tuned by hard cycling, you can probably give a good account of yourself. Unless you actually enjoy combat, though, try to avoid letting it go that far. It's usually possible.

Women may be the victims of a considerably more dangerous and despicable form of assault. Much as it pains me to admit it, a woman should think twice about cycling alone in today's world. I have no answers; the problem is a gigantic one that affects women in all activities of life, not merely on bicycles—in fact, you're probably safer riding a bike than walking down some city streets.

Weapons are mostly illegal. Given the statistics and the lousy level of enforcement, I could never bring myself to condemn or criticize any woman who carried a gun or other lethal weapon, but you have to be practical. In nearly any state, a gun on your person is good for a trip to jail. It's not worth it.

Disabling agents, such as Mace or CS gas, are legal in some states, and possibly worth carrying, since they also serve very well as dog repellent. I always carry a can of CS gas clipped to the side pocket of my handlebar bag. Check the law, because these things are illegal in many states. Chemical sprays may be useful if you have ethical objections to violence, since they do not cause any permanent bodily harm, merely a temporary discomfort and disability.

Speaking of the law, on a few occasions, cyclists have reported having had difficulties with cops—mostly small-town heat or county mounties, but a couple of bad-apple state troopers have turned up also. Usually, such hassles take the form of a lot of rambling questioning, including personal stuff you have no obligation to answer, demands to see identification, and the like. Legally, you don't have to put up with this crap, but on a practical basis, it's probably useless to object, since you'll almost certainly get hauled into the local slammer for an overnight stay just to teach you a lesson. You may sue them cross-eyed later on for violating your civil rights, but that won't fix your ruined vacation. They may also retaliate by slapping you with a citation for some nonexistent traffic violation and perjure themselves blind before a speed-trap judge. There's just no way you can win. Keep a lid on your temper, get away as quickly as you can, and when you get home, you can see if there isn't some authority or regulatory body to whom you can complain.

Every now and then, a cop may issue orders—tell you to get off the pavement, for example—for which he has absolutely no legal justification or authority. You must decide how far you want to push this. Sometimes he's just bluffing and will back down if you cite the appropriate law to him (memorizing the code numbers of state laws relating to bikes can really pay off—I even carry a xeroxed copy of the most important ones in my wallet), and, in the case of state troopers, demanding his badge number may help. Then again, in the absence of witnesses, it may get you knocked on your butt. Readers of Larry McMurtry's novels may remember the Texas Ranger who said, "Out here on this highway there's a law against anything me and my partner don't like"—a principle cherished by many badge-wearers, not only in Texas. (Don't misinterpret any of the above remarks; my own experience has been that the great majority of cops of all kinds are quite friendly and helpful toward people on bicycles, even when they may not be at all that way toward the general public. Something about a bicycle seems to shout innocence and honesty. Most cops seem to consider cyclists a breed of harmless eccentrics, like shopping-bag ladies. Our image in this country is a pretty good one—try to keep it that way, in your dealings with the people you meet.)

People worry too much about this whole problem of dealing with hostile locals; in fact, the main reason I brought it up was to put it in perspective. Many cyclists even refuse to wear helmets or proper cycling costume, or change clothes before going to a store or visiting a town because they fear they might alienate people. This is silly; if they aren't bothered by the basic fact that you're traveling by bicycle, your clothes won't matter. More often a helmet serves as a catalyst for a conversation— "You mean that thing will go fast enough that you need that?", followed by a general agreement about how badly some people drive. Being cool and avoiding conflict is one thing; skulking furtively around, hoping nobody will notice you, is merely Uncle-Tomming, which *nobody* respects.

Most trouble of this sort is like traffic: It's best solved by avoiding it. If you find a campground that's been taken over by noisy drunks, go elsewhere. (By the way, don't make the common middle-class assumption that violent or vicious behavior is confined to poor people and racial minorities. In my book, the scariest thing on the road is a bunch of boozed-up college boys from a certain type of fraternity—they sometimes have absolutely no sense of restraint whatever and will behave in ways that would appall a Hell's Angel. I suggest that you avoid public camp-grounds located near college campuses on Friday and Saturday nights; they can be bad, bad news.)

Many cyclists worry about encountering outlaw motorcy-clists. No doubt many of these people are dangerous, particularly to unaccompanied women, but I've got to say that the ones I've met while cycling have been friendly enough and usually rather interested in what I was doing. They seemed to sense that we shared, in some bizarre way, an alienation from the four-wheeled consumer culture—that a bicycle was, in a sense, an "outlaw" vehicle too.

In fact, a good friend of mine, cycling through California in the 1960s, fell in with a group of Hell's Angels at a roadside cafe, and hit it off so well with them—they were impressed that anyone would be brave enough to ride such a frail machine down a busy highway—that they made him an honorary member, an unusual distinction, if a dubious one.

Out of their saddles, into the dirt,
and thereby hangs a tale.

—William Shakespeare,
The Taming of the Shrew

CHAPTER **11**

Rough Stuff

Rough-stuff cycling—riding on unpaved roads, dirt trails, anywhere the pavement doesn't go—while a respected and venerable branch of the cycle-touring tradition in England, is still regarded by most U.S. bikies as something of a stunt. If you talk about it much around some of the more precious members of the Serious Touring Set, you may get a reputation as a wild, cowboyish, rather infantile adventurer with no regard for life, limb, or bicycle—a bit of a ruffian, actually. . . .

As I noted earlier in this book, there is a widespread notion in America that the modern lightweight bicycle is at home only on smooth, hard road surfaces. If a race, tour, or other organized ride is routed over a short stretch of gravel, or even a less-than-perfect blacktop, loud and bitter are the complaints. "If you've got decent equipment that you care at all about," I heard one fellow sniff after a slightly bumpy bit of country pavement, "it's unreasonable to be expected to ride over this sort of road." If your equipment can't take a few bumps, I thought but didn't say, it can't be all that hot to start with.

Even the small but growing subculture of dirt-road and mountain-trail cyclists in some areas, while representative of a very healthy trend, mostly seems to view off-roading as a kind of challenging sport engaged in for its own sake rather than as a natural and normal extension of cycling. Very few American dirt cyclists seem to be interested in actually going anywhere or doing any extended touring, though this attitude does seem to be changing a little. Most of them appear to be involved in a kind of pedal-powered version of dirt-trail motorcycling.

It's too bad; people don't know what they're missing. Once you learn to ride safely and easily over unpaved roads and to negotiate certain obstacles, you open up a whole fantastic world of outdoor adventure. (Learning to do this is mostly a matter of developing confidence—like learning to ride a bike in the first place, the big barrier is in making yourself believe it's possible.) Many of the finest wild and semiwild areas in the country, though well off the paved highways, are crossed by gravel and dirt roads, logging tracks, and the like, and most are easily negotiated by bicycle. Often, vehicle traffic is light or even nonexistent, and fine, private campsites are around every turn. You can travel such places with *any* reasonably sturdy, lightweight touring bicycle—you *don't* have to have a specialized "mountain bike" or cyclo-cross machine, if you're willing to use a little judgment and technique—and you can carry along your camping outfit to make yourself self-contained and independent.

I'd like to repeat something I said in the introduction: Your bicycle, improbable though this may sound, has the potential to be a full-fledged, backcountry vehicle like the canoe or pack horse, to say nothing of such wilderness-despoiling horrors as snowmobiles, trail motorcycles, and jeeps.

Don't back off from this chapter because it all seems too difficult or too hard on the bike. Sure, you'll probably want to make your first bikepacking trips along paved roads—a good idea, in fact—but sooner or later you really ought to consider expanding your horizons. If you never get off of the blacktop and away from the developed campsites and manicured landscapes, you'll be depriving yourself of the ultimate bikepacking experience—and life is too short to go depriving yourself of experiences, if you can help it.

Here's how you do it.

Bumping and Grinding ─────────

In the main, rough-stuff riding technique consists simply of very good regular cycling technique. It involves much the same skills of keeping your balance, maintaining a smooth pedal motion, and controlling the bike in such a way that it feels like an extension of yourself. You just have to pay a little closer attention to what you're doing on rough stuff. This is especially true with regular lightweight bikes with narrow-section 27″ tires; the various 26″ balloon-tire bikes are more forgiving.

The most important trick to rough-road cycling, in my opinion, is a technique I find rather difficult to describe; for want of anything better, I call it "sitting loose" on the bike. Some of the Japanese martial arts use a term that can be translated as "sinking your weight." If you sit on the bike in a very tight, rigid manner, due, perhaps, to nervousness or a desire to have full control of the machine, you actually raise the center of gravity of the whole bike-human complex. You will be much more likely to lose control or balance, and have a harder time catching yourself if you do. Your body will be so tense and stiff that the shock of bumps, holes, and rocks will be more likely to damage the bike, and if you should fall, the chances of injury increase.

You know those little novelty dolls with the round, weighted bottoms—you push them over, and they bob back up? Form a kind of mental picture of yourself as one of those dolls. *Will* your weight downwards—there's no better way to put it, that I can think of—and try to relax your upper body as much as you can without losing control of the bike. Concentrate on keeping your weight low and back over that rear wheel. Resist the impulse to lean forward onto the handlebars, or you may induce a skid.

Of course, this is not to say that you just slump there like a bag of potatoes. You must keep a good firm grip on the bars and be ready to respond to all of the bike's movements without hesitation. What is needed is a kind of *dynamic* tension, so that your body is springy and resilient without stiffness.

It is this relaxed yet dynamic physical state that allows a really fine rough-stuff cyclist—especially a champion cyclocrosser—to *flow* over incredibly difficult, uneven ground as if he and the bike had the ability to become partly liquid. It all sounds very mystical and abstruse, but one day it will come to you, and then suddenly you will feel that the bike is no longer a mechanical device you are using, but an extension of your will, almost a part of your body.

Probably it is unnecessary to advise you to go rather slowly on rough roads; few of us could get up much speed even if we tried. Keep gears fairly low, but high enough so that you can get some pressure on the pedals. This will give you more control than when you freewheel, though of course you don't have much choice on downhill slopes. Go through turns slowly, so that you don't have to lean too far—leaning is a chancy business on gravel. Avoid sudden stops—sometimes you have no choice, given the kind of thing that occasionally shows up in your path, but look ahead and try to slow down gradually when a stop seems imminent.

Be extremely cautious on steep downhills—grades tend to be very steep indeed on unpaved backwoods roads, which are usually intended for trucks and jeeps and may even have been laid out with horses in mind. Use those brakes and go down as slowly as you can; the normal perils of downhilling are intensified here. When you have to freewheel, keep your weight on the pedals to lower the center of gravity.

Going over a bump, rise *slightly*—not the honking position, just out of the saddle a little way—and put your weight on the pedals, keeping the cranks horizontal. As the bike moves under you, following the contour of the ground, keep your weight equally distributed between both feet, so that the bike can "rock" and the bump doesn't get any direct resistance to damage the frame. Your arms can also help here; as the front wheel goes over the bump, lift slightly up on the bars—*slightly,* not the "wheelie" routine—to help the wheel over the bump. When the front wheel is over, immediately rock forward onto your extended arms, elbows bent to act as shock absorbers, so that there is less weight on the back wheel as it encounters the bump. You can combine this trick simultaneously with the technique of "rocking" on the pedals. This all sounds more athletic and difficult than it really is. These movements are mostly quite small, involving shifts of weight rather than violent gymnastics.

The basic idea here is to reduce or eliminate any direct opposition of forces—points at which your body is thumping down on the bike in one direction and a bump in the road is slamming up at it in the other, so that the bike frame and wheels are subjected to possibly damaging forces. The whole technique quickly becomes automatic with even a little practice.

Much of the secret to rough-stuff cycling lies in learning to "read the road" rather than in any special riding technique. You'll have to watch the road more carefully than when spinning down a paved highway. This doesn't mean riding along with your gaze glued to the road directly in front of you. In fact, this is bad practice. You need to keep an eye on what's coming up well ahead because of the need to avoid sudden stops or violent maneuvers. Learn to read warning signs, especially when you're off even the graded gravel roads—a dark patch up ahead on a dirt track, for example, means that the ground is probably wet, while an unusually light patch may mean loose and treacherous sand. When riding along a path across a meadow where the way ahead is overgrown with grass, beware of the spot that seems unusually green and lush-looking; chances are it's wet and therefore soft. And so on.

Actually, a good, hard-packed dirt track is easier to ride than some badly potholed blacktop roads, let alone gravel. If the path is high and well drained and there has been no rain recently, dirt can be a joy on which to ride. One of my favorite off-the-road routes is a dirt road along the top of a levee. Along the big rivers of the South and Midwest, there are places where you can ride for mile after mile along the levee tops. The roads are clear and little traveled, being mostly for the use of emergency crews during floods, and you've got the place to yourself except for the herons and blackbirds. Riding on this kind of clean, hard-packed dirt is not greatly different from riding on a paved highway, except that speeds are lower.

Gravel, especially fresh or little-used gravel, is tougher. Loose, thick layers of gravel form a very yielding, sliding surface in which bike tires can slip and swerve. If a road has been very recently covered with gravel, all you can do is try to hold a steady course and speed, and hope it doesn't go on too long—which it usually doesn't. Luckily, except when it's very fresh, gravel tends to work its way into long humps and leave bare, hard dirt where car and truck tires have pushed it aside. Ride in these channellike depressions and the footing is usually secure. On occasion, you may have to "change lanes"—if a bad pothole or mudhole shows up ahead—and this must be done carefully, because when you swing across the ridges of gravel, your traction and balance are momentarily very poor.

Older gravel roads that are not well maintained tend to turn into bare earth and rock as the gravel is gradually worn or washed away. Such roads usually offer good, hard surfaces as far as traction goes but are almost always badly rutted and potholed. In mountain country with certain types of rock formations, a worn-down dirt road may have actual ridges of bedrock forming humps across it; one of these is an occasion to come up off the saddle a few inches and use the dynamic "rocking" technique, rather that just slamming across the bump. Such roads look worse than they are; your bike, after all, only makes a track a couple of inches across, and you can almost always pick a relatively clean line through even the most washed-out sections. In fact, a good rough-road cyclist can often find a fairly smooth course through spots that bounce jeep drivers out of their seats! Despite their roughness, these older roads with their bare surfaces are far easier to ride on than newer ones with raw, fresh, deeply-graded gravel, so if there is a choice of routes, your best way might be quite different from the one you'd choose if you were driving a car.

Mud is something else again. Dirt and gravel roads sometimes get muddy, and this is unpleasant, but as long as there is a hard bed right under a thin layer of mud, it's not too bad. You just have to ride carefully, much as you'd ride on a road with patches of ice. But when it comes to actual deep mud—not me. Some people are very good at riding in it. I get off and walk the bike through it. And curse a great deal. I hate mud.

The Obstacle Course

Of course, all of the preceding was based on the idea that you'd be riding the bike along something resembling a clear road, however grim the details. A few rough-stuff fanatics even go beyond this and probe into roadless country, along animal paths and logging tracks. Such bushwhacking usually involves very little actual riding. More often, the bicycle is simply pushed laboriously along, even carried over obstacles.

If you're gutsy enough to try that sort of thing, there's not much for me to add—anyway, it goes beyond the perimeters of what most of us would call cycling. The bicycle becomes just a kind of wagon or wheelbarrow. Now and then a cowpath or a fresh logging cut is clear enough to ride, but usually the brush and weeds grow over the path so deeply that cycling is virtually impossible. (Loggers, cutting a road for a one-shot operation, with no intention to return, do a very minimal job of it, just a track along which a truck can force its way—though if bulldozers have been along, you may have something that, after a fashion, you can ride over.)

One exception is abandoned farm country. In some areas, particularly in certain officially designated Wilderness Areas, the land has been grazed for years before being taken over by the government. In such places, there are often good-sized open pastures, with the ground hard packed and rocky from extended overgrazing. Old cattle paths across such pastures are very easy to cycle, though you may occasionally be stopped by thorn bushes. One of my favorite places is a stretch along the upper Buffalo in the Ozarks, now a Wilderness Area, where a person could probably spend years studying the old farm sites and fallen-down houses. I've never gone there except on foot, but I can think of several points where a competent cyclist could penetrate and ride around in dry weather.

Even when riding on less desperate roads, a cyclist may occasionally have to abandon the saddle for more pedestrian efforts. A dirt or gravel road may have been washed out, leaving a gully to cross, or there may be a fence to get over (watch the trespassing—some landowners are *very* difficult about this) or an unrideably steep gravel pitch.

Of course, nobody needs written instructions on how to walk along pushing a bicycle. (Though I'll pass along one tip—in an emergency situation that forces you to walk the bike a really considerable distance, a mile or more, take a minute, get out your wrench, and remove the pedal on the side where you'll be walking. Then the damned thing won't lacerate your shin every other step.) If you have to carry it across a ditch or other unrideable, unpushable barrier, lift it using the cyclocrosser's technique: arm through the main triangle, top tube resting on the shoulder, hand gripping the handlebars so the wheel doesn't flop around, other hand extended for balance. Usually, unless you're pretty strong, you'll have to unload the bike first in order to carry it any real distance. Now is when you'll be glad you chose a pannier and handlebar bag set that can be removed and replaced easily under all conditions—or very sorry you went for some fiddly, fragile artifice that refuses to yield to your wet, cold, muddy fingers.

Before lifting that bike, *unload,* no matter how much trouble it is, if there is any question at all whether you can handle it. Injuring your back or tearing a shoulder tendon is bad enough anywhere, but who needs it on a dirt road 20 miles back into the woods?

Swollen streams can block a road, even a fairly good one. On backcountry dirt roads with fords rather than bridges, a sudden shower can turn a minor creek into a serious obstacle. Be very, very cautious and conservative about crossing a stream with or without your bike. Wading across a simple, little, ankle-deep brook is no big deal, and sometimes you can even ride across (though it's a good way to get water into your bearings). If the stream is moving rapidly, however, especially if it's in flood, even rather shallow water can have enough force to knock you off your feet. If you must cross, it may help to wade across first without the bike—use a pole or staff to feel for the bottom and provide "third leg" stability. You can usually find a fallen limb to serve. Also rig a safety line of rope or parachute cord across the stream. Then you can go back and work your way across with the bike and the gear, using the line as a kind of handrail. Unload the bike if the water is at all dangerous; make two or three trips to get all of the stuff. If it's cold, or the water is cold, take a break afterward and fix a hot drink.

If you should fall while crossing a deep or fast stream with your bike, *save yourself*—don't hang onto the bike if you need both hands to save your own life; the bike just isn't worth it. (You can always recover it when the water recedes in summer.)

This whole stream-crossing business is very dangerous. I happen to be a pretty experienced whitewater boater, and I can attest to the fact that moving water exerts a power all out of proportion to its possibly innocuous appearance. There is such a thing as knee-deep water in which a big, strong man may be unable to stay on his feet, and it's not just the rivers, because some of those tiny mountain brooks, when swollen by heavy rain, are like fire hoses. You only need a few inches of water to drown if you can't get your face out of it—if you fall and hit your head on a rock and are alone, you might drown in a couple of inches, so wear your helmet when crossing rocky streams. Better yet, see if there isn't another route, or make camp and wait for the water to go down. If it's just a spring-rain flood, it shouldn't take long.

Actually, a broad, slow-moving river can be much simpler to cross—quite often there are shallow crossings that you can wade with little danger. I strongly suggest that you try this only with others along, unless you can clearly see the bottom all the way across.

Navigation

Rough-stuff cycling is the one branch of bicycle touring in which it is possible to get well and truly lost—not just confused and astray on the wrong road, but "where-the-hell-*am*-I" lost. While some roads follow reasonably logical routes—along a ridge or deep valley, or parallel to a stream—and can usually be followed with ease, dirt roads through forest areas often twist and wind and intertwine in a highly confusing manner. Intersections and forks in the road may not be marked, or the signs may have been defaced by slob hunters who used them as targets. And there may well be no one to ask for directions.

A first-class set of maps, a good-quality compass, and the knowledge to use both must be regarded as essential equipment for any bikepacker venturing off of the main paved highways. Ordinary highway maps do not show roads of this type, and, anyway, the scale is far too huge to be of any help. You'll have to get something in a suitable scale, showing all or most of the backcountry roads. Don't skimp or get stingy on maps. The good ones don't cost that much, and without them you can wander around the boondocks all day and never get where you want to go.

In my own state (Arkansas), the Highway Department each year issues a set of maps of the various counties—50¢ apiece currently, a bargain—showing every little dirt and gravel road, and even individual houses and buildings. Well, they show almost every road; they usually miss one or two, but nobody's perfect. You can have a ball just studying these things—you find out about whole networks of roads through areas you had thought to be relatively trackless. I would assume that other states have something equivalent, though I have never had occasion to check.

Even better are the contour maps issued by the U.S. Geological Survey (USGS). (See the back of this book for information on getting these.) Not only do they show obscure forest roads and individual dwellings, they also contain a wealth of other information on the terrain—good to know when setting up your gearing for the trip—types of land, such as cleared, forest, swamp, and so on, and even sometimes things like fence lines. On some of the newer ones in the big, detailed scale, the information is almost indecent. You have to learn to read the symbols, but they provide a sheet that explains all. Don't go into any seriously wild country without these. For sheer information content to weight of paper, they must outdo all other printed matter.

The one real problem is that these maps are, in many cases, several years out of date. In forested country, dirt roads of the type we are looking for are often cleared and graded virtually overnight—even a map correct as of January may be inaccurate by November. Abandoned roads can sometimes be swallowed by the forest in surprisingly few years. I know of a lot of these; I cut some of them myself, a couple of decades ago, and now you can hardly find them. So, if you can get something like the Highway Department maps I described above, do so, and use them as a supplement to your USGS quads. With these in combination, you shouldn't go far wrong.

This may sound elementary, but some people forget: Make sure your compass is clear of your steel bike frame before checking directions!

Rough-Stuff Bikes

As I say, any well-made, touring-type bicycle can be taken into the rough, if the rider is willing to be careful. If you get your kicks banging wildly over rocks, ruts, and humps, plowing down long, washed-out grades covered with sliding scree and gravel, trying to jump the bike over obstacles, and occasionally falling on your behind in the dirt, all with a fine disregard for the effect on bike or bod, then there are specialized machines made for this sort of thing. Or you may want to try to build one yourself. I do not put this approach down, exactly, though it does seem to raise some questions about carrying camping equipment, since I can't imagine any arrangement of racks or bags that would withstand this sort of treatment. (Also, the klutzy performance of such a bike on the highway will rather restrict your range of operation.) It's just that I don't know much about it; you're on your own.

It seems to me that many dirt-road and backcountry riders are trying to turn the bicycle into a kind of two-wheeled, pedal-powered jeep. This is fine, as far as it goes. I applaud anything that extends the potential of the bicycle, or any other environmentally sound machine. My own approach, and the only one I can really talk about with any authority, has always been to treat the bike more like a very agile, sure-footed pony, that's able to pick its way almost delicately over tricky ground. Or we could compare the two approaches to backcountry cycling with the whitewater scene—the rafter, bashing and slogging his way through the rapids, relying on the size and sturdiness of his raft to get him through, and the kayaker, threading his tiny craft through complex passages and surviving by agility and skill. Both approaches are valid; in some measure, it seems to come down to personality.

In this book, I'm primarily writing for people who are just getting into bicycle camping, and few such people will want to get involved with anything as specialized as the mountain-bike and super-trashmo scenes just yet. I believe that the average reader of this book either owns, or expects to get, a fairly basic, straightforward bicycle that's suitable for a wide range of uses, so I have oriented the material in this direction.

There may be, however, readers who are getting very interested in the rough-stuff end of things and think they might like to get heavily into it. If this is so with you, then you probably wonder whether there are modifications that you should or could make to your bike to make it more suitable for this type of riding without going to the extreme of creating a specialized machine. Conceivably, you may be even thinking of building a bike for rough-stuff camping and touring, but prefer to keep it within the basic road-bike pattern. So, while in general the remarks on bikes and their parts presented earlier are valid for this section (see Chapter One), a few points might be worth making.

Any decent frame, solidly made and with a reasonably confortable and stable layout, will do fine. The main thing is to avoid the extremely stiff, somewhat unstable, criterium-racing frame, which will be hard to handle, and certain, fairly uncommon, touring frames that have very low bottom brackets. (With a low bottom bracket, you increase the chance of hitting your cranks or chainwheels on rocks, bumps, and other obstacles, and your chain will pick up more mud.) Usually a rough-stuff bike is considered to need a long wheelbase for stability and comfort, yet it can go the other way. I use an old Gitane road-racing frame, with fairly slack angles but quite a shortish wheelbase, and I find that the added agility and quicker turning qualities allow me to pick my way through rough patches and dodge rocks and potholes. I used to do the same sort of thing with a long-wheelbase touring bike, and it was indeed more comfortable and forgiving, but I hit a lot more bumps and humps. It was like the country-and-western classic, "Give Me Forty Acres and I'll Turn This Rig Around." What I'm getting at is that something that seems to be a drawback may offer an advantage that cancels out the other, so don't worry too much about frame geometry.

A lightweight modern frame, especially one made of double-butted tubing, correctly lugged and brazed, is much stronger than it looks; it is actually stronger than the apparently rugged clunker, because the metal is of far better quality. The massive construction of the clunker is made necessary to begin with by this inferior metal. I bring this up because people are sometimes nervous about taking their good, light bikes onto rough roads, fearing that they'll damage them; believe me, any good bike is far tougher than you'd believe. The only quality frames too frail for rough stuff are those special racing frames made from very thin-walled tubing, and I hardly think anyone is likely to be tempted to take one of them off of the pavement.

If you do want to build a bike that you can use for regular touring and rough stuff too, a good starting point would be a modified cyclocross frame. (Check with any good custom-frame builder, such as Al Eisentraut or Jim Redcay.) The 'cross bike, with its high bottom bracket, long but not sloppy wheelbase and rear triangle, generous fork rake, and overall strong construction, is in many ways the ideal bikepacking frame. It is laid out so that your weight comes more over the rear wheel, which is important for balance and traction on loose surfaces, and it will have braze-ons for cantilever brakes—more of which in a moment. The main problems involve a few braze-ons that you'd probably like to have, and the unfortunate fact that many fine 'cross frames are made with Campagnolo racing dropouts, which do not have eyelets for your rack—and none of those cobbled-up substitutes is strong enough for rough stuff. If you explain your needs, any competent 'cross-frame builder can easily substitute dropouts with eyelets, and braze on fittings to anchor your carrier up top. (A very few top people can take an existing frame and braze on fittings, and even change dropouts, without ruining the temper of the metal—but don't let your buddy who got a torch for Christmas talk you into letting him "customize" your frame.)

As to the stuff you hang on the frame, most standard components are entirely adequate. Short-armed (165mm.) cranks will give much better ground clearance; you can pedal them over ground where you'd have to freewheel with anything else. Lyotard's steel platform pedals work well for this kind of cycling and are extremely strong. Many cyclocrossers take two toe clips and rivet them together for a double-strong clip that is not easily deformed in rough conditions; it's not a bad idea.

I have already gone into the gearing matter; suffice it to say that here is where you will really do well to use small chainwheels to get your low gears, give up the high gears, and use a fairly small cog cluster (biggest cog 28 teeth) with a compact racing-type derailleur. Big clusters and long-armed derailleurs are easily damaged by brush, rocks, and mud, and the long arm of the touring derailleur dangles the chain down close to the road where it gets covered with dirt and grit. Best derailleur I've seen or used for this kind of thing is the tiny Huret Jubilee, which is compact and light, though a bit tricky to install. Whatever you do, use those handlebar-end shifters; this is one situation that definitely calls for both hands on the bars at all times. I wouldn't ride dirt with anything else. Top cyclocross coaches agree.

As you've guessed by now, I think we can learn a great deal from the cyclocross branch of racing—not to be confused with "bicycle motocross" and similar kid games—and, in fact, if you're really determined to become the next Ian Hibell or cycle to the Arctic Circle or whatever, you could do worse then get into 'cross racing during the winter, just for the training. Those guys can do incredible things with bikes—and the bikes are very light, high-quality racing machines, not clunkers. (There is a probably apocryphal but still apt story about a U.S. 'cross team that showed up at the World Championships, checked into the dorm, and went down to the cafeteria, which was in the basement. They knew they were in trouble when they met the East German team riding up the stairs. . . .)

Cantilever brakes, if you can get the fittings brazed on without ruining the frame, are far and away the best for rough stuff, especially if there's any mud. They leave a lot of clearance for mud and dirt and twigs, yet develop tremendous stopping leverage. 'Crossers use them by choice, so a cyclocross frame will have the braze-ons, or should.

Steel rims aren't really necessary if you ride carefully and don't overload the bike. I ride very rough roads with a pair of inexpensive Araya alloy rims, and even my couple of hundred overweight pounds hasn't damaged them. The strength of a wheel is largely determined by the skill of the person who built it, anyway, not the materials used. So use sturdy hi-tensile steel spokes, preferably plain gauge, such as Union or Torrington. Stay away from those pretty, thin, stainless-steel spokes made for racing, because they break very easily. As for tires, use a sturdy clincher, such as Michelin 50s or Schwinn LeTours (my hands-down choice).

Your carrier must be very, very strong and solidly mounted. Here is where I really endorse those light steel English carriers, such as Butler and Karrimor. Any bags durable enough for ordinary cycle camping will be all right here—the bags themselves don't really take any particular additional strain—though you might like to pick a color that doesn't show dirt. Keep the bag size down, because big, fat, drooping panniers, especially those with buckle straps and flaps, pick up brush and dirt. Also, in view of the additional stresses imposed on the handlebars, I'd caution you to be extra conservative about loading that handlebar bag.

As for what to wear, regular cycling clothes are fine, but in brush country or on gravel roads, you may prefer to wear long pants. Bare legs get whipped by brush reaching out from the roadside, and grit and gravel thrown back from the front wheel may sting the skin. Long pants also give you a bit more protection in a fall.

Might as well pause here and say it—yes, there *is* a bit more chance of falling in this type of cycling. It's not that much higher than any other type of riding, but it does exist. The falls tend to be of the relatively harmless sort—nasty spills on rock ground can bang you up a bit, but your speed is almost always so low that you're in little danger of a really serious injury. The lack of automotive traffic on most backcountry dirt roads makes it unlikely that you'll have to worry about the worst accident of all, being hit by a car. So, on balance, rough stuff is actually safer.

Because of the chance of a fall among the loose rocks and protruding roots that abound, a full-bowl helmet should be worn in most cases. I remove mine when riding on rockless dirt, such as one of those levee roads, but that's about the only exception. For rough stuff, I like the MSR; the big scoops of the Bell sometimes snag overhanging limbs and twigs, though this is admittedly a rather picky point.

Bata-type cycling shoes, or joggers, are the logical choice for rough stuff. Cleated racing shoes do not work well at all. I've tried them—when I was racing, occasionally I used to yield to temptation while out on training rides and go haring off down this or that dirt road in full racing regalia. (You really learn to ride that kind of stuff when you're doing it with narrow, hard, expensive silk tubular tires!) It never failed. Sooner or later I had to get off or put my foot down, and the cleats instantly got jammed with mud, dirt, or gravel, while bits of topsoil filtered in through the vent holes in the shoes and guaranteed some blisters on the way home. Mud is especially bad for cycling shoes; I pretty well ruined a pair of Adidas racing shoes, which are not cheap, in the Delta country of Arkansas and Mississippi.

Just one more thing, while we're off the road: *Never ride your bike on a hiking trail.* I mean a real hiking trail. In some places, the authorities have routed hikers down "trails" that are merely old dirt roads, and you may feel free to cycle them at will. In most places, nobody says anything if you take a bike places where "vehicles" are not supposed to go. It is generally recognized that bicycles, being silent, slow, and odorless, are not what the regulators had in mind. I've cycled in several officially designated "wilderness" regions, closed to cars, motorcycles, and horses, and nobody's ever bothered me about it—though I suppose an officious official could get tiresome if he wanted.

But a genuine hiking trail, made for the use of people on foot, should be left to hikers. They don't have many trails in this country, whereas we have thousands of miles of highways and streets to cycle; it's pretty unfair to invade their limited and shrinking territory. There is a worse problem: erosion. The hikers, with their lug-soled boots, already cause enough trouble, so that the famous Appalachian Trail needs to be renamed the Appalachian Trench in some areas. Bicycle tires chew up the topsoil in a particularly destructive way, creating little channels down which rain water and snow melt can pour, quickly eating away soil to form big ditches and gullies. Your innocent little bicycle track can, in time, turn into something as ugly as the Alaska Pipeline. Stay off the hiking trails with your bike—though if it's for a short distance, it might be okay to walk along and *push* the bike; without your weight, the tires won't dig in very deeply. If you see another cyclist about to make this mistake, get over there fast and explain the reasons to refrain. If he won't listen, then tell him there's a rabid bear on the trail.

*I only know one way of finding
out how far one can go, and that is by
setting out and getting there.*

—*Henri Bergson*

CHAPTER **12**

The Trip

So now you're ready to go do it to it. No doubt you feel it's about time. Where, then, to go? Perhaps you already have a destination in mind; indeed, you may have had a destination in mind before you began reading this book. By now you must have some idea of whether it's going to be a practicable goal, and what it's going to take for you to get there.

If you haven't yet chosen a destination, think over what you know of the geography of your region. Remember, we're talking about something with a lot more range than your feet—any area within a radius of two or three hundred miles of your home, provided you have the time and there are places to camp along the way, is within striking distance. You can just straddle your bike in front of your own house and hit the road. Even lacking campsites along the way, two or three stays in motels shouldn't be too painful financially.

If your part of the country has any special points of interest—famous mountains, waterfalls, natural formations, or National Parks—these might seem ideal, but be a bit cautious about seeking out well-known tourist attractions. You can find yourself in the equivalent of rush-hour freeway traffic just getting

234

there, and when you do arrive, you'll probably find that the heavy volume of public use has forced the authorities to set up labyrinthine regulations about where and when you can camp, build a fire, go potty-potty, and, probably, look at the scenery. ("Visitors with names beginning with A through M may look at the waterfall with the right eye only from 8:00 to 12:00; those beginning with N through Z—" Don't laugh, it's probably being printed up already.)

Anyway, heavy use is hard on the environment. We are, as we have so often been told, loving to death the few remnants of wilderness our forefathers didn't murder. There are once-beautiful hiking trails that have been worn into ditches a foot below the surrounding ground level, rivers that sometimes contain more canoes than water (one of my favorite rapids has recently been renamed "Take A Number"), and snowy slopes that resemble 42nd Street. Your bicycle's range and versatility should allow you to be more selective and to avoid the crowds.

One outstanding bikepacking possibility in many areas is the National Forest system. These forests are often crisscrossed with networks of very well graded dirt roads for the use of forestry crews (and, let's admit it, the timber hogs that your government has sold *your* trees to—if you visit any National Forest, be ready to see some things that will make you burn), and often you can camp pretty much where you please. The Forests are far less well known than the Parks, so you'll have less tourist pressure to contend with.

Consider your destination in the light of your time frame. A few of us can go just about when we like and stay as long as we please, but most people have only certain times available for extended trips—a vacation or break from school or work. This might be a very poor time to visit some places. Summer might be unpleasantly hot and dry, or spring might bring torrential rains. Also, tourist traffic varies wildly according to season. Some of the most heavily visited spots are virtually deserted during the off season. (Some public campgrounds and other facilities, too, are free of charge during the off-season months, though they charge very hefty fees in peak periods.)

Something I'd like to toss in here that's been bothering me for several chapters now. Don't be too heavily snowed under by the "backcountry" aspect of this book. I have tended to emphasize this side of bikepacking, suggesting equipment and techniques suitable for relatively wild country. (I avoid the term, "wilderness," here. Often applied to any reasonably unpopulated bit of woods or hills, this word properly should be restricted to true roadless areas in which human artifacts and vestiges of habitation are at a minimum. There are very few true wilderness areas left in the U.S., except for Alaska—and a gang of greed-heads are doing their best to invade that—but some places come pretty close. My point is that "wilderness," in the strict sense of the term, is not really accessible to bicycles, or anything else with wheels—nor should it be.)

I've gone into these things because I want to make sure that the potential of the bicycle for this sort of thing is understood. That doesn't mean that you *have* to go scrambling off into the blue on some lonely goat track. You can have a lot of fun, and even—if you absolutely must—some "meaningful experiences," and never get off of the pavement. There's a lot of very beautiful country out there, and some of the best parts are crossed by paved roads. Not all public campgrounds are revolting, littered, noisy Winnebago ghettoes; there are several in the Ozarks that I quite often use, and, except for weekends, I usually have them to myself.

To me, wild country is the only place really worth being, and everything else is merely to be endured; but then I am a native of such country, and it's natural that I would feel that way. I certainly don't want to give the impression that I am trying to impose my own interests on anyone else. In fact, I strongly suggest that most people confine their first bikepacking trips to paved highways and campgrounds until they get a little experience. Many people have been disappointed and even turned off by trying too much too soon.

The essential thrust of this book is to help you get out and have a good time. I'm certainly not trying to set up some kind of woodsier-than-thou status hierarchy; there's enough of that around already. Go where *you* want to go, not where somebody thinks you ought to go. As the old mountain men said, find out which way your stick floats.

Info

Usually you don't have to be CIA material to get information for your plans; the resources are abundant. The library is an obvious starting point. Check, also, state parks-and-tourism departments. Write their offices, or, better, visit them in person, and you'll wind up with a truckload of brochures, maps, information on public campgrounds, and addresses of other organizations that may help. Federal offices in charge of National Parks or Forests are another helpful resource. The Forest Service puts out some pretty good free maps, though, withal, highly inaccurate ones in many respects. (The important thing about Forest Service maps is that they show which land is private and which is public—very important in finding places to camp and avoiding trespass problems.)

One thing to watch out for when checking with public agencies: There are several different departments and bureaus involved with public lands, and each of them tends to pretend that the others don't exist. A map or list of public campgrounds compiled by the state may not show federally owned sites, and vice versa. The Forest Service, which is a branch of the Department of Agriculture, frequently fails to show on its maps campgrounds maintained by agencies of the Department of the Interior or the Army Corps of Engineers. (By the way, don't overlook the last agency—they may do horrible things to rivers, but they do operate some excellent public campgrounds, often free, along the major rivers over which they have authority. They've got lots of free maps.) Check with all of the relevant agencies, and you may find some surprises.

Private organizations, such as historical societies, regional environmental groups like the Sierra Club or Ozark Society, Audubon Society chapters, and regional tourism and promotion organizations run by business people, all should be consulted if there's any chance that they know something you don't. It won't hurt to put up a little note on the bulletin board at school or the outdoor shop explaining your plans and requesting information from anyone who's been there, too.

Above all, don't forget bicycle clubs! There must be *some* organized cycling group in your state. They can tell you more than anyone else about which roads have less dangerous traffic, what towns have hostile cops, even where the dogs are. Another cyclist knows more than anyone else can about your problems and needs. Many regional cycling associations have even put together cycling guides to their areas, some quite sophisticated.

Getting There

Even if your objective is a relatively wild area in which you plan to cruise the back roads, you'll still probably have to do a certain amount of open-highway cycling to get there. (Unless you carry your bike on top of a car until you get to the area of interest—some people do that; I've never tried it.) Picking a good route is the most important way in which you can minimize trouble and maximize the fun on this part of the trip.

It might seem that a cyclist should always seek out the older secondary routes and stay off the main highways. Sometimes this is true, but not invariably; some of those narrow, potholed two-laners have astonishing volumes of traffic. Some of the wider, more modern roads are actually safer for cycling, even though they have more and faster traffic. The lanes are wider, so there's room for vehicles to pass you safely; the police keep a better eye on things—thus reducing the chance of trouble—and people who live along such highways tend to curb their dogs, or the dogs don't live long. While it might seem that scenery would be better on the older road, in fact, newer highways tend to be laid out and landscaped with some attempt toward eye appeal, while the older routes are often lined with junkyards, abandoned motels, decaying billboards, and gravel pits.

You can predict a certain amount about traffic patterns if you can get some idea of the economy of the region. A town with large factories, or a railhead or grain-elevator center in farm country, will have a good deal of truck traffic. (In farm country, some information on growing and harvesting seasons will be invaluable, since it affects the nature of the truck traffic.)

College towns are usually pretty quiet on weekdays, but on weekends the roads in and out of a college town may be fairly terrifying. Friday afternoon is especially bad. On the other hand, college towns are good places to look for bike shops, if you need to buy something.

A topographic contour map is ideal for getting a picture of the terrain to be expected. (Bear in mind that you can handle a good deal more truck traffic on a flat, straight highway than on a winding mountain road.) If you don't have such a map, there are other clues: Railroad lines, shown on most maps, will follow the easiest grades between points. If a road is shown to twist and turn in a series of violent switchbacks, it's almost certainly going up or down a steep mountainside. Remember that, while you might want to avoid hills on your route, flat country can be even worse if the wind is up—and it usually is.

Speaking of wind, weather is a subject that all long-range bikies need to study. It's far too complex to go into here; enough to say that you should at least be able to judge the likelihood of rain and the probable direction of prevailing winds at a given time of year. If nothing else, there's the weather forecast on TV and radio.

The availability of places to camp along the way will certainly influence your choice of routes, unless you plan to stay in motels for this part of the journey. Here again, you can get information from public agencies. More about places to camp in the next chapter.

How Far, How Fast?

The common question, "How far can I ride in a day?", is as meaningless as "How long is a rope?" There are so many variables there that I could use up the whole rest of this book just listing them. Anyway, it's not just a question of how far you can ride, but how far you want to ride. A few people don't like to stop until they feel they've really exhausted themselves, but they usually go into racing. Most of us, on a noncompetitive ride, prefer to stop while we still feel like living—not to mention the need to put up the tent, fix supper, and so on.

In any event, you've got to have some idea of your expected daily mileage before you can plan your trip. A common error, and a source of much disappointment and difficulty, is to assume that you can make the same kind of mileage that you usually rack up on a weekend out-and-back bike ride near home. A cyclist who rides a couple of those "century" rides may even expect to be able to cover 100 miles a day on his or her camping trip.

It doesn't work that way. For one thing, those casual rides and club runs are usually made with an unloaded bike. Even if you followed the advice in this book and made a lot of rides with your camping kit, chances are that the total load was still lighter than what you'll take on an actual trip—little things sneak in there at the last minute.

For another thing, the whole ambience is different. You can cover quite a few more miles when you know you'll be finishing up at home, with a hot bath, a handy kitchen, and a bed, none of which you will have to unpack or assemble—and, chances are, somebody else to do the cooking. Your training and fun rides are usually made over familiar roads, a psychological advantage, and if you do an out-and-back loop, you may have the wind behind you at least part of the time (whereas, on the road, the wind will be from dead ahead at *any* given moment—Bikepacker's Law #2). The training ride is usually something you do on Saturday or Sunday, with a whole week to rest up or make short rides before and after; on the road, you've got to be able to keep up this pace every day. When you finished that century, do you think you could have gotten up the next morning to do it again?

I suggest the Rule of Halves as a conservative approach. Estimate your basic, typical mileage from your normal home-area, bare-bike, club, or personal rides, the distance you have established from experience that you can cover in a day without total exhaustion. Take half of this, and you'll have an idea of what you can comfortably do on the open road with a loaded bike on a day-to-day basis, leaving time for making camp, breaks for meals, stops to view scenery, and so on. If you can ride a club century run in fair comfort, ending the ride tired but not exhausted, 50 miles will be well within your powers for a daily average on a bikepacking trip.

This is assuming that the terrain is similar in both cases. If the place where you're going is very hilly and your riding has mostly been on the flat, cut this estimate in half again. You can also cut it in half for dirt roads or rainy weather.

When you get right down to it, you can't beat experience; when you've made a few of these trips, you'll have a much better idea of your own capabilities and will be able to plan your later trips more accurately.

One good rule: Make your first day's ride short, no matter how strong and fit you are. It gives you a chance to get everything shaken down and your muscles loosened up. Chances are that you'll discover something about the bike or other equipment that needs adjustment, and this will leave you plenty of time to work on it. (Always remember to leave yourself time for this—working on a bike by candlelight simply isn't practical.) Even if you're in the 100-mile-a-day class, a 30-mile first day isn't absurd at all.

Be conservative in your planning. Don't set yourself a series of Herculean tasks. Instead, plan for slightly less than your maximum each day. If you leave yourself time for flats, breakdowns, dogfights, and the like, these things become mere irritations rather than disasters, and you'll get to camp feeling energetic and happy rather than dragged out.

If all of this seems to be incompatible with your plans—if you're going to have to go your limit every day to reach your goal and get back in the time you've got—then I suggest you reconsider the whole project and file it under Chew, Biting Off More Than You Can. Go somewhere nearer home. Or use your car, or get somebody to drive you, to chop off some highway miles. At a certain point, an experienced person may, indeed, go for broke in this manner, but anybody who is qualified to cut it that fine shouldn't have to read books about it.

Getting Ready

Training for a camping trip is not at all a bad idea. You don't have to set up the kind of rigorous program a racer follows, but you'll certainly have a better time of it if you'll get in shape first. Try to ride your bike every day, even if only a little. Go on longer rides when you can, and remember what we said about carrying your outfit to get used to it. If you're preparing for a hilly trip, ride some hills. Start with a bare bike and gradually add weight until you're up to your full kit. If several of you are going together, try to ride together often, so that you get used to each other's styles and idiosyncrasies. This last can save everyone a lot of bad scenes.

If you can get into it—and not everyone can stand the boredom—a program of calisthenics and light weight exercises will be helpful. Be sure to work on the shoulders and arms, as these muscle groups must work hard to control a loaded bike, especially on rough roads. Jogging and running will build your wind, but be sure that you don't damage your knees with improper shoes on excessively hard surfaces, such as sidewalks.

When you've got your outfit assembled and your body in good shape, try a few overnight camping trips. Surely there's some kind of campground, park, or other recreational area within easy cycling distance of where you live. It doesn't have to be anything all that great or exciting. All you're after right now is the training and experience.

Don't scoff at these little overnighters; they are very valuable. You get the cycling and fitness training, you get practical experience in using your camping equipment in the field—and, believe me, little things like putting up your tent and operating your stove get a lot harder away from your backyard—you test your gear and learn its weak and strong points, and you get in some practice getting everything broken down and loaded onto the bike in the morning. You also find out about things that you need and don't have, and perhaps things you're carrying that you don't really need.

On these trips, carry more than you actually need. Choose a time of good weather in case of trouble, but carry the full tent, fly, and sleeping bag anyway. Take a little extra food. Carry the makings for a really good, hearty meal that has to be cooked with some care—something considerably more sophisticated and cumbersome than you'd bother with on the road. Then, when you get into the long-range stuff and have to simplify, the bike will seem lighter and the work simpler by comparison. If you're not used to spending nights outdoors, a good home-type meal will help your morale.

You will also find, I suspect, that overnight camping trips of this kind are great fun in their own right. In fact, given the range and speed of the bicycle, you could see quite a bit of country without ever spending more than one or two nights outdoors per trip. Despite the give-'em-hell atmosphere of this book, there's really no law that says bikepacking *has* to be a long-range, long-term business. Probably a majority of American campers of all kinds do nearly all of their camping this way—overnighters and the odd, long weekend—and get in only one longer trip each year. There's nothing wrong with that. Some of the nicest outdoor experiences I've ever had have been on overnighters.

Since I'm on the subject, let me extend that thought a little. If you really want to become an expert outdoors person, the most important thing is to get outdoors as much as you can— whenever and wherever the chance appears. If you wait around for opportunities to go on long wilderness expeditions, unless you have some really unusual breaks in your life, you're never going to become very experienced—most people just don't have the time, money, or connections. Grab what you can get whenever you can get it, and don't be picky or assume that things like local weekenders aren't worth the bother. If you study the habits of really skilled outdoor people—except, perhaps, those who actually live out in the woods or the like—you'll find that they are very hard to locate on weekends. Friday evening or Saturday morning, the backpack goes into the trunk, or the kayak goes atop the car, or, by God, the bike is rolled out of the house, and they *go,* even if they have to be back tomorrow morning. Many even cut classes or lie to the boss and take off during the week when the weather is just too nice . . . which is why so many of them stay broke, but never mind that.

For obvious reasons, a book of this nature has to be primarily oriented toward the longer trip in more remote country. It's not the only game worth playing, and I hope nothing I've said has led anyone to think otherwise. I go off on long solo trips of various kinds pretty much whenever I like, but I still ride out of town now and then, on nice afternoons, to a little park by the river, so close to the city that I can see the lights. I spend the night and pedal back next morning. It's something I value highly.

Groups

This book has been solo-cyclist-oriented because that's how I operate, but many people prefer to travel in groups of two or more. On balance, there's a lot to be said for it. It's certainly safer—dogs and humans are less likely to bother you when you outnumber them, and motorists are more careful in passing a group. In case of an accident or illness, somebody can go for help, and if there are three or more of you, someone else can stay with the victim. In some emergencies, first aid needs to be administered by another person.

A group, too, can get individual loads down quite a bit. They can share a stove, pots, first-aid kit, even a tent if they get along well, and this means each person carries less. This is a definite plus.

Of course, there are many people who simply enjoy the company of other people—indeed, I suspect this is true of the majority of people. They tend to be bored and lonely when alone, and such people had better travel in groups, or they will get depressed. Even types that are less gregarious often find it a bit demoralizing to spend several days and nights alone—especially nights in the woods with no other campers around—and when things go wrong or you feel tired, the loneliness can get pretty overwhelming. Even loners like the author feel it occasionally. (It's probably the reason most loners are such fanatics about wildlife—the birds and animals are sometimes the only company we have.)

Groups can be bad news, too. It is very important, if you're going to get a group together, to make it a compatible one. Little personality conflicts tend to be magnified over a long trip, especially when everyone is tired, wet, or otherwise uncomfortable.

Anybody who gets on your nerves in town will drive you to thoughts of homicide in the woods.

These things are particularly important on a cycling trip. I'm not sure why—perhaps it is the basic isolation imposed by the bicycle, as contrasted to the teamwork involved in paddling a canoe, for example—but bicycle travel seems to put more of a strain on interpersonal relationships than any other form of outdoor activity. There are people I enjoy running whitewater with, or hiking with, with whom I cannot stand to cycle. Tempers can really flare.

One reason, probably, is the way the bicycle's efficiency magnifies differences in human strength and stamina. A slight difference in body strength and oxygen uptake between two hikers, for example, will seldom create any real difference in walking speeds—things like the trail surface and the amount of weight carried will tend to force them to match their pace. Paddlers, too, usually travel at about the speed of the current, regardless of power or skill levels. Bicycles, however, are very special machines. A cyclist who is only a little bit stronger, fitter, or more experienced than his companions can very easily motor off up the road and leave his friends miles behind. If he isn't careful to hold back and stay with them, there can be considerable bitterness—they may consider him an arrogant show-off, and he may make it plain that they are holding him back. Even unspoken thoughts like this can make trouble.

So the group must have at least roughly similar aims. A hard-driving, hell-for-leather type, obsessed with mileage and speed, is sure to come into conflict with a laid-back, dawdling observer of wild flowers, unless they can work out their differences before the trip. Of course, if they adopt the right attitude, each can learn from the other.

It is not necessary that everyone have the same level of expertise, if the more experienced members are willing to take it easy and help the novices, and if the novices, in turn, will refrain from being oversensitive. Sometimes a single experienced cyclist leads, or simply rides with, a group of others who are relatively green. The experienced person must be careful not to fall into an authoritarian posture and begin ordering everyone around, but rather be diplomatic and kindly in giving advice. Not everyone can do this.

Then again, not everyone can take advice graciously, either. Nobody want to ride with a novice whose insecurity and touchy ego interprets all guidance and suggestions as personal attacks. Going along with the guidance of more experienced people is a sign of maturity and intelligence, not a surrender of dignity.

Considerations of ideology or prejudice have no part in these matters. Occasionally one encounters a "male chauvinist" type who assumes that all women are his inferiors, or a militant feminist who will not accept any advice or help from a man lest she seem to be copping out, or older cyclists who think they should be deferred to on grounds of age alone, or younger ones who assume everyone over 30 is senile. Even things like economic and social status—and, God help us, racial prejudice—have been known to rear their exceedingly ugly heads. There is no excuse for it—any of it—and people who behave in this way have only themselves to blame when nobody asks them on trips. The only thing that counts in the outdoors is what you know, what you can do, and how responsible you are about doing it—*not* your sex, age, social status, race, or anything else—and anyone who believes otherwise is merely a damned fool.

Since there are many cyclists who don't camp and campers who don't cycle, it's very possible that the group may include highly expert cyclists with little or no knowledge of camping, and others whose cycling expertise is minimal but whose background in backpacking, canoeing, and the like makes them entirely at home around things like tents and pressure stoves. In fact, the latter type usually do better on longer trips. Hotshot bike jocks who are lost around camp sometimes eat and sleep so poorly that their cycling soon deteriorates as well. The skilled camper will manage to eat and sleep well, and saddle sores and leg cramps are a lot easier to take when you can look forward to an enjoyable evening in camp.

A mixed group like this can have a fine time if they work it out so that each person can contribute what he or she is best at; then everyone has a feeling of worth, and also gets to learn from others, so that the trip is a mutual, growing experience. Sometimes this results in rather comic shifts in the pecking order. The big, powerful bike-buster who led the pack all day is suddenly transformed into a helpless tyro, holding stakes and carrying water for the skinny girl on the cheap bike who could barely keep up on the road.

Except when skill levels make job allocations inevitable—obviously if the group includes a doctor or nurse, that person gets the first-aid kit—you should arrive at prior arrangements about camp chores, or there may be hard feelings. In a mixed group, men often assume that the women will do the kitchen work, but nowadays that is far from a safe assumption. (Saying it out loud may be distinctly *un*safe!) Take turns, rotate jobs, assign permanent positions—do it any way you like, but work out some kind of understanding before you hit the road.

Sharing equipment is something else that must be agreed on ahead of time. People vary in their willingness to share certain things. Be sure you don't get into an "I thought *you* brought it" situation. Make out lists, and be sure everybody gets a copy and knows what he or she is supposed to bring. If there are going to be any cash expenses involved, work out the details before starting—arguments over things like paying for the gas for the guy with the car, for example, have led to the permanent destruction of friendships.

Male-and-female duos (or quartets, sextets, or oversextets) can have a lot of fun on and off bikes, but they can also have some very grim scenes if some sensitivity and understanding aren't brought to bear. A big, strong man often forces the pace and hustles his smaller companion along. He may be trying to show off his muscles and exert dominance—mixed groups that are not paired off on any definite basis are often plagued by this kind of exhibitionism. Probably, however, he genuinely fails to realize that what he considers a very easy pace may be close to maximum effort for someone else, especially for someone whose bike probably isn't nearly as well designed to fit her anatomy as is his. Remarks like, "Come on, you can do it," or "This isn't fast," are like gasoline on a fire.

This kind of situation can be irritating even between two men of different strength levels, but it rarely reaches the boiling point because the emotional factors involved are less complex. Most men grow up with the basic assumption that they'll be competing with other men in many situations. Also, a certain type of banter and mockery is understood between most men to be a form of encouragement, and essentially affectionate. Yet women quite justly feel angry at remarks they consider belittling, insensitive, or patronizing. If she then responds with heated words, the day can turn into a very long one.

Men must try to remember that women get a good deal of patronization and putdowns in their daily lives, and this makes them a bit touchy about criticism by men; a little extra consideration wouldn't hurt. Women, on their part, need to remember that the big fascists don't *mean* any harm; it's just that all of those muscles back up into their skulls and numb their brains.

Keep in mind, though, that there are lots of hard-riding women around, and plenty of out-of-shape men. Sometimes, the male member of a mixed duo tries to assert a dominance and leadership for which he is in no way qualified. Damn it, if she's a better cyclist or knows the area better, put her up front and listen when she talks.

If I had a dog that would lie where
my bed is made tonight, I would kill
him and burn his collar and swear
I never owned him.

—George Bradley

CHAPTER **13**

A Place
for the Night

River people like to kid about playing the Campsite Game. This is supposedly played by holding out for the ideal, perfect campsite. The idea is that as it grows late and the group has to look for a place to camp, you wait until someone else suggests a spot, then find fault with it until everybody agrees to go a little farther and look for something better. Since any campsite has some flaws, you can keep this going until it's getting dark and everybody has to camp in some absolutely dreadful spot. Then the game-player complains all evening about what a lousy campsite the others have chosen. (We are indebted to river guide Gaylord Stavely, author of the fine book, *Broken Waters Sing,* for codifying this important game.)

Seriously, though, folks (he says, picking up the mike, as the band begins the intro to *I Did It My Way*), if you want this trip to be fun rather than an exercise in masochism, you'll start looking for a campsite early on, well before you get really tired. Stumbling around in the dark, trying to cook and set up the tent is about as much fun as a pinched nerve, and fatigue doesn't improve the situation. Anyway, most people like to spend an hour or two exploring their surroundings—looking at birds and wild flowers, and so on—after getting off the bike for the day.

What do you want in a campsite?

It should be level—at least, there should be a level area big enough in which to sleep and fix meals—and high enough to be well drained in case of rain, yet not so high and exposed that wind will be a problem. Trees will be welcome for shade and breaking the wind, as well as aesthetic value and interest, and a ground cover of grass or dead leaves will be more pleasant than bare dirt or rock (though in dry weather, it may be better to stay in less inflammable areas). You'll want to be sure that there are no cattle around that can wander through camp, knocking things over and stepping on you, and in warm weather, you'll certainly want to avoid thick vegetation that can harbor ticks. A source of clean drinking water is vital, yet you won't want to camp near a still or slow-moving body of water that breeds mosquitoes. Of course, you want the area to be fairly clean and free of trash and litter, and without a lot of crowding or obnoxious neighbors. It's also nice if there's a scenic view, an interesting natural phenomenon such as a waterfall, or other source of stimulation and enjoyment.

Sounds good, right? Now, try and find it. Such places exist, but not in profusion. Usually you'll have to do the best you can. Fortunately, the greater range and speeds of the bicycle can simplify the problem. A good cyclist can check out 15 miles of road in the time it would take the average backpacker to cover 2. And, unlike the paddler, the cyclist can turn around and go back if he decides that last spot was the right one after all!

Here is another good use for those topographic maps. Contour lines show you where flat areas are found, an important consideration in mountain country. An ordinary road map may show a highway coming very close to a river or lake, and you might assume that this means you can camp there and get water easily, perhaps fish, and even swim. When you check your trusty USGS quad, though, you might learn that the road runs along the edge of a 200-foot cliff with the water at the bottom and no way down!

Even without contour maps, you can do some predicting. For example, when a river makes a sharp bend, especially in mountain country, the inside bank will tend to be rather flat and low, sometimes with open gravel bars or beaches, but the outside of the curve is very likely to consist of cliffs or steep banks.

Advance information of this kind can save you considerable disappointment and extra riding. When you see a promising spot, haul out the maps and consider carefully whether this isn't likely to be the last one for a good long way. It's very frustrating to have to backtrack 15 miles to a spot you passed up because you thought there might be one down the road with a better view.

In cooler weather, especially when the days are short, remember that things like mountains and cliffs can knock an hour or so off of your sunshine time. If you camp where there's a big rising landform off to the west, it's going to get chilly and dark a lot quicker; if there's a hill to the east, it will be that much later in the morning before the sun begins to warm things up. Consequently, if you're traveling along a meandering river valley—and many roads follow such valleys—it may be better to find a campsite along a stretch running east and west rather than one running north and south. Remember, too, that places that get more sunshine also have heavier brush and thicker forest growth, and therefore it will be harder to find a clear area to make camp.

Wind movements and weather patterns are also affected by terrain. In most parts of the country, a hill to the north will break some of the chillier winds, and, of course, cold air tends to flow down hillsides in the evenings. You can really go quite deep into this business of terrain and weather and so on; it's fascinating, and repays its study well.

Of course, a primary requirement for any campsite is that you be allowed to camp there in the first place. This isn't always all that straightforward to arrange. New bikepackers sometimes set out with the assumption that they can just bed down anywhere they like, but in fact, landowners have become increasingly touchy about trespassing, and a few are downright psychotic. There is no state in the U.S. where a landowner has the right to employ lethal force—either the use of a deadly weapon or even pointing it—but plenty of proprietors firmly *believe* they have such a right and will attempt to exercise it. If a landowner threatens you with a gun while you stand on his land, he is breaking the law, but if you stand there and argue the point, there is an excellent chance that he will shoot you—he then may go to jail, but that won't do you any good. In Texas he'll probably get away with it. *Don't mess with landowners!* Something about the ownership of land seems to make some people authentically crazy.

It is, however, often possible to secure permission to camp on privately owned land. Some more possessive proprietors are quite willing to let you put up your tent on the back forty, just as long as you acknowledge their ownership rights by asking properly.

When you ask a farmer or other rural proprietor if you can camp on his property, anticipate some of his most probable worries. Explain that you have a small stove and so will not be building any sort of fire or chopping down young trees, that you will be careful to close all gates so that stock doesn't get out (a common complaint), and that you will leave the site clean. Quite often, the landowner is sympathetic toward neat, low-impact campers such as yourself; he's mostly concerned with keeping out the kind of slobs who cut wire, leave fires burning, throw garbage around, and so on.

Make sure he understands that you're on bicycles—something about bikes seems to carry a connotation of innocence. Lots of people will welcome a couple of bikepackers, even though they'd call the police if you were on motorcycles (or, worse, hitchhiking). Assure him that you aren't carrying any kind of firearms; offer to let him check.

I camp mostly in Federal lands, so my experience in these matters is limited, but friends report (and my own small experience confirms) that very few landowners will turn you down if you approach them in the right way. Rural people are mostly hospitable—in fact, a couple of times I've had to explain that I *wanted* to sleep in the woods and wasn't doing it through hardship; they wanted to put me up at the house! The ones who can be nasty are the city people who retire or make a pile and get a place out in the country. They bring their urban attitudes of suspicion, defensiveness, and possessiveness with them, and you may never get past the Dobermans to ask them. The hell with them; ride on down the road and find some *real* country people.

Camping regulations on Federal lands are an absolute can of worms. There are so many different departments, agencies, and bureaus, and so many different classifications and special regulations, that you can only check out the situation for each area on an individual basis—generalizations are worthless. There are places where you can simply camp anywhere you like, and others where you can camp only in officially designated campsites (also known as camper ghettoes), and some that are closed to all campers, period. Some wildlife refuges are closed to campers during certain months and open for use—in designated campsites only—during others. Permits are being required in some fragile or heavy-use areas; in some cases you have to have a fire permit and in some you are not allowed to build an open fire at all. The only safe approach is to write to the supervisory agency, preferably the local office directly responsible for the area concerned, and request enlightenment. Then, carry a copy of the answer with you. If they've misinformed you, or if you are bothered by an officious ranger or other official who tries to make up his own rules, you've got it in writing for your own protection.

Campgrounds

We've been assuming that you will want to camp "in the woods"—in an undeveloped, wild area, or at most in a stretch of farm country. Since few cycling trips are made entirely within public-land boundaries, however, and landowners cannot be relied on to give permission for camping, most cycle campers from time to time have to camp at designated or developed campgrounds, whether public or private.

This isn't necessarily horrible or even unpleasant. Some public campgrounds, especially the so-called "primitive" kind found in some National Forests and along some rivers, can be very nice indeed. A cleared area with a couple of fiberglass outhouses, and, perhaps, a water pump and a few grates for fires, isn't "wilderness," but it's as close to wilderness as is a heavily-used spot in a popular "wild" area where a hundred campers have built fire rings and the trail is worn to a ditch. From the viewpoint of environmental impact, the campground is a great improvement.

The people you do run into at these less-developed campgrounds tend to be more pleasant company—the really noisy, obnoxious types tend to gravitate toward places with flush toilets, electrical connections, playgrounds, and the like, which is another reason to avoid those spots.

The elaborately developed sites are usually awful, full of noisy people in elaborate, gas-wasting, road-hogging, air-befouling motor homes and trailers, frequently with hordes of children whose behavior is enough to make you think King Herod might not have been all that bad. The whole atmosphere of such a place is totally contrary to what most cycle campers are looking for, and the only reason to stay there is if it's the only possibility within range, a situation that does come up from time to time. If I were on the road and had no alternative to camping at a crowded, noisy, overdeveloped place like this, I would seriously consider checking into a good motel instead; the motel would be more restful and probably not much more expensive. At most of these developed places, they soak you a fat fee for camping there, even though you will not be using any of the facilities, such as electricity, gas, or septic dumps, or creating wear on the roads, which is what the fees are meant to pay for.

Still, a blanket condemnation is not entirely fair. In the off-season months, these places are virtually deserted, and then they can be strangely pleasant, if a bit eerie. The snack bars are closed, the playgrounds and tennis courts are silent and deserted, and the elaborate pavilions are occupied only by nesting birds. It's not a wilderness experience, God knows, but there's a kind of satisfaction to it, all the same.

Some of the private campgrounds aren't too bad if you've got no alternative. They're usually a good deal cleaner and better policed than the public ones, anyway. The fees usually aren't any worse than the more expensive public campgrounds, and certainly less than motels.

Camping

Assuming you've found a spot, the first thing to do, unless it's raining, is to pull out your sleeping bag and fluff it up, so that it has a chance to air out a little before you get into it. If it's raining, of course, the tent goes up first. Get the tent up early anyway; then you've got somewhere to toss small, easily lost things that you'll need during the night, such as your flashlight.

If there's a choice, pitch your tent or tarp on a raised spot rather than in a depression or at the bottom of a slope; then you won't have to worry about getting flooded out. A quick study of the ground should show you where the water's been running off. *Do not dig a trench around your tent.* This is totally indefensible, ecologically, in that there is nothing that promotes erosion and gullying faster than digging ditches, even small ones, in the delicate ground cover. Do not cut any living plant or tree, and if you have to move large rocks, note where they went so that you can replace them. The idea is to make a minimal impact on the place. Even in a public campground, there's no excuse for leaving scars.

Do not engage in "campsite engineering"—making neat little benches with rocks and logs so that you can all sit around the campfire and sing old songs. Don't create big fire rings, erect frameworks of green poles to hang your clothes and your cookpots, or any of that Boy Scout business that used to be taught in summer camps and shown in campcraft books. A few people are still promoting the engineering approach—there actually appeared, a couple of years back, a brand-new book that consisted almost entirely of pictures and diagrams showing you how to make your campsite elegant with furnishings made from limbs and saplings. Among the things shown were clothes racks, lean-to shelters, even ladders. People who promote practices like this, especially when they involve cutting living trees and bushes, should go through life with a throbbing headache just above the left eye.

One bit of digging is necessary, however, if there are no toilet facilities—digging a hole to bury solid human wastes. Don't dig too deep—just a few inches—or the recycling process won't work well. Carry a light plastic or aluminum trowel for this purpose. The basic rules go back to Moses (Deuteronomy 23:13, if you're curious). This practice must be followed even for relief stops along the road—you are no more justified in making a mess in the woods by the highway than you would be doing it in camp.

As for what you do after you set up camp, it's up to you; you may want to walk around the area, or you may prefer simply to sit and rest and watch the sun go down. If you do go walking around public campgrounds or take the bike for a joyously unloaded ride, you'd better keep an eye on your stuff or take some sort of measure to discourage pilferage. Out in the real woods, the problem is not acute—though I have heard some depressing stories—but in an area where people drive in and out frequently, particularly if there is a town of any size nearby, your bicycle and other possessions can sprout little feet and walk away when your back is turned. The tent, sleeping bag, and suchlike items are not likely to be ripped off—though it does happen—and usually you can safeguard them simply by closing the flaps of the tent in such a way that it is hard to see whether or not there's anyone inside. If you're alone, you'd better take things like your camera with you even when you go to the toilet. As for your bike, there are people who will screech up to where you left it leaning against a tree, toss it into the back of their pickup truck or car, and be off faster than you can say, "This is the act of a cad and a bounder."

So most bikepackers put up with the weight of a cable and lock—not the monster kind meant to discourage professional-grade, urban thieves, just something to slow down the not-so-good ol' boys. If they want to steal your bike badly enough to cut a cable in broad daylight in a public spot, they probably wouldn't hesitate to clonk you on the head and take it away from you. Neither eventuality is at all likely. Just carry something to deter the casually larcenous; anything more serious is too heavy and not likely to be really effective anyway.

When breaking camp in the morning, clean up after yourself. That doesn't mean just hit the high points, it means obliterate the signs of your presence as if you were an escaping prisoner being tracked by a death squad. Pick up your own trash and some of the last guy's. Replace any rocks or logs you moved. Kick loose leaves over the place where you filled in your sanitation hole and other places where you may have disturbed the ground. Pick up everything, even little bits—be especially watchful for bits of food wrappers. Nothing in the world burns me more than finding a tossed-aside wrapper or bag from a packet of freeze-dried food or something from a health-food store. Anybody who knows enough to buy that kind of stuff in the first place damned well knows better than to throw it on the ground. People who build fires sometimes try to burn food wrappers, discover that there's a layer of unburnable foil in there, and then go off and leave the blackened foil to clog the fireplace or ugly up the clearing. Burning fully combustible trash, under safe conditions, is a good practice; even if garbage containers are provided, you might as well lessen the load on the disposal process. If there turns out to be foil in there, though, take it out as soon as it cools, and the hell with whether you get your fingers a little smudged.

Do not bury uneaten food or, worse, cans. Animals come and dig the stuff up, and it's bad to get animals thinking of humans as a source of food. With bears, it creates a danger to humans, and in all cases, it creates a danger to the animals. Raccoons are something of an exception; they are so intelligent that they already know perfectly well about your potential as a grocery provider. They will very professionally go through all of your stuff in search of munchies, and nothing can be relied on to stop them. The old hang-the-bag-from-a-limb trick works about as long as it takes a fast 'coon to haul the bag up hand-over-hand. Hands are what they've got, and they are the damnedest burglars in the woods. They can operate zippers and buttons, and open doors. In fact, a family of raccoons once unzipped a backpack zipper I'd been unable to unstick for a week . . . .

When you are ready to go, stop and go back and look over your site one more time. This will help to prevent you from leaving something behind, which most of us do from time to time. What's more important, it may reveal something that you failed to clean up or render harmless—a dropped wrapper, an unfilled toilet hole, a smoldering fireplace. Not only should you want to correct such oversights, but if the ranger finds it, he may come after you and force you to go back and take care of it, and give you a fat fine, too.

Walk and ride very softly and carefully on this battered planet. It has taken just about as much abuse from our species as it can stand.

*The third NINE, undivided, shows
one from whose buttocks the skin
has been stripped, so that he walks
with difficulty.*

—*The* I Ching

CHAPTER **14**

Keeping
Everything Running

This isn't a book on bicycle repair and maintenance, let alone a first-aid manual. You should familiarize yourself with the relevant procedures from other sources before going (see the reading list), or make sure to go with someone who does know these things. Just to get you started, I'll pass on a few tips on the basics; after that, it's your ball.

The Motor

Right—that's *you. Saddle sores* are the most common cycling trauma. They aren't funny; they can turn the trip into a torture marathon and make you seriously sick. The best cure is prevention, which is accomplished primarily by cleanliness. Wear proper shorts with chamois or terry insert, and wash them *daily*, with a good hand soap, or, better, an antibacterial medical soap, if you can get it (try Hibiclens Surgical Scrub—expensive, but death on germs). Clean your body carefully, too. Take along a lot of those little Handi-Wipe towels and discreetly wash the crotch and buttocks area during your noon break.

Some have written that plastic saddles harbor fewer germs than leather and therefore will cause fewer sores. Just goes to show that you can get some people to believe anything. Your own skin, to say nothing of the shorts, will teem with germs anyway, and who in God's name rides with bare skin in contact with the saddle?

Adjusting the saddle correctly will go far to correct this problem too. In particular, many people set the saddle too high, so that they rock from side to side and rub the skin raw.

Should a saddle boil develop, it is important to stay off the bike until it heals—another good reason to leave extra time in your schedule. Treat the boil by cleaning it with alcohol or surgical scrub and applying a good topical ointment of the antibiotic type. If you can't avoid riding for some reason, apply a thick gauze pad—a woman's sanitary pad is perfect—and lower the saddle a bit to compensate for the thickness.

Regularly rubbing the area with alcohol will toughen the skin.

If you have a real saddle-sore problem, despite all of the correct precautions, then it is likely that something in your body is lowering your resistance to infection. You may be undernourished or coming down sick, or you may need to slow down and take it easy. Any simple infection that refuses to heal is a sign of more deeply seated problems.

Numb hands are the curse of the long-distance cyclist, and there are no easy answers. I have arthritis in my fingers, and I suffer terribly at times. Set the bike up so that you don't have too much weight on the hands. Wear gloves, thick ones, There are various wraps and sleeves to pad the bars; I cut strips of thin foam from an old Ensolite sleeping pad and wrap them around the bars, securing them with duct tape and covering them with regular handlebar tape. Some people have had good results with air-conditioning-duct insulation foam. Also, a front wheel with a low-flange hub will transmit a bit less vibration.

Shift your hand positions frequently. Unless the road is rough, ride one-handed a lot, wiggling the fingers of the free hand and changing hands often, to get circulation going.

Abrasions from minor falls are as nasty for campers as they are for racers. Treatment consists of cleaning the injured area with a disinfectant (disposable towels are available), applying a topical ointment, then covering the area with a bandage to keep out road dirt. If the injury is on the leg—and it usually is—it will be very hard to keep it clean. Ideally, you should stay off of the bike until it heals, but if this is impossible, at least change the bandage frequently and keep the area as clean as possible. If there is the slightest reason to suspect more severe infection, abandon the trip and get professional medical treatment immediately.

Sunburn is no more of a joke than any other first-degree burn; it can make you seriously sick. Prevent it by using a good lotion containing PABA or a similar sun-blocking agent, and by regular controlled tanning before the trip. If you just don't tan, but burn and peel, then use more lotion and keep exposure minimal. Seek shade along the road, plan the ride so that you can do most of your riding in the morning, and camp in shady spots. If you get sunburned, stay out of the sun for a day or two, and wear long-sleeved shirts and long pants. (Anyone who sunburns easily should carry a set of these as basic gear, in any temperature.)

A well-stocked first-aid kit is a very important item; there is a discussion of this in the back of this book. No first-aid gear is of any value unless the user is competent—unskilled, uniformed efforts at first aid can do more damage than the original injury. You also need to know where to stop, what operations should not be attempted by nonprofessionals in the field. If you've never taken a first-aid course, do so before going camping. The Red Cross offers classes in most communities.

A backpacker or paddler often operates in such remote country that he has to be able to deal with really major medical emergencies—river and mountain guides have had to set fractures, perform appendectomies, and deliver babies. Such situations are rare for cyclists. In a group, one can ride for help. If you're alone and can't do this—and don't try to ride when you're sick or hurt—you're usually near enough to a road so that you can try to wave down help. In this paranoid, self-centered age, few motorists would stop for their own mothers, but if you leave your bike lying where they can see it, sooner or later somebody— usually a truck driver, a hunter, or some kind of cop—will stop. If you are in really rough backcountry, you'll need a more complete first-aid kit and more extensive knowledge of how to use it.

All of this morbidity shouldn't discourage anyone. Cycle camping is a very safe sport, and nearly all of the common problems can be prevented with a little forethought and care.

The Bike

You don't have to be a master mechanic, but you do need to be able to keep your bike running if you don't want to have to carry it home. This is mostly a matter of keeping things clean and making small but vital daily adjustments and checks. Mechanical systems usually break down because they were improperly adjusted or allowed to get out of adjustment.

Any bikepacker should have the tools and the skills to perform the following operations correctly.

1. Repair flat tires, including removing and replacing wheels, and maintain tires at correct pressure.
2. Adjust derailleurs, front and rear, including shift levers.
3. Adjust brakes and replace worn shoes.
4. Adjust stem, seatpost, saddle, and bars, and tighten all of these to prevent slippage.
5. Lubricate all open lubrication points that use oil (does not include hubs, bottom bracket, and headset—any real cyclist should know how to strip, clean, regrease, and reassemble these bearings, but it's primarily an indoor job).
6. Replace broken cables for brakes or derailleurs.
7. Replace broken spokes and keep wheels trued.
8. Adjust all bearings for play.
9. Keep exposed mechanisms, such as chain, derailleurs, and cogs, free from accumulations of dirt.
10. Regularly check all bolts, screws, clamps, and the like for tightness, and tighten if necessary.

Broken spokes are a particular annoyance, though if you have really well built wheels, you may never have this problem. (In all modesty, I haven't broken a spoke in five years, and the last time I did, I was badly overloaded and riding cheap wheels. I build my own wheels, but I have had guidance in this from professionals and have built wheels for a living.) Replacing a spoke is easy unless you break one on the right side of the back wheel. Due to the peculiar strains imposed by the multispeed-cluster arrangement, this is precisely where they break almost always—in fact, I've never seen one break anywhere else. The problem is that the freewheel cluster is in the way and has to be removed. (Aagh.) Pulling a cluster is a job even in the shop, especially 34-tooth granny cogs, which really get torqued on there. It's hard to get enough leverage to break the freewheel loose from the hub, except with a very big wrench, too big to carry on the bike. (The freewheel remover itself is just a little tiny thing.) I must admit I've never encountered a freewheel that I couldn't get off with a 6" or 8" crescent wrench—I've never even owned a crescent bigger than 8" and, when I was racing, I used to have occasion to pull a freewheel two or three times a week. I'm heavy enough to use my foot to stomp the wrench handle and break the freewheel loose. Obviously, somebody who weighs 100 pounds will have less luck.

A length of pipe slipped over the wrench handle will give you the needed leverage—maybe you can find something in a ditch or at a farmhouse. Failing this, walk to a gas station or house and see if you can borrow a big crescent. If all else fails, and you're a good mechanic, very carefully disassemble the freewheel—don't try this unless you can do it easily and smoothly in the shop—and this will let you get at the spoke hole.

Some cyclists take an over-long spoke, bend the end into a kind of S-like kink, and work this into the hole. They say this will hold enough tension to allow you to ride to the nearest big-wrench owner. I've never tried this myself. I've seen some pretty weird-looking emergency repairs in which a piece of spoke had been forced into the hole, bent back on itself, and then used as an anchor point around which to twist the end of the broken spoke. It is not something I'd rely on myself, but it's better than riding a wheel with a spoke out, which will permanently ruin the wheel.

If you keep breaking spokes, you're overloaded or you've got a lousy set of wheels. With properly built wheels and reasonably strong spokes—not those thin little stainless jobs—broken spokes should be very rare on anything but extremely bad roads.

Remember to carry along a little can of oil, and use it regularly. Sewing machine oil is good, but vegetable-base oils like 3-in-1 gum up too badly. In rainy weather, lubricate exposed parts like the chain *daily*.

It will help greatly if you will carry a thin, light sheet of plastic—a painter's drop sheet—and cover the bike on rainy evenings. Don't cover it unless it's likely to rain; dew can condense inside one of these things and get your bike just as wet as the rain would.

I'd like to close this chapter with a list of ten basic rules, most of which have already been mentioned in this book. You will note that there is a common principle; a little reflection may suggest other implications—and not just for cycling.

1. Eat before you get hungry.
2. Drink before you feel thirsty.
3. Find a campsite before you become exhausted.
4. Shift down before it becomes too hard to pedal.
5. Apply the brakes before you enter a turn.
6. Slow down before you build up dangerous levels of speed.
7. Check the map before you get lost.
8. Fix things before they break or fail.
9. Treat minor injuries and illnesses before they become serious.
10. Get out of the sun before you get dizzy, and out of the wet and cold before you get chilled.

Have a good trip.

The Bikepacker's Laws

Bikepacker's Law #1: The biggest, fastest, meanest dogs live halfway up the longest, steepest hills.

Bikepacker's Law #2: The wind is always from dead ahead at any given moment.

Bikepacker's Law #3: Anything that can get into the spokes, will.

Bikepacker's Law #4: At any unmarked fork or intersection, if an accurate map is not used, the wrong alternative will always be chosen, but the mistake will only be discovered at least two hours later.

Corollary A: On back roads, in an area for which accurate maps are not available, the chance of any given intersection being shown on the map is in inverse proportion to the seriousness of the consequences of taking the wrong turn.

Corollary B: The likelihood of any guess being correct is in inverse proportion to the confidence of the guesser.

Bikepacker's Law #5: The chance of finding any given item at a rural store is in inverse proportion to the need or desire for said item, times the square of the distance to the next store.

Bikepacker's Law #6: The competency, sobriety, and courtesy of vehicular drivers is in direct proportion to the width of the road, but in inverse proportion to the average speed at which they drive.

Bikepacker's Law #7: The chance of getting any zipper to work smoothly is in inverse proportion to the urgency of need involved. (Exception: This Law does not apply to any zipper operated by a raccoon, especially if there is important and irreplaceable food inside.)

Bikepacker's Law #8: The attractiveness, cleanliness, and peace-and-quiet level of any public campground will invariably be in direct proportion to the availability and proximity of alternative places to spend the night.

Corollary: The noise level maintained by the people next to you, and the lateness of the hour to which they keep it up, will be in direct proportion to your need to get up early next morning.

Bikepacker's Law #9: In any group, the eagerness with which any member volunteers to do the cooking will be inversely proportional to his or her ability to produce edible meals.

Corollary: The single member of the group who most consistently and reliably turns out savory, mouth-watering meals will be either a macho male who considers cooking women's work, or a feminist who assumes she is being made to slave in the kitchen because she is a female, and no amount of reassurance from other group members will help.

Bikepacker's Law #10: It always rains the day you buy your new bike.

Repair and
_____Maintenance Checklist

The following items should be carried on trips of real length, especially in remote country. On shorter trips, cyclist can adjust to fit needs, according to his own judgment and experience.

Crescent wrench, 6″ or 8″

Screwdriver to fit adjusting screws and bolt heads (more than one may be required—some derailleurs require Phillips as well)

Pliers, small pair (not really necessary for bike work, but handy in camp also)

Utility knife

T-handle or socket-type wrench to fit any bolts not accessible with crescent (a 3-way, Y-shaped wrench sold in bike shops is ideal)

Allen wrenches as required (5, 6, 7mm. sizes are most common)

Cone wrench to fit hub cones

Crank tool for cotterless crankset (extractor and tightening wrench—in some models these are one tool, in others separate items)
Freewheel tool
Spoke wrench
Chain rivet extractor
Tire repair kit
Spare tube(s)
Spare brake and derailleur cables, one each
Spare brake shoes on long mountain trips
Spare spokes, 4 (if you need them all, you've got a pair of lousy wheels, but they're handy for other things such as roasting wienies)
Assorted spare nuts, bolts, and screws, as well as spares for small, easily lost parts such as quick-release spindle springs
Can of light machine oil, small
Tube of Loc-tite or equivalent, small
35mm. film container full of white grease for bad-weather runs
Double-tube epoxy set, small (wrap tubes separately and carefully)
Old toothbrush (for cleaning chain, etc.)

The pump might also be considered a tool. Many cyclists like to carry a small pressure gauge to keep their tires at correct inflation. This is probably a good idea, though veteran bikies tend to trust their thumbs to check tire pressure. Dunlop makes a small gauge that is highly regarded.

Get only good-quality tools; cheap tools chew up expensive bike parts and, therefore, are far from cheap. Be sure that the tools fit your bike—metric sizes are complex, and freewheel and crankset tools, in particular, come in a bewildering range of types and sizes, mostly noninterchangeable. For example, threads may be entirely different between Japanese and Italian bikes, and French bikes usually don't match *anything* else, except for a few Swiss ones. (Incidentally, if you're trying to choose between two bikes, one French and the other British, Japanese, or American, and all else is fully equal, then take the nonFrench one. French bikes are beauties, but parts are hell to get—British and Japanese bikes use the same threads and sizes as Schwinns in most cases.) See Sutherland's book (see reading list) for an explanation of all this.

No tool is any better than your knowledge of how to use it. If you can't be bothered to learn to do the job, don't bother to carry the tools.

Do not assume that you can borrow tools from others in a group, unless you talk this over beforehand. A group may as well share a crescent wrench, but finer tools, such as allen keys and cotterless-crank tools, tend to be personal, and some people don't like to share them. It's also very possible that your bike may not have the same components and take the same tools as your friends'.

Camping
Outfit Checklist

I am always suspicious of published checklists; a person's outfit is an individual and highly personal affair, and no two people will have the same ideas or needs. For the most part, I think any person reading this book carefully should be able to arrive at his or her own list and at least have an adequate starting point from which a final outfit can be evolved with experience. However, it is considered incumbent on the author of a book of this nature to provide some sort of basic checklist, and I bow to tradition.

What I have done below is listed my own outfit as I carry it on a fairly typical, mild-weather camping trip (early fall—warm days, slightly cool but not cold nights, occasional heavy rains), in country where food can be obtained at least every two or three days. *This is an example;* it is *not* meant to be a set of requirements for others.

I have also listed weights (important ones were measured on a postal scale, while I guessed about a few small items, and I've broken down the load according to where I carry it on the bike, in order to demonstrate how the weight may be distributed.

Panniers

Bleuet butane stove, full	1 lb.	8 oz.
Butane canister for stove		10 oz.
Pots, 2 (light aluminum, supermarket type)		8 oz.
Plastic cup		1 oz.
Spoon		1 oz.
Butane lighters		2 oz.
Air mattress, short, featherweight		8 oz.
Tent stakes		8 oz.
Flashlight, loaded, with 2 spare batteries		5 oz.
Candle lantern and 4 candles		8 oz.
First-aid kit		10 oz.
Cycling shorts, spare pair		10 oz.
T-shirt, spare (usually one T-shirt is a long-sleeved type)		5 oz.
Sweatshirt or long-sleeved flannel shirt (wool in cool weather)		10 oz.
Long pants or sweatsuit pants (light wool pants in cool weather)		12 oz.
Light down vest (only in cooler seasons)		10 oz.
Socks (1 spare pair of light socks for riding, 2 pairs of heavier socks for nights—the second pair of socks is seldom in my panniers. Instead, I usually tie them to bag straps to dry out after being washed)		6 oz.
Moccasins		10 oz.
Toilet paper (half roll)		6 oz.
Basic toilet articles (soap, toothbrush, comb, etc.)		8 oz.
Sewing kit		2 oz.
Iodine for purifying water (second bottle in first-aid kit)		1 oz.
Nylon parachute cord, 50 ft.		3 oz.
Small notebook		2 oz.
Sketch pad or Morilla Block, and pocket-size watercolor set		12 oz.
Food (staples such as margarine, coffee, sugar, cereal, plus dried foods for 2 to 3 days, *up to* maximum of about 10 lbs. at start of trip or immediately after replenishment stop)		

Maximum total carried in panniers is between 20 and 25 lbs.

Atop Rack

Sleeping bag, Hollofil mummy	4 lbs. 8 oz.
Tent fly (or tarp, if tent isn't carried)	12 oz.
Tent poles	8 oz.
Folding water jug, empty (under securing strap)	5 oz.

Total atop rack is about 6 lbs.
Total maximum weight supported by rear carrier assembly is approx. 25 to 30 lbs.

Handlebar Bag

Tent, small forest-type	2 lbs.
Cable and lock, light	1 lb.
Tools	1 lb. (??)
Maps (will vary widely in weight according to area)	8 oz. (?)
Snacks, sunburn lotion, small sheath knife, small can of Mace spray, compass, etc.	12 oz. (?)

Handlebar bag contents tend to vary most for obvious reasons; total should not run over 5 or 6 lbs. Small camera sometimes carried here will add about 12 oz. or so.

Rain suit (approx. 1 lb.) is tied to the back of the saddle; various items such as cap, wallet, folding knife, etc., are in the jersey pockets. The rider is wearing the other pair of shorts, other T-shirt, jersey, helmet, gloves, and riding/walking shoes.

Total weight of equipment and supplies carried on bike should not go over 35 lbs. under normal circumstances; 30 lbs. is more usual except at start of journey or when leaving store with full load. Of course, extra pounds may be carried for short distances, as, for example, when carrying heavy items from a store to the evening's campsite, if a short ride.

The outfit described is not entirely realistic; some items are listed for completeness, but, in actual fact, it is very unlikely this entire list would apply to any given situation. For example, in weather cool enough to call for a down vest, long pants, and heavier socks for nights, insects would probably be no problem, so the tent would not be carried; in weather warm enough for insects to be bothersome, I carry and wear only shorts, using rain pants or knitted leg warmers if mornings are chilly.

Variations tend to cancel each other out in this way. A Coleman Peak 1, liquid-fuel stove weighs more than a Bleuet and takes up more room, but with this stove, fuel is carried in a bottle clipped to the frame, and therefore the butane canister's bulk and weight are eliminated from the pannier contents.

The weights of the frame-mounted items (pump, water bottle, lights), the bags, and the rack have not been figured in, since they are indispensable, and most makes weigh about the same. As to bike weight, I have no idea whatever.

I probably forgot a few small items, but what the hell.

First-Aid Kit

I am even more nervous about making specific suggestions in this area; I am not a doctor (failed premed, but that was long ago . . .), and there are, no doubt, many readers who know much more about first aid and medicine than I do. The following list will give you the basic idea if you're really lost, but remember that, as with the tool kit, none of it is of any value unless you know how to use it properly.

Adhesive tape, 1" wide (be sure this is waterproof)
Sterile gauze, 2" wide, 1 roll
Sterile gauze pads, 3" square (3 or 4 for ordinary use, half a dozen or so for rough stuff)
Butterfly closures, half a dozen
Assorted band-aid-type dressings, especially the wider kind—1" × 3" (remember that a large dressing can be put over a small injury, and, if necessary, trimmed, but a too-small dressing will not cover a long gash or broad abrasion, so lean toward the larger sizes)
Disposable disinfectant wipes (try to get medical prep pads—ask your doctor)

Moleskin, 2 sheets (yes, cyclists do get blistered feet)

Ace-type elastic bandages, 2″ or wider, 2

Antibiotic or topical ointment "triple antibiotic" kind if you can get it

Disinfectant soap (remember, person administering first aid must wash own hands first; Hibiclens Surgical Scrub or hexachlorophene—the latter is a prescription item— Hibiclens works better anyway)

Iodine (for water purification—also a first-aid item)

Aspirins (Percogesic tablets are a more effective painkiller and relaxant, probably the strongest nonprescription painkiller around—you may want to take them as well)

Antihistamine capsules, Contac, etc. (in cold or wet weather or for those prone to colds or hayfever—do not ride while taking these)

Throat lozenges

Antacid tablets (I suggest Pepto-Bismol; they help control nausea and diarrhea as well—take more than you think you'll need, as the change in diet and environment tends to upset stomachs the first couple of days, even experienced ones)

Muscle embrocation (Ben-Gay, etc.)

Folding scissors (sold at fishing shops)

Tweezers

Small-gauge needles, 2

Razor blade

The kit should be stowed in a small, plastic, snap-lid box and then wrapped in a watertight plastic bag. Contents should be neat and organized, so that you don't have to rummage around in an emergency. Determine on a particular place to carry the kit—usually an outside pannier pocket—and always keep it there. On group trips, everyone should know where it is kept. It should, of course, be carried by the group member with the most training or experience in medicine and first aid.

If one member of the group is clearly the logical choice as "medic"—a doctor, nurse, policeman, or fireman trained in emergency medical procedures; a graduate of Red Cross or other first-aid courses; an ex-military medic, or the like—that person should not only carry the first-aid kit but should ride last in the group. Groups tend to get strung out on bikes, and if there is a crash or other accident on the road, it is better if the injured person can simply wait for the group medic to come along, rather than have to have someone ride off up the road after the first-aid person and bring him or her back. This could save very valuable time. For some reason, doctors who cycle tend to be very hot, fast riders who love to get out ahead and burn up the road, so it may be necessary to do some serious talking about this point.

Even if no member is particularly skilled in first-aid techniques, the kit still should be carried by the last person in line, for obvious reasons, just as the man or woman with the maps goes up front. If you want to trade positions, trade the stuff, too.

First-aid supplies are very dangerous if used improperly. Do not attempt anything beyond your training and skill; with bicycles available, there is rarely any valid reason why you can't *go for help,* and get the victim to a doctor. Only on truly remote trips or in special situations (if, for example, flooded streams have temporarily closed the only routes to the outside world), should you attempt anything beyond the most elementary first aid—the stuff listed above is primarily there to treat minor cuts, abrasions, sorenesses, and discomforts.

There are many, quite good, small first-aid kits on the market, sold in drugstores, sporting-goods stores, outdoor shops, and the like. If you get one, check the contents. Sometimes they sell you a lot of stuff you don't really need, while leaving out essential items. The best kits I've seen are those made up by Indiana Camp Supply, Inc., P.O. Box 344, Pittsboro, Indiana 46167. This firm is headed by Dr. William Forgey, author of *Wilderness Medicine* (see reading list), and they have an absolutely incredible line of medical supplies for outdoor use. This is the only source I know of wherein you deal with people who are knowledgeable in both the medical and outdoor fields. So check it out.

_____ # Further Reading

There is very little good literature on bicycle camping per se. Most of the books that appear to deal with the subject are actually about bicycle touring, with plenty of useful information (or, depending on the book, wild misinformation) on bikes and how to ride them, but not much you can get your teeth into when it comes to real camping.

One exception—the only one I've seen that I really liked—was Raymond Bridge's _Freewheeling_ (Stackpole, 1974). This book is now totally out of date, and the parts dealing with the bicycle were pretty inaccurate even when written. Yet, it's still very much worth reading if you run across a copy. Unlike nearly every other author of bike books in the early '70s, Bridge was (and is) an expert outdoorsman. The book contains plans for a simple pannier set that might be of interest to those on budgets.

Other than this, there are a number of books available that deal with various matters relating to bikepacking. I have listed some good ones below, arranged according to the parts of this text to which they seem best related.

Introduction

Background and Inspirational

Full Tilt, by Dervla Murphy (Murray [London], 1975). Not really about bike camping, it's the story of an Irish nurse who rode her clunker from Ireland to Afghanistan, alone, and doesn't seem to have felt that she was doing anything all that unusual.

King of the Road, by Andrew Ritchie (Ten Speed Press, 1975). Far and away the best book on the history of the bicycle—the only good one I've ever seen, in fact; most are dreadful. Read it even if you aren't normally much of a history buff. After you read about how much ground the old-timers covered on those clumsy-looking machines of theirs, you will have a better appreciation of the potential of your own modern bike.

Chapters 1 and 2

Hardware

The constantly changing nature of the market and the technology makes it impossible to be very detailed in discussing bikes, clothing, and other accessories. New makes come out, old favorites unaccountably disappear, Federal agencies tinker with various, largely bat-brained regulations, and manufacturers often make major changes in well-established products.

The best way to keep up on this subject, then, is through magazines rather than books. *Bicycling* magazine (33 E. Minor St., Emmaus, PA 18049—widely available at newsstands as well) is currently the only general cycling magazine in the U.S., but tries hard not to act like it. Most issues contain very detailed technical articles on various new developments in cycling. Author of this book also writes a column on, oddly enough, bicycle camping.

Here's one book of possible interest: *Bicycle Frames,* by Joe Kossack (Anderson World, 1975), a small booklet well worth perusing if you are thinking about going the custom-frame route. Its orientation is mostly toward racers or high-speed tourers— Joe Kossack was once my racing manager and made no secret of being wholly unsympathetic about the idea of carrying a lot of stuff

around on a bike, let alone sleeping in the woods—but the booklet
is still a very good study of what goes into a custom frame, and
why.

Chapters 3 through 6, and 13

Camping

America's Camping Book, by Paul Cardwell (Scribner's, 1973).
Don't be put off by the title; this is a good one, with plenty
of patterns and plans for making your own equipment—
some very good tent designs—and some good information
on bicycle camping, too. They should bring out an updated
edition.

The Budget Backpacker, by L. A. Zakreski (Winchester, 1977).
Good tips on making your own lightweight camping gear, or
acquiring it cheaply. Plans include a set of bicycle
panniers, and, although they are too small, the basic
pattern could easily be adapted by anyone with some
imagination and a grasp of the requirements.

Camping and Woodcraft, by Horace Kephart (Macmillan, 1917—
frequently reprinted). Should have put this one under historical background, of course; it deals with a bygone era in
camping, when people cut tent poles and built log cabins
and so on. Yet, Kephart was far ahead of his time in his
grasp of the freedom afforded by going light, and his
literary style is a joy to read, even now; strictly a nostalgia
trip, though—don't try to *do* it the way he describes!

Harsh-Weather Camping, by Sam Curtis (David McKay, 1980). In
the required-reading category for anyone going outdoors;
Curtis writes with great skill and knowledge about the
problems of heat, cold, snow, and rain (the latter being of
tremendous importance to the cyclist). Quite a bit of material on cycling can be found here, in fact, as well as general
camping equipment and techniques, clothing, and so on.
This is an absolutely outstanding book.

High Peaks and Clear Roads, by Raymond Bridge (Prentice-Hall,
1978). Same guy who wrote the old bike-camping book,
and he's obviously learned a lot more about cycling since
'74. The cycle-camping section of this book is a considerable improvement. This book is of particular interest to
people who want to do various kinds of camping—

backpacking, cycling, kayaking—as it deals with all these and tells you what equipment is most versatile. It's very general, though.

Joy of Backpacking: People's Guide to the Wilderness, by Dennis Look (Jalmar Press, 1976). A pretty good little book, marred or enriched, depending on your viewpoint, by a certain tendency toward ideological polemic (as you might guess from the subtitle) and the author's strong Sierra-and-Rockies background. It does show a very commendable sympathy with those with money problems, and good suggestions for solving them.

Light Weight Camping Equipment and How to Make It, by Gerry Cunningham and Margaret Hansson (Scribner's, 1976). Another useful reference for those who may want to try making their own gear.

The New Complete Walker, by Colin Fletcher (Alfred A. Knopf, 1978). The definitive backpacking book; Colin Fletcher is to the backpack what Jacques Cousteau is to the Aqualung or Jeff Cooper to the pistol—that is, not only has Fletcher illuminated the subject for others in a readable manner, he has also led an authentic intellectual and philosophical revolution that changed the whole nature of the field. The book is now very outdated in terms of technology—hardly any of the remarks on equipment are valid now—and Fletcher's own interest in solo hikes in mountains and deserts makes the book of limited relevance to other camping situations—low-altitude forests, for example. Backpacking is not cycling, so why, then, the must-read recommendation? Because Colin Fletcher understands the most important things—how to keep weight down, how to deal with little but important bits and pieces, and, above all, *what it's all about*—and, if you read this book, so will you.

Chapters 7 through 12

Cycling

Many books have been published on cycling in this country in the past ten years, at least 75% of which were and are so bad as to boggle the mind. During the "bike boom" of the early

1970s, it was possible to sell just about anything having to do with bikes, and many writers did so; some were cynical hacks out to make a fast buck, others were sincere people who simply weren't qualified, but they all turned out a lot of garbage. So, be warned if you go trying to read up on cycling—there's a lot of genuinely bad stuff around, and some of the most successful titles have been among the poorest in terms of accuracy.

The Bicycle Touring Book, by Tim and Glenda Wilhelm (Rodale, 1980). I don't entirely agree with all of the authors' ideas by any means, but this is still a very good book on bicycle touring, and any reader of this book will find it of great value in planning and preparing for a bikepacking trip. Authors do seem to worry unduly about the opinions of the general public; I mean, who cares what a lot of whuffo's think? (A whuffo is someone who stands on the sidewalk and says, "Whuffo' you ridin' that thing, boy?") But a good book, withal, the best I've seen on general cycle touring.

Bike Tripping, by Tom Cuthbertson (Ten Speed Press, 1972). A witty and appealing little book, easily the best literary product of the early bike-boom days. Cuthbertson examines various aspects of the cycling scene—traffic, dogs, weather, theft—with great humor and considerable insight. The section on wind is easily the best I've ever encountered. There is also a chapter by Al Eisentraut, the great frame builder (God created the world in the beginning, except for bicycles; He left *them* to Eisentraut) on frame design and construction.

DeLong's Guide to Bicycles and Bicycling, by Fred DeLong (Chilton, 1978). Rather dry and very technical in places, but a very thorough study of general cycling problems. I don't share DeLong's ideas on in-traffic cycling or Federal regulation, but, basically, this is a good book.

Effective Cycling, by John Forester (self-published, in frequently updated editions). Very dry reading, crude illustrations, flimsy binding, and a tendency to preach in the most dogmatic terms. A controversial figure in the cycling world for many years, Forester seems to find it hard to recognize that there might be other valid ideas besides his. But this book does contain the very best, most complete study on cycling in urban and suburban traffic that has ever been written. If you have to cycle through any sort of urban area at all, you ought to read this one (but only the part on riding in traffic—Forester's advice on certain other matters, notably lubrication, is not in agreement with the thinking of most contemporary cycling authorities and mechanics).

Everybody's Book of Bicycle Riding, by Thom Lieb (Rodale, 1981). Helpful information for the beginning cyclist. Lieb's articles long have graced the pages of American cycling magazines, and this book is a good one. It's very basic, but it does not commit the usual sin of oversimplification. If you're still new to cycling and want a general manual, I suggest this one.

Richard's Bicycle Book, by Richard Ballantine (Ballantine, 1978). A popular paperback, brought more or less up to date now. Ballantine writes very well indeed and the book is a joy to read, except for an unfortunate tendency to quote a certain sleazo American cycling author named William Sanders. Technical section is not entirely accurate (Richard, for example, has somewhere picked up the idea that bar-end shift levers have to have their cables run through holes drilled in the bars, which is not true, and the equipment described is mostly early-1970s stuff), but no matter; Richard's great value lies in his total fearlessness in telling you the un-prettied-up truth about drivers, dogs, thieves, and so on, and in his very real love for the subject that permeates every page.

Chapter 14

Matters Medical and Mechanical

Anybody's Bike Book, by Tom Cuthbertson (Ten Speed Press, 1971). A simple and enjoyable guide to the basic operations of bike maintenance. It's not a complete shop manual, but a good starter.

Glenn's Complete Bicycle Manual, by Harold Glenn and Clarence Coles (Crown, 1973). Still pretty much the basic bike mechanic's manual. If you have any mechanical aptitude, you can figure out how to do just about anything you might need to do to your bike with the help of this book. If you have little or no mechanical training, experience, and aptitude, you might do better to start with Cuthbertson's volume. The photos in Glenn's make it much easier to follow complex operations.

Sutherland's Handbook for Bicycle Mechanics, by Howard Sutherland (Sutherland Publications, 1981). A complete guide to what fits what—threads, sizes, and so on. This book is absolutely necessary in making any changes at all to any bicycle, because so many different parts are incompatible—different countries use different threads, some freewheels won't go on certain hubs, and the like. It's especially important in making up wide-range gear setups because it tells you the capacities of various derailleurs and also gives you some good tips on how to get the best performance from them. The book also gives spoke lengths, bearing-ball sizes, and a mountain range of other information. It should be owned by every home cycle mechanic.

Wilderness Medicine, by William Forgey, M.D. (ICS Books, 1979). A thorough and complete guide to emergency medicine for the outdoorsperson. In fact, it tells you much more than any average cycle camper will ever have to know. It's available from Indiana Camp Supply, a mail-order house that also sells the supplies and equipment needed for backcountry first aid. I think enough of this one that I hesitate to list any others, though *Being Your Own Wilderness Doctor,* by Bradford Angier, is quite good, as is Wilkerson's *Medicine for Mountaineering.*

_____ Useful Addresses

Mail-Order Suppliers

Bikecology Bike Shops, P.O. Box 66-909, Los Angeles, CA 90066. A big and successful mail-order operation, somewhat given to making extreme claims for their merchandise, but a good source for a lot of cycling gear. They carry a line of excellent Bob Jackson touring frames at a low price.

Bike Warehouse, 215 Main Street, New Middletown, OH 44442. Good selection of touring equipment, low prices.

Cannondale, 35 Pulaski Street, Stamford, CT 06902. Outstanding bike bags—you can't go wrong here. They also have some fine clothing, sleeping bags, and tents.

Eastern Mountain Sports, Inc., 14209 Vose Farm Road, Peterborough, NH 03458. Wide range of fine outdoor equipment, with *honesty* in their catalogs.

Eddie Bauer, Fifth and Union, P.O. Box 3700, Seattle, WA 98124. Cadillac trade—very expensive, fine-quality gear, especially down clothing and sleeping bags. If you can afford it, this is really good stuff.

Indiana Camp Supply, Inc., P.O. Box 344, Pittsboro, IN 46167. Source for first-aid supplies and much, much more, from books to tents to candle lanterns.

L. L. Bean, Inc., 2651 Birch St., Freeport, ME 04033. Something of a tradition. They've moved more toward clothing in recent years, but they still carry lots of fine equipment at decent prices.

Mountain Bikes, Box 405, Fairfax, CA 94930. Super-clunkers and rough-stuff bikes.

Palo Alto Bicycles, 171 University Ave., Palo Alto, CA 94302. Used to be mostly a racing shop but lately has begun carrying good touring gear.

Organizations

Bikecentennial, P.O. Box 8308A, Missoula, MT 59807. Still very much in business, running group cycling tours, some of which include camping. They're also a source for excellent tour guides, books, and other information for cycling in various parts of the U.S. Write them.

League of American Wheelmen, P.O. Box 988, Baltimore, MD 21203. The 100-year-old organization for touring cyclists in the U.S. Its waters have been muddy of late, owing to factions within, but this does not change its status as the premier American cycling organization for the nonracer. The monthly *Bulletin* contains useful information on tours, technical matters, and legislative developments.

Maps

For areas east of the Mississippi, including Minnesota, write to the *Branch of Distribution, U.S. Geological Survey, 1200 South Eads Street, Arlington, VA 22202.* West of the Mississippi, including Alaska and Hawaii, the USGS address is *Box 25286, Federal Center, Denver, CO 80225.* A single order for both eastern and western maps may be placed with either office. You first will have to write for the free index map for the state in question, which will show you which quadrangles you want. They also provide a free guide to map symbols.

Author

The person responsible for this book lives at 316 W. 21, Little Rock, AR 72206, and welcomes all feedback, suggestions (anatomically possible or otherwise), hate mail, indecent propositions, gifts of real estate, and so on, but makes no guarantee to respond to any of it.

Index